THE MAGIC WORLDS
OF BERNARD MALAMUD

SUNY SERIES IN
MODERN JEWISH LITERATURE AND CULTURE

THE MAGIC WORLDS
OF BERNARD MALAMUD

Evelyn Avery, Editor

State University of New York Press

Published by
State University of New York Press, Albany

For information, address State University of New York Press,
90 State Street, Suite 700, Albany, N.Y., 12207

Production by Kelli M. Williams
Marketing by Michael Campochiaro

Library of Congress Cataloging-in-Publication Data

The magic worlds of Bernard Malamud / Evelyn Avery, editor.
    p. cm.—(SUNY series in modern Jewish literature and culture)
    Includes bibliographical references and index.
    ISBN 0-7914-5065-1 (alk. paper)—ISBN 0-7914-5066-X (alk. paper)
    1. Malamud, Bernard.   2. Novelists, American—20th century—Biography.
3. Jewish authors—United States—Biography.   4. Jewish fiction—History
and criticism.   5. Humanism in literature.   6. Jews in literature.   I. Avery,
Evelyn Gross, 1940–   II. Series.

PS3563.A4 Z75 2001
813'.54—dc21
[B]   2001020148

10 9 8 7 6 5 4 3 2 1

TO THE MEN IN MY LIFE
DON, PETER, AND DANIEL

Contents

What should I call it? I pondered, listing and rejecting titles such as *Bernard Malamud's Fiction* (too prosaic), *Bernard Malamud and the Critics* (too harsh), or *The Many Worlds of Bernard Malamud* (a possibility but too vague). Titling a manuscript seems more difficult than naming children, though in both cases the effects are generally indelible. As usual, author Bernard Malamud provided the answer. Taken together his works consist of different worlds, the shtetl, the university, the ballfield, New York ghettoes, rural Vermont, Italy, and Russia. Separated by education, class, age, and sensibilities, as well as settings, the characters, nevertheless, are often touched by the author's magic, offered a "new life" in the guise of the old, and transformed emotionally or spiritually into different, usually better people. In works where the magic fails, as in *The Tenants* or *God's Grace*, its presence is still felt, highlighting the absence of grace. "The Magic Barrel," I thought, embodies the tensions, struggles, and above all the redemptiveness of Malamud's fiction.

"Magic" and "Worlds" capture the essence of his landscapes. It is Bernard Malamud who must be thanked for inspiring this book as the warm, personal recollections of the man and the penetrating analysis of his work testify.

And I must thank my contributors for their cooperation. Their willingness to revise and meet deadlines was itself inspirational. I would like to thank Ann Malamud for encouragement and interest and my husband Don and sons Peter and Daniel for their ongoing support.

Finally, I would like to acknowledge the contribution of Towson University's Faculty Development Fund, which provided me with release time to work on the book, the Dean's fund for manuscript preparation, the English Department Chair, Clarinda Harriss, for enthusiastic embraces, and the department secretaries, Nancy Zellinger and Deana Johnson for the skills which I lack. I also am grateful to SUNY's production editor, Kelli Williams for her patience and assistance, and to James Peltz and Sarah Blacher Cohen, SUNY editors, whose support transformed my manuscript into a book.

Evelyn Avery

In an age that prizes diversity, Bernard Malamud's voice is uniquely universal. Though he combines the tones of Eastern European Jews, struggling immigrant Americans, bumbling academics, ghetto blacks, and even talking animals, the author has an extensive audience that cuts across ethnic, regional, and national boundaries. In the best literary tradition, Malamud, a humanist, uses the particular to express the universal. While such characters as Morris Bober, Willie Spearmint, and Sy Levin are ethnically identifiable, they experience "what it means to be human," to struggle against evil impulses and act on the good. The blend of universal themes, unforgettable characters, and a distinctive writing style has made Malamud popular with general readers as well as scholars. The recipient of two National Book Awards, the subject of numerous books and studies, the inspiration for The Malamud Society and national conferences, Bernard Malamud is recognized internationally as a major author. The son of Russian Jewish parents, he drew upon his immigrant Brooklyn background to people his early work, *The Magic Barrel* (1958), *The Assistant* (1957), and *Idiots First* (1963). The struggling "little Jew" even appears in Oregon and Italy, often as the conscience of the general community. Despite however, the use of specific settings and dialects, Malamud resists the ethnic label. He has described himself as a "writer who happens to be Jewish." Like William Faulkner or Nathaniel Hawthorne, whose regional worlds speak to all readers, Malamud has created an ethnic community with universal values. On the surface, however, not all of Malamud's fiction can be described as ethnic or Jewish, for in *The Natural* (1952), *A New Life* (1961), *Dubin's Lives* (1979), and *God's Grace* (1982), he experimented. He left New York City with its refugees, victims, marginal types and explored Europe, New England, Oregon, and a post–nuclear holocaust island. Readers familiar with Malamud's

"Jewish" fiction, for example, may be surprised by the "exotic" *God's Grace*, but will discover in these essays that all of his fiction is connected and is part of his distinctive vision.

Authored by scholars from diverse academic, theoretical, and literary backgrounds, the essays in this volume can be divided into three broad categories: Malamud's life, individual writings, and comparisons of several works. Thus, Part I contains Paul Malamud's recollections of his father, Daniel Stern's account of his close friendship with the author, Joel Salzberg's evaluation of the Bernard Malamud-Rosemarie Beck correspondence, portraits by his colleagues Nicholas Delbanco and Alan Cheuse at Bennington College, and Chester Garrison and Warren Hovland at Oregon State, and a eulogy by Cynthia Ozick.

The second section contains Sanford Pinsker's reflection on *A New Life*, Walter Shear's study of *Dubin's Lives*, Edward Abramson's Buddhist reading of *The Assistant*, Karen Polster's analysis of "The Last Mohican," and David Mesher's examination of *God's Grace*.

Part III explores patterns in Malamud's fiction, in which Lillian Kremer investigates Yiddish archetypes; Eileen H. Watts examines the Holocaust legacy; Alan Cheuse analyzes "Romance and Desire"; Victoria Aarons studies structure and style and Evelyn Avery compares the kindred *neshamas* of Bernard Malamud and Cynthia Ozick. A final essay by Daniel Walden focuses on Malamud's moral characters, while Eileen Watts presents a comprehensive annotated bibliography of works about Malamud written between 1993 and 1999. Taken together the essays examine the Jewish, American, and universal aspects of Malamud's art, applying fresh approaches (such as Buddhist) to old favorites such as *The Assistant* and a Biblical perspective to Malamud's futuristic *God's Grace*. I feel particularly fortunate to be able to include several intimate essays by those very close to Malamud. In a vivid, moving memoir, Paul Malamud remembers his dad in Oregon, a disciplined writer and teacher but also a caring father, reliable colleague, and courageous activist in the face of injustice. In the son's memoir we see the father's wry smile, his delight in nature, the classroom, and his social circle. Contrary to the image of *A New Life*, the Malamuds enjoyed Oregon, maintaining their connections there after they returned East. Part of a longer work about himself, this essay focuses on his father and reveals the affection between father and son.

Affection and respect also characterized Malamud's relationships with friends. An extensive correspondence, edited by Joel Salzberg, illuminates the friendship between Rosemarie Beck, artist, and Bernard Malamud, writer. From 1958 when they met at the Yaddo art colony until 1970 when "their lives moved in different directions," the two maintained a lively, somewhat irregular correspondence, the flavor of which is captured in Salzberg's article.

On a different level Bern, as he was called by friends, is fondly remembered by his colleagues at Oregon State where he taught from 1949 to 1961. In Paul Malamud's 1993 interviews with Chester Garrison and Warren Hovland, they recall less familiar sides of Malamud—the comedian who enjoyed pranks, the outspoken faculty member who questioned bureaucracy, the gifted intellectual who relished poker games with the guys. Still, many viewed him as the "New Yorker," the intense Easterner whose "nervous drive" set him apart from his seemingly easygoing colleagues. A decade later Malamud returned East, but not to New York. Instead he settled in rural Vermont, where he taught at Bennington and met Alan Cheuse and Nicholas Delbanco, who became lifelong friends and, after his death, editors of *Talking Horse: Bernard Malamud on Life and Work.* In an essay on "The Magic Barrel," Delbanco recalls family gatherings with the Malamuds, sharing "picnics, weddings, funerals, collective occasions," and support in times of need. Malamud called Delbanco "his protege," a tag he willingly accepted.

Although Delbanco admits he "can't pretend to critical distance [about] an author he love[s] and admire[s]," his study of Malamud's story, "The Magic Barrel," benefits from the personal involvement. A template for later fiction, "The Magic Barrel" blends "fact and fantasy—a magic—realism," characteristic of Malamud's writing and imagination.

There is more to Malamud's work, however, than magical realism. As Eileen Watts illustrates, in "The Lady of the Lake" and "The German Refugee" the author's Jewish consciousness, his immigrant background, and his historical awareness are reflected in his fiction. Thus, "The Lady of the Lake" is a "sort of allegory of the Akedah"(Abraham's sacrificing of Isaac), attesting to Malamud's familiarity with and interest in Jewish lore and law. The ironic and tragic "German Refugee" reveals an author sensitive to the horrific complications of the Holocaust for victims and survivors.

While Watts explores the influence of Jewish history on Malamud, Edward Abramson suggests a uniquely Buddhist interpretation of *The Assistant.* Those readers used to a Judeo-Christian perspective may be surprised initially by the different terminology and imagery, where the grocery becomes the "monastic training ground," and Morris and Frank assume a "master-pupil role." Ultimately, however, Abramson reconciles East and West and enriches our appreciation of *The Assistant.*

The West, that is the American West, fascinates Sanford Pinsker as he explores America's "frontier," specifically Oregon, in Malamud's "academic novel," *A New Life.* In his freewheeling essay "Malamud's New [Academic] Life—and Ours," Pinsker locates the novel in a historical context, viewing *A New Life* as part of a venerable genre, which it transcends. Part of "Malamud's complicated moral vision," the novel is also credited with humor, courage, and stunning descriptions of the Northwest.

Another intellectual is the subject of Walter Shear's sensitive psychological study, "The Lives of Dubin," in which Dubin, a biographer of D. H. Lawrence, experiences a "midlife crisis," but, unlike many contemporary protagonists, overcomes it. While incorporating major critical views, Shear's portrait of the aging, tormented Dubin on the verge of disintegration is insightful and moving.

Light years removed from New York, Oregon, or Vermont, *God's Grace*, set on a remote island inhabited by primates and one human being, inspires David Mesher's Talmudic-like essay, "Gorilla in the Myth: Malamud's *God's Grace*." Contrary to some critics, Mesher argues that Malamud's last complete work "is [his] most Jewish novel." In an impressive exegesis, supported by Torah references and Malamud's other works, Mesher credits *God's Grace* with religious affirmation in the tradition of "The Mourners" and "The Magic Barrel."

Like David Mesher, Lillian Kremer views "Malamud's fiction as permeated by Jewish themes, characters, and history." She is particularly impressed with the *lamed vov tzaddikim*, thirty-six anonymous righteous men from Jewish legend" who often appear as teachers of morality and spirituality in Malamud's fiction. In her review of Malamud's background, Kremer cites the influence of Yiddish and Hebrew writers such as Sholem Aleichem, I. L. Peretz, I. B. Singer, S. Y. Agnon, and Amos Oz whose "ethical Jewish wisdom and collective historic memory" inform Malamud's works too.

On a different note, Alan Cheuse reminds us of the romantic and sexual side to Malamud's writing. Whether in *The Assistant*, *A New Life*, or *Dubin's Lives*, Malamud's men get more than a spiritual education. In this sprightly essay, Cheuse depicts love and lust intertwined as the characters struggle to reach their hearts' desires.

Sadly, as Daniel Walden indicates, Malamud's protagonists fail to achieve their hearts' desires but in their struggles, they become " 'menschen,' common folk elevated by decency and morality."

Finally Victoria Aarons's study, "Tropic Suspension in Bernard Malamud's Fiction," examines the "chiasmus . . . a figure [of] subtle ironic self-parody." Through artful diagramming of sentences and phrases, Aarons illustrates the effectiveness of Malamud's style, which balances parallel structures that are also "opposites, antithetical," a form consistent with the "ideological tensions and contradictions of American Jewish fiction" and its insecure characters. Her analysis weds structure and content, ranging over a number of stories and novels.

Although Malamud's fiction speaks for itself, knowledge of the author, his personality and experiences, enriches our appreciation of his writing. In my own case, professional and personal interest in Malamud dates from 1958, when I read *The Assistant* and marveled at its insights into human nature. As the daughter of a poor Brooklyn grocer, I identified with the characters and setting, commiserating with Helen Bober, a part-time student with a bleak future. I identified Morris and Ida with my own parents slaving in the store, but even at eighteen, I understood that the novel transcended its parts. While the details engaged me, the theme, a recurring one, altered my perspective. In simplest terms, Malamud's fiction, even with the most naturalistic settings, offers characters choice, some degree of control, an acknowledgment of their free will. If only in response to grim fate, Malamud's characters learn moral behavior and even love, so central to Judaism and civilization.

Even as I read Malamud's fiction, I was making personal and professional choices—to major in English at Brooklyn College, to marry and teach in East Africa, and soon after in a Brooklyn ghetto, and to enroll in the University of Oregon graduate English program, not far from Oregon State where Malamud had taught and written *A New Life*. When *The Tenants* appeared in 1971, I was writing my dissertation on Richard Wright and Bernard Malamud, comparing black and Jewish writers. Was Malamud writing my life? I wondered as I wrote him an unabashed fan letter, which was followed by a meeting at the University of Oregon where Malamud had given a reading. Later, at an English department dinner reception, I observed him, a study in contrasts, reserved in appearance, balding, with a fringe of gray hair, a brushlike moustache, and eyeglasses. Wearing a suit, he looked more like a businessman than an artist or intellectual. Nor did his modest demeanor, his soft voice, and attentiveness to others prepare strangers for his firm views. He refused, for example, to be labeled an ethnic or a Jewish writer. When one of the English professors reminded him of his statement, "All men are Jews," Malamud explained patiently, "I never expected anyone to take it literally. It's a symbolic way of showing how history, sooner or later, treats us all." To the chastened professor's request for an autograph, he good-naturedly agreed, suggesting that in the future the scholar "should read an author's novels, not the critics' fiction." Nor were Malamud's values limited to literary criticism. When he overheard my advisor worry about my pregnancy delaying my thesis, Malamud suddenly chimed in, "Life is more important than art, mazel tov." He extended his hand to my husband and patted my shoulder.

For the rest of the evening, we talked about literature, his writing, and our respective Brooklyn childhoods. Asked about influences, he pointed to Russian writers such as Dostoyevsky and Chekhov and American authors Nathaniel Hawthorne and Henry James (interestingly, my thesis advisor, Christof Wegelin, is a Jamesian scholar who has written on Malamud). I asked Malamud about the influence of Yiddish and American Jewish writers on him. "Of course," he responded, "I am familiar with Sholem Aleichem and fellow-writers like Saul Bellow and Isaac Singer. But I don't think they have influenced me." He acknowledged that some of his values and even details came from his family background, from his father who was a hardworking, honest but poor grocer, from candlelighting and holiday traditions, Yiddish words and accented English which contributed to his "Yinglish" style, but he emphasized that his family had stressed morality and not religion. He also reminded me that "while all authors use autobiography, for [him] that's only a jumping-off point."

When I asked him about critical reception to *The Tenants,* he expressed disappointment. "The critics tend to confuse fiction and life. They looked for a political statement; but I write literature not propaganda. Some even have viewed the ending as bleak while I offer reconciliation before it is too late."[1] *The Tenants,* he disclosed, was a response to Richard Gilman's *New Republic* essay supporting the "black aesthetic," where only Blacks could write and critique black literature. *The Tenants,* I thought, reveals Malamud's fear of being typecast as a parochial Jewish writer; it questions the purpose of literature and the relationship between the artist and his community. At the heart of *The Tenants* is the struggle between the intellectual Jew and the passionate Black, each incomplete and unable to assist the other.

Nor was the novel Malamud's first exploration of the subject. Years before, he had written "Angel Levine" (1955) and "Black Is My Favorite Color" (1963), which revolve about Blacks and Jews. Malamud's background, which included childhood experiences with Blacks from a nearby neighborhood and later contact as a teacher in Harlem, formed a basis for his fiction. He wrote me that he felt sorry for "poor Jews and poor Blacks, unfortunate people generally . . . [but] he admired the pretty black girls in brightly colored dresses . . . and vital skilled black basketball players." Combined with a sense of "the other man's strangeness," such emotions contributed to *The Tenants.*[2]

The correspondence was followed by a summer visit to his home in Bennington where he taught for half the year. My family and I were greeted by a handsome, sprawling white house, tall lush evergreens, and the writer dressed in casual slacks and a short-sleeved shirt. His welcoming air charmed our children, Peter (ten) and Daniel (four) who were invited to snack on root beer and cookies and explore his home. He dismissed my concerns about his rugs and vases by labeling them "just objects." While the boys played on the spacious back yard, we chatted about his fiction which he described as primarily imaginative and only loosely autobiographical. As an example he cited *A New Life,* which satirized the provincial Oregon college where he had enjoyed teaching and made good friends. Before we left, Malamud shook hands with our children. Looking seriously into the eyes of Peter, our ten year old, he said, "I like the way you handle life." To Daniel, our four year old, he said, "your mother made the right decision five years ago, "an allusion to my thesis advisor's reservation voiced at the Universityof Oregon dinner reception.[3]

Five years later in the summer of 1982, when I visited Bennington again, he looked tired and pale, suffering from the aftermath of a stroke that left one arm weakened and his speech slightly slurred. He was relieved to have finished *God's Grace*, despite his illness, though he warned me that I probably would not like it.[4] Although he was partially right about my first reaction, I have since reevaluated the novel and recognize its power.

Unfortunately Malamud did not have the opportunity to complete his last novel, *The People*. I was privileged to host him and his wife Ann at Baltimore Hebrew University where he received an award for distinguished Jewish writing and dramatized portions of *The People*.[5] As his voice rose and fell, reflecting different characters, and an occasional chuckle escaped, it was clear that the author was enjoying himself. It was also evident that *The People* reflects old patterns and new directions. By transforming a Russian Jewish peddler into an American Indian chief, Malamud reverses the process by which a Christian character such as Frank Alpine (*The Assistant*) identifies as a Jew. When the protagonist, Yozip Bloom, asks, "What can I do for my people?" he is worried about Indians, not Jews, from whom he feels estranged. Actually, the Indians and their plight provide "what he had lacked in his former, lonely life." Why should this "shtetl" loner embrace Native Americans? Why should this greenhorn commit himself to tribal life? Perhaps, suggests Malamud, Indian life appeals to Yozip as a member of the lost tribe of Jewish Americans searching for their identity in the new world, a quintessentially American quest.

"The reader must feel free to choose," Malamud had once said about interpretations of his work. That evening the Baltimore Jewish audience embraced the author as one of their own. From his early works, Bernard Malamud had resisted the ethnic label, but like Yozip, he had been adopted to represent a tribe of wanderers, the tribe of American Jews. That night in Baltimore was the last time I saw Bernard Malamud, who died several months later. The friendship begun in 1970 ended in 1986 when I learned the bad news just before my Malamud seminar was to meet. Although fifteen years have passed I miss him, as do countless other friends and devoted readers.

Having entered the new millennium, social and cultural forces seem poised at the abyss. With morality taboo, and truth questionable, relevance rules. In an age that deconstructs, Malamud's voice does not. It speaks clearly, imaginatively, with the weight of ancient traditions and the understanding of modern conditions. While we miss his presence, his fiction reminds us of our capacity for love, compassion, and justice, which makes the center hold.

Notes

1. Bernard Malamud to Evelyn Avery, dinner reception at University of Oregon, August 1972.

2. Bernard Malamud letter to Evelyn Avery, July 8, 1973.

3. Avery family visit with Malamud, Bennington, VT, July 10, 1977.

4. Bernard Malamud to Evelyn Avery, Bennington, VT, July 13, 1982.

5. Bernard Malamud, Baltimore Hebrew College, Baltimore, Md., November 1985.

Part One

THE AUTHOR

Chapter 1

MALAMUD IN CORVALLIS
Memories of Dad

Paul Malamud

From a Child's Perspective

Around 1950 Dad wrote many letters to colleges across the country, seeking full-time work as a teacher. When he received an offer from Oregon State College in Corvallis, my father, mother, and I (in my twos) took the transcontinental train west. Then, as now, Corvallis was in the heart of the Willamette Valley, about a two-hour drive from the Pacific Ocean. The valley was a landscape of hills covered with wheat and Douglas fir forests, bounded by the Coastal Range toward the west and the higher Cascade Range eastward, a sharp contrast from Brooklyn and Manhattan where Dad had spent his life.

Editor's Note: The following two chapters contain Paul Malamud's childhood recollection of his father when the family lived in Corvallis, Oregon, where Bernard Malamud taught at Oregon State College from 1949 to 1961.

Chapter 2 contains interviews or "conversations," as Paul calls them, with Chester Garrison and Warren Hovland, colleagues and good friends of his father.

3

Of the newcomers to Oregon State, some were Easterners who wanted to make a new start or find a job or move out to where there was lots of empty land, after the war. Others, like my father, had survived the Great Depression. It was a generation of survivors. Now, they wanted to read books, to find out about music and art, and have the good life they'd been denied. In particular, some were serious about reading.

The younger faculty, with their similar experiences and aspirations, may have become something of a clique—with grievances against the more conservative senior faculty. The new community gave my parents, themselves ardent New Dealers, people with whom to share their political ideas, their reading and social lives. Social lives at that point meant dinner parties, lots of them, as well as some visiting among women during the day.

The wives brought their husbands along to dinner, so families got acquainted. My mother began to cook well. Some of my earliest memories are of dinner parties. My mother would laugh and refer to Corvallis as "the center of the universe—ha ha," meaning that it was almost like that, then, for a little while. People were ostensibly informal, and would often leave the house unlocked, even if they went away for a weekend. Children ran in and out of other peoples' houses.

My father seemed like a vast presence to me when I was quite small. Whatever he had been earlier, by the time I knew him in the early nineteen fifties he seemed a happy academic. He had a heavy blue-green beard shadow, and wore rimless spectacles. He was fond of Shetland sweaters and corduroy jackets. He was professorial, given to orderly thought and habits.

It was a quiet town—at the end of every street, one could see hills with fields of grain and stands of oak. They might as well have had covered wagons on them—in the recent past, doubtless they had. If you went into the country, you'd see an occasional old wagon wheel, bleached and rusting, lying on the ground.

That was probably his first impression—seeing those hills covered with dark green Douglas fir trees interspersed with golden-brown fields of hay or grass visible past the edges of the town as we walked along the half-deserted streets, so different from Manhattan. Most of Corvallis consisted then of shingled or planked bungalows dating from the earlier part of the century, and the college was in this part, uptown. Monroe, a side street that slashed diagonally through Corvallis, led to the downtown, a main street in the typical style of small towns of the era. The town ended at the river.

Dad's job paid something like $3,000 a year. Such a salary covered food and housing, but, apparently, during the summer some college faculty were concerned about their ability to make ends meet.

When we moved, my parents gave up the friends of their youth and the New York City area. They were lucky in where they landed. Academic life was in flower. There were many young faculty coming to Oregon State and they quickly made friends. Above all, the war was over, and everyone was in the mood to celebrate. Everyone had access to food, cigarettes, and booze. Many of the younger faculty at OSC were World War II vets, supporters of Roosevelt and the New Deal who had been educated on the GI Bill. Some of them were cultivated as friends.

He was at the college—a few blocks away from the houses where we lived at that time—frequently. When the time came for him to come home, I would often hang around the living room, waiting for him to walk through the door. If it was raining, I could watch for him through the windows, usually, in that climate, dotted and streaked with lines of rain. If not, I might go out on to the sidewalk and wait there. Finally, I'd see him walking toward the house with a firm, relaxed stride, homburg on head, his long, brown raincoat, which went down to his rubbers, flapping in the wind, exposing his tweed jacket and tie, paper under his arm. My young sister, Janna, and I would rush to him, pulling on his coat, shouting, hugging him welcome.

He was a warm-spirited man, and he could get quite angry. In general, his anger melted quickly. As I got older I must have realized he was basically sensitive, gentle and kind, erudite, and humorous. He had a way of talking about the ordinary events of life that turned them into stories. People were his entire life. He loved Charlie Chaplin. Even visits to doctors could be fun—sort of special occasions—if he took me there. We'd often play tic-tac-toe on a piece of paper in the waiting room.

When I was quite young, Dad would occasionally invite me to take a walk with him and confide a few details about his own childhood. As the son of a poor grocer in Brooklyn, he grew up, more or less, in the kind of environment described in *The Assistant*. He told me that when he was a young boy, he had gotten pneumonia—this would have been in the teens of the century—and had almost died. The doctor had been about to pronounce him dead, but his heart began beating again. He said his father, Max, a grocer, had been so delighted he had gone out and bought for his son, Bern, a set of *The Book of Knowledge*, the children's encyclopedia of its day and that was his first introduction to the world of knowledge and learning. Aside from that, he had few toys, I believe, perhaps a stick acrobat that swung back and forth and up and down on strings between two wooden sticks. He certainly did not have a good life as a child, and I think he was pleased to be able to bring up his own children in a peaceful, pleasant place.

He said that in his youth he had to work behind the counter, serving customers and carving up deli meat. If he was slow, he said, Max would get angry and shout at him in front of the customers. His own mother died when he was young. When I asked him if his stepmother had done anything good for him, he thought for awhile and said, "She helped me get out of the house." Once when he was older—I presume an adolescent or college age—he walked toward the family store, and saw his father, Max, sitting beside the front window. His father looked up hungrily—hoping for a customer. At that point, he said, he saw his father as a human being and forgave him for what he had not given him (and presumably decided to get out of Brooklyn forever).

Basically, Dad was a storyteller. He had the gift of taking the day's experiences and turning them into stories, to amuse his family at dinner. As he sat in his armchair afterward, he would rub his slippered feet one against the other while spinning a tale that amused and pleased him. He was sharply observant about human incidents and details of behavior. He had a hearty sense of humor, especially in his thirties and forties. When I was young boy, he enjoyed taking me on his lap and telling me stories—as he later did with my sister. One group of stories was about an evil witch called Cycorax, another about a penguin named Penny whose misadventures were rather like those of a silent movie comedian. Dad's comic sense had obviously been influenced by the silents, probably Chaplin in particular, whom he greatly admired, and in the fifties in Oregon he helped start a campus film society where I saw Chaplin shorts and features for the first time. He was delighted when his children showed a sense of humor.

He had a slow, deliberative, cautious manner. He made notes about everything—reading, writing, teaching, personal matters—in a peculiar, crabbed hand that was difficult to read. Sometimes in the morning when he was shaving, he could call out to me or to Mother and ask us to note a word or phrase on a writing pad, so that he would not lose it. I'm sure whatever he was working on was on his mind most of the time. He tended to read the way he wrote—slowly but thoroughly, underlining all kinds of key words, phrases, or thoughts he considered important. He did this in his teaching, as a way of preparing a text—but even when not teaching he would underline articles and passages in books that interested him. He was saturated in words and language.

Early in life, Dad must have developed a feeling that high culture and the life of the mind were the only escape from a mundane existence—and he obviously brought this with him to Corvallis. He must have known he would not go back to the financial poverty and social deprivation of his childhood, but he wanted to continue to get away from it, as far as possible. He read constantly. He listened to the local classical radio station—KOAC—and as I fell asleep I would hear the first bars of the theme from Handel's Water Music, which introduced the program. I went to sleep to this lulling music—or to the shrieking and laughter of guests at a dinner party downstairs—and sometimes awoke fitfully to wind blowing, making the wooden windows bang in the sashes, and usually to the patter of rain.

He and my mother, thanks to her vast energy and stamina, created an orderly family life. Other families in that postwar community ate dinner informally—we were sometimes advised—when they felt like it, in front of a television set, but we sat down around the table at 6:15, because he and mother felt strongly about that. After dinner, he'd put on a dull-colored sweater or a patched corduroy jacket and read in his arm-chair, a modest affair of a Danish-modern frame and two foam cushions, while listening to classical music.

Occasionally, very occasionally, my mother and I would visit him at work. The part of the English department where he had his office was a glorified quonset hut that had been constructed in World War II—one-story, long and narrow, with two parallel wings joined by a third at one end, with a cream-colored shingled exterior and a corrugated roof. The corridors, which had linoleum floors and green plywood walls, seemed to me to be the haunts of rather important people. One could hear tingling, clever, adult laughter coming from the room with the coffee machine. Occasionally, his colleagues would chat with my mother in the hall or pay attention to me. Once or twice we watched him teach. Standing in his tweed jacket in a cream-colored barn-like room lit with fluorescent fixtures he looked avuncular, humorous, authoritative, and very much in charge of his class. After that, I felt that being a teacher would be my goal, and it was for a long time.

Dad insisted I read. He constantly praised me when he felt I was imaginative or humorous. He refused to buy a television set until the late nineteen fifties. Many men in the community hunted, fished, and hiked. Dad wasn't the least interested in this, and I did not understand why he wasn't eager to do these things. I didn't like his lack of active involvement in the real world, as I saw it. However, he did appreciate the natural beauty of Oregon.

His interests and focus and perhaps political views put him at odds with the community in other ways. When he had come indoors after work and was standing in the dining room, coat still on, eagerly opening the mail, he complained to my mother about an occasional very senior colleague (no doubt unimaginative, passionless, cold—a Republican). He sometimes found his students vapid, callow, and dull, and poorly prepared for reading and writing. But it was not embittered, frightened griping, it was more like intellectual outrage—he and my mother were young and had life ahead of them; and he had his friends and allies on campus too.

Then—as now—freshman composition students couldn't spell three-letter words. Dad could become fascinated by the mental processes of his students, including one young woman who believed the Devil was some-where in the real world, always lurking behind a rock, ready to tempt, or attack her. He would explain to me and my sister carefully, patiently, that such people were not bad—they were ignorant and uneducated. The value of education was the tenet of his life, and whatever success he had as a teacher probably came from this belief.

He could be outspoken. He once told one of his bosses to his face that he "had a heart of corn flakes." For some reason, they didn't fire him, maybe out of a certain decency, or because he had a family or because he had friends and allies at the college, or because he was a published writer, or because they may have respected his guts.

At parties, when the name of Senator Joe McCarthy came up, his voice would rise in anger and a lot a people would talk at once. In that sense, they—that is, fifties liberals—seemed part of a beleaguered, righteous cir-cle. My parents and their friends believed in such institutions as the League of Women Voters. Their heroes were Franklin Roosevelt and (briefly) Adlai Stevenson. In those days, liberalism had a genteel, high-minded quality, different from popular culture.

One of my earliest memories is of the election of 1952. I was sitting on the polished pine floor of the downstairs dining room of the house we had then, and my parents seemed especially excited. They had taken the radio from its shelf alcove and had put it on the dining room table—there was a man's deep voice on it and occasional sounds of crowds cheering in the background.

I could not understand what the announcer meant, but my parents were pacing around and laughing nervously. "He's gonna get it," said my father "he's gonna get it." This seemed to continue for several hours, but as the night wore on, my father's "He's gonna get it" got weaker, and in his and my mother's voice, I heard plaintive disappointment. "Of course, of course," said my mother in the matter-of-fact tone. "Of course he was going to win." The warmth and enthusiasm of the room partly evaporated. I asked what had happened, and my father explained that a man called Stevenson was trying to beat a man called Eisenhower in an election.

"What's an election?" I asked. "An election," said my father, "is where two men want to be a leader, but they want to do different things. Say, one man wants to build a bridge and another man doesn't want to. Then, the people have to choose which of the two men they want—the one who wants to build the bridge, or the one who doesn't."

"Who do you want to win?" I asked.

"We think that Stevenson is the better man, dear," said my mother.

"Why?" I asked.

Dad interrupted. "Because he's better-educated and has a better sense of humor. He's a more gifted individual."

"And who are most people for?"

"Eisenhower."

Later, as it became clear that Stevenson was going to lose badly, my father lamented, "Oh, schlook," and threw up his hands in disgust, and then sighed, shrugged, and went off to read a book. He had, however, taught me something. He liked teaching.

The "college people" were beginning to paint their walls off-white, prefer Danish-modern furniture, and purchase hi-fi's, then being invented, as opposed to using flowery wallpaper, retaining the bulbous furniture of the thirties and forties, and listening to small record players. Both my parents read books—that above all is what defined their group, far more than their inadequate income.

Everything interested him: his writing, his wife, his children, his correspondence, the people he came into contact with during the day, and what he read in the news. At best, his voice would leap over the dinner table in joy, or in combat, but frequently with humor and always with passion. He was rarely bored or blasé or polite. He was interested and passionate and incisive and sometime brilliant, and always involved with the people he talked to. His friends came to dine with him and my mother not merely because she was a good cook and energetic person; they came because he was himself. And many of their friends were young and full of energy too so their dinner parties were lively.

In late winter, Dad bought tickets to the college basketball games, perhaps hoping his children would enjoy the real, all-American childhood he had missed—though he himself was capable of surreptitious pleasure in these forays. (And it is true as a boy he had seen much baseball at Ebbetts Field.) About once a month for a few years, my father, sister, and I—and occasionally my mother—would drive to the stadium, lit with floodlights, and walk through the rain, our breath a gray mist, into the enormous, echoing, yellowish wood gymnasium with its smell of varnish, popcorn, and sweat. We would quickly claim bleacher seats. After about ten anticipatory minutes, the band came running out onto the floor, and a hush fell. Then, to the strains of the Oregon State College fight song, the players came running out onto the floor. Most of the college faculty stood at this point to humor the gladiators, but not my father, who made his stand against the sheeplike good-fellowship of the community, refusing to pretend that his heart swelled with pride at the entry of the home team. He was an adult (he had a point there) and wasn't going to stand up for a bunch of college boys.

The other team's band came out on the floor. When both teams had been lined up and introduced by an announcer with a carnival-barker voice, the lights dimmed, and a sudden, reverent hush fell. Far away, high in the stratosphere of green girders and black, cavernous roofs, one could see the American flag, a pinpoint of red and blue, spotlit, and next to it, the Oregon State College flag, an orange "O" on a black field. Everybody, including my father, stood. There would be a roll of snare drums and the band would crash into the anthem, wobbling and squeaking, especially in the clarinet passages, but loud. After the last bar, there would be a sudden hiss, swelling into a roar. A whistle blew, rubber sneakers thumped the floor, and the game was on.

My father had not learned to drive until he got to Corvallis, and he wanted me to start when I was still young, so I would be better at it. As I got older—old enough to see over the dashboard—on Saturdays or Sundays sometimes we would drive a little way out of town in our green 1952 Oldsmobile, the successor to a green 1952 Plymouth, until we were on one or another deserted asphalt road surrounded by woods, in the silent afternoon, when there would be no other cars.

I was elated at this privilege. He would squeeze against the gray felt-padded door and I would sidle up close to him, first holding on to the steering wheel as he guided it, then beginning to turn the wheel myself. We went slowly, first just along straight stretches of highway—rarely seeing another vehicle—then taking gentle curves and going up and down hills. Finally he let me push on the gas pedal. For boys at that time and place, wheels seemed the main goal of childhood—I will never forget my pleasure at being allowed to drive a real car instead of my bicycle or at best a kiddie-cart. As time went on, we'd go farther out and then, in continuing defiance of the law, as I was about ten years old, change places so I sat in the driver's seat and drove. I looked forward ardently to these privileges, relishing the unaccustomed feeling of power.

He encouraged me, maybe by example, to take an interest in the outside world, whatever form it took, and to be intellectually aggressive in school. A great treat was going with Dad to the Natural History Museum, a small and odd collection of Western paraphernalia in the basement of a yellow adobe university building on the edge of town. We'd walk there on occasional Sundays when the weather was good. The first display case—the largest one and the one that first met the eye, was full of pioneer ladies' hoop skirts, masks of Northwest Indians—animal faces— green or black with yellow teeth, with eyes painted on or inset by wooden balls—or semi-human faces with scars, knobs, and war paint, straight faces and twisted faces, with black, bushy hair. Above all, in a wider, sunny hall at the end of the museum, stood a row of old stagecoaches, large and brown or black—enormous contraptions of wood and canvas standing empty like mummy cases. There were glass cases of pistols, percussion cap rifles, arrowheads, and tomahawks. My favorite exhibit however was the rocks. We'd walk through black velvet curtains into a small booth. Standing alone on a pedestal was a four-sided glass case containing white and gray rocks. We pushed a button—the booth went dark, then a purple light came on overhead and the rocks in the case glowed with brilliant fluorescent spots: reds, greens, and blues, the colors seeming to run down the sides of the rocks like liquids. In Corvallis, in the fifties, this was major entertainment.

Frequently on weekends, we would drive westward across a low range of mountains to the Pacific coast, a shorter distance away. I loved and hated these trips. I hated them because I got sick. The curves on the coastal road were atrocious, and I would often feel nauseated as the clunky vehicle slowly skidded around them. Sometimes, when my parents permitted, I was allowed to sit in the front seat, hanging my head out of the window to catch fresh air.

We got into the car and drove along curving roads, climbing higher and higher into the fog. For the most part, our only companions on the road were log trucks, inching their way along, great red lights blinking in the fog and enormous tree trunks on their flatbed trailers jiggling ominously, kept from slipping off and crushing us only by a thin length of chain. Finally, after an hour or two of foggy creep, we went down until we found ourselves driving alongside a large, black estuary with pine forests on both sides. "It's okay now, we're past the curves," my father said helpfully. We passed a solitary cabin where bait was sold. The fog of the mountains had dissipated, but now we were touched by tendrils of fog from the sea. We got to a small town with pink and white wooden houses and suddenly were on a bridge stretching over a great, wide bay.

Finally, we arrived at the empty beach, near the town and bridge: miles of gray and white sand with no one else on it. The green bay water was cold, and good for wading. Behind each beach were orangey sandstone cliffs peppered with small, gnarled trees and shrubs, the gnostic guardians of the place, and at its base lay piles of driftwood, twisted and bleached. I am quite sure nothing this magnificent or so suggestive of psychological autonomy and freedom had been easily available to Dad during his boyhood. But, partly by chance, he had it by then, and it made a difference in his life, as he could now look back on his existence in New York with a new perspective. This combination of present and past, "emotion recollected in tranquility," may be one reason his writing blossomed in those years.

Chapter 2

RECOLLECTING BERNIE
Colleagues at Oregon State

Interviewed by Paul Malamud

Chester Garrison

I came here to Oregon State University in the fall of nineteen fifty-four, and do not remember meeting him, but unquestionably we got together, recognized each other, and began forming a friendship very quickly.

By the end of the first month that we were here, we were invited to the Malamud house, which was customary, because they (Ann and Bern) were always interested in welcoming newcomers and in finding out about them. So I think unquestionably what brought us together—that is particularly Bern and myself—was that we were both Easterners. He was from New York; I was from just across the river in Jersey City.

So that established in this far country—which it certainly was at that time—a kind of rapport in which Easterners were finding each other and kind of clinging to each other. I was brought up in the area where my major associates were either Irish or Jewish, so that helped out, I think, too. I felt at home, in other words. And I think that he felt at home with me. This I mention because Corvallis is a small town. While he made the jump all the way from New York to Corvallis, Oregon—this Eden

13

according to the local people—I made the steps gradually so that I became accustomed to what was going on out here. It's not that Bern had any reason to feel discrimination against him for being Jewish—in the mid-nineteen fifties there simply weren't that number of Jews around for anybody to discriminate against in town—there were very few—however, there were an increasing number who had joined the faculty—so I think it was mainly a matter of our both being Easterners.

Aside from that, we'd both been to Columbia where he had gotten his M.A, and I was still working on my Ph.D. Since he had written his Master's paper on the poetry of Thomas Hardy, and I was dealing with my dissertation on Thomas Hardy, there were all kinds of reasons why we should get together, and it worked right from the beginning. We became fast friends very quickly that first year, and remained that way.

Bern stood out as a New Yorker. He was outspoken, as New Yorkers are, compared to people in many other parts of the country. I think out here it's desirable, or was desirable, that one be nice and not seek confrontation and think things over before kind of maneuvering for a position; but if Bern saw something was wrong, he spoke out immediately at meetings, or if it was an administrator, he spoke out immediately to that administrator. He was not an administrator's love-child by any means. And particularly the chair of the department was a person who came from Colorado and was easygoing and liked to have his own way and did not believe in confrontation. Bern confronted people, with good reason. I've never known him to do it out of indecency. It was simply a matter, "You're wrong, let's argue about it." And he would bring things up in department meetings which many other people would let slide, and certainly which the department chair found absolutely wrong from his point of view. So one of Bern's characteristics, which was his own as well as being characteristic of Easterners, is to assert one's kind of property or stance and say to anyone else, "This is wrong," and have direct eye-to-eye conflict. This was to his credit, and it was something I was accustomed to, so I found nothing wrong with it, and if we ever did argue, which was not too often—we usually discussed—but if we did argue, we both held our own and it might sound fiery to other people but it was just our backgrounds coming out.

Q: What kinds of issues did he become involved in?

A: Well, unfairness. For instance, there was one young man in the department. He was a poet of sorts who was politically oriented and he did something which irritated the department chair, and also would have irritated anybody on the administrative staff of the university, which was very conservative. So that person—on a Friday afternoon—was given a dismissal just right then and there for the entire year, and the person went to Bern and told him, "Look, what am I to do now." Bern immediately stepped right into the gap and consulted with the administrators and told them they were all wrong. By Monday, I think the administrators pulled back somewhat and the person was given an extension to the end of the year and I suspect that at that point it wasn't so much a matter of dismissing him—it was a matter of that person wanting to get out of here.

So that really represents his willingness to confront, but there are other aspects of it too. He came out here and discovered that the things that he liked to do were not available, particularly seeing foreign films—they just weren't on campus. So what do you do? If you want to see foreign films, you start a foreign film society, which he did. And before long the foreign film society caught on. I joined in on the group that ran it, and in fact, at the first meeting I went to, Bern had just received the announcement that he had a grant to go to Italy (in 1956), so I was made chair in his place because all the other people in the group had their specific jobs—one was in charge of equipment, one was in charge of selling tickets and so forth.

So he did it for two years, and I also was accustomed to seeing foreign films, so I ran it for eleven years after that. The point is that he looked around and if he felt that something was desirable and he wanted it, he would start that committee. He liked music. He thought he would like to have some chamber music. Well, he didn't actually start it but he got the thing rolling and surely enough it worked—as a matter of fact, one thing that got it working was that the foreign films had been so successful that there was money to underwrite it. Right now (1993), it's still going on after all these years. It's simply a part of the community, very successful, very well attended, and having only the top-ranked traveling performers of the country.

So again I'm saying Bern—when he went after something—it was partly because he thought it was right or he thought it was desirable and it very often worked.

He asserted himself both in individual and institutional issues. In the case that I gave (of the poet) that would be fairly typical. Increasingly, as Bern was out here, people felt that if something was wrong and nobody else was going to speak up, they would go to him. They would consult with him. Very often, if he felt it was wrong, then he was most certain to speak up and annoy the department chair to no end.

I don't remember many of the institutional issues. We did have meetings—of what was then called the Lower Division—it's now the College of Liberal Arts. Bern was always interested in anything that dealt with culture, and its furtherance.

Q: Why wasn't he fired outright?

A: Probably because he argued better than the department chair. I'm sure the department chair would have been happy to have gotten rid of him along time before he left. But the family—Ann and Bern—were very sociable. They got to know—as I guess we did too—most of the people within the liberal arts area. Bern made himself known, was known, and he had plenty of support. For the department to dismiss him would be questioned by outsiders because there were so many ties established, and because of the things that he had done. And then of course his reputation was growing as a writer.

Now, when I came here in fifty-four Bern had published *The Natural*. I had never heard of it. I don't like baseball, never did, and I hadn't heard about it, but a friend of mine two years later who came here in part accepted the job because, "Oh, there's Malamud there—I want to get to know him, I like his novel." But his reputation was growing as he published more and more and then he got the National Book Award with *The Assistant*, and that would have made it difficult for the administration to fire him, and I'm mainly speaking of the department chair. His name was around, not only in the liberal arts area. He was known. It would be difficult to drop him without cause.

Q: What was the milieu like there, then?

A: I had taught on three other campuses before—Ohio State, the University of Louisville, and the University of Colorado, each time coming further West. There's no question that in coming here (to Oregon) it was even further away from New York, not only geographically, but intellectually as well. Oregon State wasn't a university then, it was a college, Oregon State College, which was oriented to agriculture and, last of all, the liberal arts. So what happened was that anybody who was in the liberal arts clung together—that is, we associated with each other. It was a very active group, growing all the time, and full of very interesting people. We had an enjoyable social life—in fact it became increasingly intricate, so much so that when we (Garrisons) finally moved from the middle of town up to the hilltop we're on now, we had to cut back our social involvements. It was getting to be too much. But there was this group of people who had comparable interests, and they had established themselves as a kind of compound within the confines of the area. So I'm not complaining about Corvallis, because

I've loved it and when I retired I would think of no other place to go. It has become increasingly more satisfactory as a place to live— that is, for the kind of people that we are—and part of that is due to Bern and people like him.

By the time I came out here, I had experience as a teacher—and, like all teachers, I had certain stories to tell or certain ways to perform in class—sure-fire jokes and so forth. But out here, all my jokes fell flat, because of the lack of sophistication of the students. They were nice people, they were good people, but they were way out in a rather bucolic area and their sense of humor was nothing I had run into before. But gradually I found where the ground was and could build on it.

When Bern went East for one of his prizes, I took over his lit course, and I'm sure from everything I heard that he was a very successful teacher. In particular, he taught a course in imaginative writing in the evening, which drew a lot of older people—women who were tied up during the day and some men. They were people I was more likely to meet and get reports from, and even today those people who were in that class always spoke favorably of him, and thought it was just a great experience to be with him.

I don't have too many opinions from students—but I never questioned that he was thorough, that he was fair. There were perhaps cultural tensions. Many of the students out here—and I've experimented with this—are appalled at the *New Yorker,* the magazine. I made a habit at the end of the first quarter of freshmen comp to hand everybody a copy of the *New Yorker* magazine and then tell them to write a theme about it, not about the entire magazine, but to pick out one aspect of it and write about it. I know what would be coming: One, I knew that there would be great dissatisfaction with the magazine. It wasn't like *Popular Mechanics* or *Time Magazine,* or whatever, but then I also know that it would be the best set of themes I would get, because so many of them would be perplexed or even angry at the kind of a magazine I'd asked them to read. Three-fourths of the students would usually get a half or a whole grade better in that theme than they'd been getting all along, because they were so emotional about it.

What I'm saying is that Bern was a New Yorker and would strike some people as being very strange, and they would have trouble adjusting to him. And I'm sure that some people might have disliked him, because of not understanding. But I have no feeling of any general discomfort with him. There was his background, and his New York manner—I had people tell me that my manner was something that they had difficulty adjusting to.

Both your parents were fascinated by people—Ann and Bern wanted to know all about people—and they were constantly seeking people, entertaining newcomers to town, discovering additional friends, and, always, they had that comparable fascination which put them almost in tandem with each other. If there was any way in which those two people were alike, that was it. They were both unusually outgoing.

With Bern, there was a slight intellectual slant. He was about four to six years older than I, and he was brought up—and was probably more conscious of having been brought up—in the Freudian age, that is, when Freud suddenly became popular with American society. I still feel that a good deal of his writing was oriented towards the Freudian exposure he had in his formative years. He was constantly looking, constantly "analyzing" people. There are a few people who were made a little bit uneasy about that—perhaps they thought, "Well, if I tell too much of myself or speak too much it's likely to end up in a book." I always felt Freud was in the background. It was a part of him, it should have been. I'm not saying he was an absolute Freudian—that's not the point. It was a part of his age. That made him distinctive. [He was also interested in peoples' personalities as a novelist who focused on characterization—ed.]

Q: Do you remember any revealing anecdotes about him?

A: One day I was teaching in an ex-army-barracks building, a quonset hut with a rounded metal top that had been moved onto the campus from Camp Adair, when all of the sudden there was a surge of students. I had a one o'clock class, which anybody knows is a difficult class because it's right after lunch, and students' stomachs are beginning to churn and make them a little bit sleepy. This building, because of its low ceiling and lack of many windows, was a warm building on a spring day.

One day, I noticed in about the third row a student asleep, which was not too unusual. I also knew that he worked hard at noon and he came directly from work into my class. So I, of course, never said anything about it. I just made a mental note. So at the end of class, when the bell went off and the class was dismissed everybody got up and moved out; and this boy was so tired out that he didn't even hear anybody go. So Bern came in early—he was teaching the two o'clock class—and I kind of put my finger over my mouth until he got to the front of the room and I pointed out the student. I said, "What are we going to do about this?"

He said, "Well, let's just leave him there and see what happens." I departed. So his class filed in—they noticed the student. They looked at Bern, and Bern waved, apparently to say, "Let it go." He announced, "Look, we have a visitor here who is all tired out, so if he wakes up pay no attention to it, don't laugh, don't do anything." And they all settled in, and he started teaching, and the boy slumbered right on. Well, about two-thirds of the way through the class, the boy suddenly woke up. He suddenly realized that I was not up in front, that another teacher was there, that his friends were not around him, and his impulse first of all was to grab his books and start to run—but he was in the middle of the row—in the middle of the class. Rather than do so, he slumped down and sat through the rest of the class—and went out when the class went out.

I think that shows compassion. I think it shows humor. I think it shows—in a way—the way his mind might work that somebody else's might not.

I would say that most people—that is, people who knew him possibly less well—would suggest that Bern was highly serious, very serious, and always dealing with serious problems of various kinds. Now, that was not always true, because he certainly had a very fine sense of humor, and would show it, but you had to lean into it, you had to hear it, and I would say the average person wasn't even exposed to it.

I was always curious that Bern, of course, didn't drink very much. He drank wine and only occasionally would have a small scotch. My own analysis of it was that Bern admired the intellectual process, and would not like in any respect to be freed, or to have the clamps off of self-control. One time apparently somebody did put some extra liquor in what he was drinking, and he became enlivened by it, and became very amusing. I was not there at that point. But he opened up more than he was accustomed to in public. I think again it demonstrates what kind of a person he was—he believed in self-control. This, of course, was in keeping with the way he conducted his whole life style. He taught on Monday, Wednesday, and Friday. Those days were dedicated—for Bern—for either teaching, consulting with students, or grading, and that was that. But Tuesday, Thursday, and Saturday—this is a matter of discipline that amazed everyone, that he was able to maintain—it was a matter of his writing. When he was writing in his room [office] in the department with his door closed, if anyone knocked on the door, that person got a cool reception—sometimes a "Who is it?" through the door, and saying, "I'm busy." Or whatever, so that very rapidly the staff knew that if you're going to go see Bern and rap on his door, remember the calendar and what day of the week it was. I'm not exaggerating on this one bit. He was disciplined, and he wrote on those days, and nobody was to get in the way.

Q: Why do you think self-control was important?

A: That's the way he got things done. That is certainly, his drive was to write novels, and that's the way he got novels done. Other people were not anxious to write novels:they might have other concerns—getting a dissertation finished, writing of a different nature, even playing golf. The chair of the department very often disappeared in order to play golf—that was important to him, that's where he placed his importance. But Bern was going to write, and as you undoubtedly remember, he had a daily routine, also of writing—and that is he would be at his desk at nine o'clock in the morning. Even if he didn't know what he was going to say, he would sit at his desk—he told me this—he would have paper and pencil in front of him and then suddenly a word or two or phrase or sentence might wander in. The first writing of the day would come out, and then that would lead to something else and lead to something else, and off he would be for the day. Well, he quit at noon or slightly after, had lunch very often, sometimes went home, and came back again. He edited in the afternoon till about four o'clock or so, then went home and had a nap and then it was supper time and evening was devoted either to reading or entertaining. You can remember that, can't you? I never heard of his ever writing in the evening—writing was a morning occupation. Afternoon was going over it and rewriting it possibly so that it was in handwriting that Ann could type from. Nobody else I've ever known has had as strong a control of himself as Bern did.

If one wants to have an inkling of his early life, I believe *The Assistant* is the key to it, because he did live above a grocery store [in Brooklyn in his youth]—his father was a grocer. One time that he and I disagreed I said, "Well, I really thing *The Assistant* is misnamed. My way of reading it is that the assistant is not the outstanding person in the book—it's the grocer—so I would call it *The Grocer* rather than *The Assistant*." He balked at that—he didn't agree with me at all. He obviously didn't think that that was a good argument. I've always felt that the grocer must have been a very close, loving, and respectful demonstration of his father.

In writing—and this is a matter of his writing process—he had various people in town who would be specialists in one thing or another, and he would very often consult them, particularly writing his academic novel. He used to call Larry Blaney, who was in horticulture, in order to make sure anything he said about flowers and trees was accurate. He called me up one night, at nine or ten o'clock, and said, "What car was that that you came to Corvallis in?" I said, "It was a Hudson." He said, "Well, do you have a picture of it?" I said, "Yes, I'll hunt around for it." So I showed him a picture of the Hudson. He never told me why he wanted it, but of course, it's the secondhand Hudson that was driven by the central character in *A New Life* to the coast. The only explanation I had for why he wanted that was that that person in going to the coast was being exploratory, and Bern must have been taken by the title "Hudson" because of the explorer Hudson.

It seemed to me this is the way he put things together. But he wanted the picture because he always, if he was going to describe something, wanted it to be accurate. Just as he had called Larry Blaney for flowers and trees, he would call me for furniture because I restored furniture, and he would call other people for various aspects.

Once Walter Foreman—the Director of Composition—had a strange experience. He went to the coast and stopped his car near a farmer who asked him to tie a string around his tooth and pull it out. He told Bern about this. Bern absorbed it, and it appeared as something that happened to the protagonist of *A New Life*. When Walter chided him about it, Bern had completely forgotten where he picked the story up. He used life, but he used it to advantage.

Another thing about *A New Life* that strikes me—there's a rather amazing inclusion of nature and appreciation of nature which he didn't have much opportunity to have before he lived here in Corvallis. Before that, he was enclosed by a city, for the most part. So people very often in reading *A New Life* comment, "Well, what a feeling this writer has for nature"—when the characters go on walks into the hills and so forth. This area was different for him—it was a bridge.

Warren Hovland

Bernie came to Oregon State just about the same time as I did—late forty-nine–fifty. This was a period right after the war. A number of veterans had come back. It was my first teaching job, just having completed my Ph.D. at Yale, and I believe it was Bernie's first college teaching job. We both had young families. In fact, his daughter, Janna, was born just about the same time as our son, Jeremy, and both had the same obstetrician and pediatrician at that time in Corvallis.

We were still really "Oregon Agricultural College," as it were, and it was our fortune to come to a place that was just open to becoming a real university. It was, I think, Bernie and a few of us who were really working hard to help make that possible. What is now the College of Liberal Arts was at that time called the Lower Division. We used to ask, "Lower than what?"—it had a pretty low position in the order of things. There was a real lack of understanding of the humanities and liberal arts; and Bernie was a part of this group that felt we could do something to change that.

Oregon State is stuck in rural Oregon, and I think this was a real contrast to New York City for Bern. He loved the countryside—he loved the flora and fauna. He loved to walk—he walked to work. Some of that picture certainly comes through in *A New Life*. But this was a real change of lifestyle for him.

What he did was to work with a group to create a number of things that carried on to enhance the liberal arts and the humanities. He was a part of the group that planned the first surge of Liberal Arts Lectures, that brought faculty and lecturers to discuss the role of the humanities and so forth. He started the Foreign Film Festival, which continues today. It was a new thing to bring foreign films to Oregon State. [I remember his thrill at showing, and mine at watching, Chaplain's *Gold Rush*—ed.] He was a great supporter of a group that my wife and I and others in the English department worked on called "Reader's Theater." This was a community group, not run by the college, kind of an arts theater. We did read Moliere and Sophocles and Ionesco and Shaw out loud, so that was something to raise the understanding of the arts. This led to the formation of the present Arts Theater in Corvallis. With him and others there was a new interest in chamber music and a series which continues today.

Bernie was a disciplined writer—a very hard worker. His writing habits were such that it required a tremendous discipline, and it was known in the department and the community that when he was engaged in his writing, that was sacred time, and no one was to disturb him from that. As a teacher, I think he found students really unprepared for the kind of scholarship and discipline that he was used to and demanded. Although he was patient with them, I think he was disappointed at the level of their background and expectations. He did, however, offer courses in creative writing for older people in the community through some night courses, and was much appreciated for that.

He was a generous friend. I think he had a tremendous capacity for friendship. I suppose one of the things that attracted everyone to Bernie was his sense of humor. I don't know all the origins of it. There was in his spirit a kind of Hasidic joy in life, and it was coupled with a sense of irony—this tendency to blithely put his finger on pretense and so forth— perceptive observations of people around him—details—that comes through, of course in his writing. But as very generous friends, he and Ann provided hospitality for many young couples and they entertained graciously on limited resources.

I'd say that his philosophic and spiritual orientation was basically humanistic. I think throughout his writing and thinking he was probing the question, "What does it mean to be a full human being?" and I think he continued to point out the human potential, and attempted show that though we may all of us be bumbling and a bit of a schlemiel, we were always able to recognize something of our best self. Showing that potential, he pointed out that people could always be better than they are.

I do remember also that we joined with him and other friends for Seder festivals in the Memorial Union with the Hillel group, and although he didn't identify himself as part of any particular religious community I've always felt he was a deeply religious man.

Bern didn't really like to travel very much, but he made frequent trips to the coast—and some of his expeditions to the coast ended up in his writings and in our memory. What Sue and I treasure are the memories of the family visits.

I remember traveling to Seattle with the Malamud family in our car, because Bernie didn't like to drive long distances. I remember that weekend because that's when both the Malamuds and the Hovlands saw *Wild Strawberries* for the first time. Then, of course, our daughter, Anne, was baptized when she was four years old—and we asked Bernie and Ann to be godparents. That was in Randolph, Vermont, in nineteen sixty-four, and Bernie suggested the Yeats poem, "For My Daughter," which is a beautiful expression of any father's feeling about a daughter.

As new books emerged from his pen there was always a copy to us and he was most gracious in our reflections and responses to them.

A kind of funny incident that we recall—a lunch at Mo's in Newport [a small town near the Oregon coast] with Bern and Ann. Afterwards, he said, "I'd like some ice cream." Well, there was a Dairy Queen kind of outfit that had a list of twenty-eight flavors, and Bern in a very light-hearted mood composed a kind of an opera, in which he made use of these twenty-eight flavors as the characters in his little skit.

•

Chapter 3

REMEMBRANCES
Bernard Malamud

Cynthia Ozick

In 1976 I answered the telephone and heard privately an instantly recognizable public voice. I knew this voice with the intimacy of passionate reverence. I had listened to it in the auditorium of the 92nd Street Y reading an as yet unpublished tale called "The Silver Crown," a story so electrifying that I wished with all my heart that it was mine. Since it was not, I stole it. In my version, I described the author of the stolen story as "very famous, so famous that it was startling to see he was a real man. He wore a conventional suit and tie, a conventional haircut and conventional eyeglasses. His whitening mustache made him look conventionally distinguished. He was not at all as I had expected him to be—small and astonished, like his heroes."

His voice on the telephone was also not what I had expected. Instead of bawling me out for usurping his story, he was calling me with something else in mind. He had noticed that the dedication to a collection containing the stolen story was to my daughter, who was then ten years old. "Joy of my life," I had written. "I have to tell you," he said, "that I understand just how you feel." And he spoke of his own joy in being the father of his own children—but in such a way that it was clear he understood love as something both particularized and capacious, belonging to every-one. The more you have of it yourself, the more you see it everywhere. A magic barrel. When after a while we hung up, I recognized that I had been visited through this awkward instrument by an angel. I had been blessed, anointed, by an illumination of generosity fetched up out of the marrow of human continuity. Malamundian annunciations are not overly fussy, and are sometimes willing to materialize as birds or talking horses or even on the telephone.

After that, it became possible to say hello on occasion, face to face. But I always found this difficult. His largeness afflicted my courage. This, after all, was the very writer who had brought into being a new American idiom of his own idiosyncratic invention; this was the writer who had in-troduced the idea of blessing—a virtue as insight, virtue as crucible—into the literature of a generation mainly sunk in aestheticism or nihilism or solipsism. The last time I saw him on a public platform—he was standing before the historic lectern at Cooper Union—he was reading from a work in progress, and since this was not so long ago, I imagine a grieving table upon which an unfinished chapter liturgically murmurs its loss. That meticulous and original hand will not come again. The reading at Cooper Union: a straight back, a straightforward voice, tricky cadences hidden in it, an audience intensely alert to the significance of its own memory, taking in Presence and sending back the hunger of its homage. Afterward, there was, as always, the knot of admirers at his margins. But I fled him, afraid of so much light.

Consequently, I never learned, or never dared, to say "Bern." So I set-tled on "Maestro," and it seemed just right, not merely because it reflected the stories with Italian landscapes but because he is, and always will be, one of our Masters.

Is he an American Master? Of course. He not only wrote in the Amer-ican language, he augmented it with fresh plasticity, he shaped our En-glish into startling new configurations. Is he a Jewish Master? Of course. Some people appear to be confused by why he resisted being called a Jewish writer. I think I have this figured out, and it may be simple enough. It troubled him, and he was right to be troubled, that the term *Jewish writer* sometimes carries with it the smudge of so-called ethnicity, a cataloguing of traits or vulnerabilities in place of meaning. *Jewish writer* is a usage that often enough smacks of parochialism. And when it is put to that purpose it is a plain lie. The Jewish spirit is the opposite of ethnicity or parochialism, and this cry out of Sinai is all over the Maestro's work. It is everywhere.

"The important thing," Morris Bober says to Frank Alpine, "is the Torah. This is the Law—a Jew must believe in the Law . . . This means to do what is right, to be honest, to be good. this means to other people. Our life is hard enough. Why should we want to hurt somebody else? For everybody should be the best, not only for you and me. We ain't animals. This is why we need the Law. This is what a Jew believes." Artists are never equivalent to their own characters, this goes without saying; but it is also true that to separate certain characterological strains from the blood and lungs of their maker is to do violence to the force of authorial conscience. Morris Bober is the whole soul of Malamud's sacral knowledge; no one can gainsay that. And in his own language, in the preface of *The Stories of Bernard Malamud,* he wrote: "And let me say this. Literature, since it values man by describing him, tends to morality in the same way that Robert Frost's poems are 'a momentary stay against confusion.' Art celebrates life and gives us our measure." So if this Maestro of humanity protested the phrase *Jewish writer,* it was the imputation of parochialism he was, with furious justice, repudiating. Whoever thinks of Jewish writers as "ethnic" has long ago lost the origin, intent, and meaning of our civilization; or, worse yet, believes that conscience and mercy are ethnic traits.

I danced with him once. We linked arms—wasn't this in Donald Barthelme's living room in the Village?—and twirled together. It was a wedding party, and the only music available was in the strong throat of the Israeli writer Matti Megged, who sang in Yiddish, a song about a frolicsome rabbi with certain affinities to Old King Cole. The Rabbi Eli Melech calls for his fiddlers, his drummers, his cymbal-players; his phylacteries fly from him, his robes; he goes rollicking with the sexon, he cavorts, he carouses, he drinks! To this tune the Maestro and I danced, arm in arm, and will do it again, I trust, when the International PEN Congress meets at last in the Garden of Eden, in Paradise.

He wrote about suffering Jews, about poor Jews, about grocers and fixers and birds and horses and angels in Harlem and matchmakers and salesmen and rabbis and landlords and tenants and egg chandlers and writers and chimpanzees; he wrote about the plentitude and unity of the world. And that is why, in his memory and for his sake, I want to recite the Shi'ma, which calls us to listen to the indivisible voice of Unity, of Allness—that Unity and Allness in whose image all mankind is made, wellworn words that are found on the living and dying lips of every Jew

שמע ישׁדאל יי אלהינר יי אהד

[Hear, O Israel, the Lord our God, the Lord is One]

—that comprehensive vision of mercy under whose wings we stand. May the memory of this great and humane Master be blessed and forever green. As it will be, as long as there are readers.

Chapter 4

MALAMUD
Seen and Unseen

Daniel Stern

There was something of a chasm between experiencing Bern Malamud as a friend and as a writer. I have rarely seen a clearer proof of Proust's remark, "The person you see is not the person who writes the books." And yet, and yet . . . I remember thinking, after we met, after we became close, that he was mysterious as a human being as well as an artist. There was much given and much held in reserve. He was available, helpful, richly involved in a friend's life. And yet there was always some held back, private—something perhaps he was not even aware of. I think he felt, with his somewhat austere vision of life that friends had somehow to earn each other. I think, except as an artist, he was not entirely available to himself.

Quite late in his life, Malamud began receiving even more honors than he had as a young writer. Typically he received these with a certain irony mixed with pleasure. He confided to my wife that they were "like rocks falling on my head." One of the more mysterious remarks from a mysterious man and writer.

His special concerns were suffering, pity, redemption and the magical possibilities of joy. Once, when we played chamber music at our home, performing the great Schubert C Major Quintet with two cellos, Malamud walked up to me when we'd finished and said, "Danny—you don't know what we felt sitting there, listening to the music, *tormented by joy.*" A perfect Malamud contradiction.

I was reminded of this when, in the first hours after his death I turned, as I usually do in times of pain, to poetry—remembering the lines Auden wrote which he could have written as a description of Malamud's whole creative enterprise:

> Sing of human unsuccess
> In a rapture of distress.

The reverse of Malamud's remark, "tormented by joy." It cuts both ways.

His special territory is also the comic distance between our yearnings, our ideals and the comic disappointments we endure in their pursuit—as well as the presence of the magical in everyday life. To this end he often uses the mythic, the legendary, as tools to take measure of that distance.

He also uses his uncanny gift for the condensed poetics of deceptively plain language. Consider the opening lines from his story "Idiot's First":

> The thick ticking of the tin clock stopped. Mendel dozing in the dark, awoke in fright. The pain returned as he listened. He drew on his cold embittered clothing, and wasted minutes sitting on the edge of the bed.

The iambic accents of that first sentence, the clarity of the image, the daring choice of the word *embittered* to describe a man's clothing—and in passing in a word, his life—this is a master at work.

By the time I met Malamud he'd already published *The Natural, The Assistant,* "The Magic Barrel," and *A New Life*—and was known in the smaller literary circles as an important artist. *The Magic Barrel* had won the National Book Award in 1957. (Bern told me privately that he'd received exactly thirty-five dollars for the title story from the *Partisan Review,* a sum, he added, that was quite welcome to a struggling writer. He was not complaining.) By the time he published *The Fixer,* a few years later, he was more widely known. It was, for a short while, a best-seller—Malamud's first and only best-seller—it won the Pulitzer Prize and was made into a film starring the British actor Alan Bates. The screenwriter, a formerly blacklisted writer named Dalton Trumbo, sent him a copy of the screenplay. When Bern asked why there wasn't more of the humor of the book in the movie, Trumbo replied, "We didn't want it to be too Jewish."

The Fixer, as many know, was based on a famous case of the nineteenth century—the Mendel Beiliss case. The accusation of ritual murder made against the poor Jewish peddler turned it into a case that became famous all over Europe. Malamud had heard about it as a child and it haunted him. Interestingly enough, when my wife and I would make one of our visits to the Malamuds' house in Bennington, Vermont, where he lived and taught for many years, the guest bedroom had bookcases—as did most of the rooms—and there I saw a great many books on, of all things, the Dreyfus affair. It seems that Bern had been considering the Dreyfus affair for a long time, instead of the Beiliss case. I think his choice of the lesser known case was an instance of the perfect pitch writers need in choosing their subject matter. The Dreyfus affair, written by about everyone and chewed over in every language, would have dwarfed Malamud's bitter, linguistic irony. The Beiliss case was his—to make his own.

Three of his works were made into films: "Angel Levine," *The Fixer*, and *The Natural*—this last, the only successful film, at least in terms of the public. Malamud actually saw it twice and told me he thought it was a good movie, though it was not, as he put it, *his* book.

The Natural was filmed by and with Robert Redford. And here, too, Bern felt it was not "his book." But paradoxically, and you could always count on him for paradox, he liked the film and saw it not once but twice. "Angel Levine" was, he agreed, botched by a very good director, Jan Kadar (who had directed a small Jewish classic, *The Shop on Main Street*), with a potentially extraordinary cast including Zero Mostel and Harry Belafonte. No one could explain what went wrong, but it was considered by Malamud and his friends, as well as the movie community, to be a failure. Elliot Gould held an option for years and years on *A New Life*. It has never been made.

We talked a lot about Hemingway's attitude toward the filming of his works. They couldn't change what was on the page—you take the money and run—and hope for the least embarrassment possible. I should say not "run" but walk" because you learned quickly that, to be a friend of Malamud's, *you walked!* With little consideration given to the difficulties. I have walked with that man in the rain in Vermont, in the snow in New York—in country cold and city heat. And—with the walks came the talk—the gradual unfolding, each time, of a most private man—the delicate circling of sensitive subjects—followed by the startlingly bold questions dealing, sometimes in an astonishingly direct way, with the people we cared about . . . subjects we were passionate about . . . and, always, inevitably, arriving at the bedrock: the question of writing.

He was, as everyone knows, a man compelled. He hit that study every morning and wrote and wrote. His attitude toward revision was quasi-religious. If you didn't revise you were short-changing the work, yourself and the reader. Not long before he died, he confided to my wife that he basically took three years on a novel: the first year he got the story down. The second year he revised and organized into its final form.

The third year he perfected the language, so that it said everything he wished it to say.

He was a time-haunted man; it was if he knew his clock was ticking faster than some other men's, and faster than all the work he had to do. I think of Keats' lines: "When I have fears that I may cease to be/before my pen has gleaned my teeming brain"—and I think, whether Bern consciously thought that, he lived and worked as if he did.

Sometimes a short story would trouble him over one small detail. He would ask people, question them, intently as to experiences and motives. But he told me that after he wrote *The Fixer*, which took place in Czarist Russia, he took a trip to Russia and when he came back he didn't have to change a word. So much for research versus imagination.

I think that, toward the end, when he was exploring deep new territories, as with *God's Grace* and "The People," he may have felt a little uncertain. But only in his anxieties. I think he struggled more with these last books than earlier, because he was striking out into bold new areas. He once called me when I was living in Los Angeles and he was beginning a new book. "I don't want to write," he said, "another Malamud character." I think he was referring, indirectly, to the categories and pigeonholes in which some critics placed him. The new book was *The Tenants*, a bold new approach which, I believe, has not received the full acclaim it deserves. It is not only a daring attempt to deal with the problems between Blacks and Jews; Malamud was drawing a map of the mysterious creative process of writing. I think that he was and is one of the few major voices in mid- to late-twentieth-century writing. In particular he remains one of the handful of great short story writers of all time.

To understand what writing was to Bernard Malamud you have to go back to the generation before him—the generation of Yeats and Joyce. Here was a man to whom—as to them—the act of imaginative writing enclosed all the metaphysics, politics, and yes, all morality. (Though he was not one for the moralistic—if you were moralistic you had a lecture not a work of art.)

He came as close to making a religion of art as is possible; a religion of suffering and comedy, taking the Jew as his starting point for what was most human in humankind. All men are Jews, though not all men know it—perhaps his most famous and mysterious line. This Jew he took through many incarnations, legendary, fanciful, and fantastic. Friends of mine who had read his books and then met Bern were often amazed that this wild imagination was encased in a neatly turned out man who seemed more schoolteacher than artist. Let alone an artist who had invented a unique Bestiary which included a Talking Horse who longed for freedom, a victimized Jewbird named Schwartz, and a gorilla becoming gradually human and Jewish at the same time.

I too was amazed time and again. From what deep source came that magician's art—that wild joke at the heart of cruel existence? That pratfall lurking around the corner where lovers embrace?

He took on—like it or not—the thankless task of being a kind of artistic conscience for me—as, no doubt, for many others. I wrote to him, once, in a difficult period in my work—I was in pain and I guess pain makes children of us all. He wrote back in consolation and patience, and patient consolation makes parents of us all, if only for a moment. He wrote:

> Maybe its that time of life. We all hunger to know what's next and the answer seems to reside within. The self plays with matches, ignorance burns and the self in flames is not easy to contend with. But to get more, better, from the self you have to give more, better to life. You base a comic character on the self and learn from his performance. . . . What is basic to living (living good rather than well) must be fought for first and forever. But make resolutions without punishing yourself beyond reason. And enjoy your life because it respects you. . . . You are rich and fragile at the same time . . . the "you" is for me, too.

This letter, many years ago, from a man who had been rewarded perhaps less than any major writer in America, up till that time. It's easy to understand why it gave all of us who loved and admired him so much pleasure when the appreciation of his work grew and grew in these final few years. The last time we spoke, he told me with a kind of marveling that young people were writing him and saying: "Mr. Malamud, your work has changed my life . . . or, because of you I'm going to be a writer." The world woke up; the BBC wanted an interview, Japan beckoned, the Italy in which he'd lived years before gave him a major literary prize. Awards, honors—it all seemed to happen at once. And he followed the paradoxical advice he'd given me: he enjoyed his life because it respected him.

He was a kind of true North; an absolute integrity about the conduct of life, and a clear, though never simple, idea of what it takes to be a Mensch. It takes courage. It takes love. It takes *everything!* In his daily conversation as in his writing the word *human* was invested with a value as in no other writer I can think of, Menschlichkeit . . . human-ness.

He once wrote to me: "To write seriously today requires, it seems to me, unending courage. Poor writers. Bravo uns."

Chapter 5

ON *THE MAGIC BARREL*

Nicholas Delbanco

I first met Bernard Malamud in 1966. I was an ambitious boy of twenty-three, with a debut novel about to appear and the self-confident conviction that I could and should replace him while he took a leave of absence from his teaching job. He was leaving Bennington College for what turned out to be a two-year stint in Cambridge, Massachusetts; I drifted into town and was hired—astonishingly, I still believe—by elders who saw something in this junior they might shape. By the time the Malamuds returned, I was happily ensconced as their near neighbor in Vermont; over the years we grew close.

The relation was avuncular; though Bennington's faculty is unranked, Malamud was much my senior colleague. It was and is a small school and town, and the Language and Literature Division seemed very small indeed. We attended committee meetings and movies and concerts and readings and poker games together; we shared meals and walks. When I married, in 1970, the Malamuds came to the wedding; when they gave a party we helped to cut the cake. With no hint of condescension he described me as his protegé; I asked for and took his advice. My wife's daybook bulks large with collective occasions: cocktails, picnics, weddings, and funerals shared. In times of celebration or trouble—when our daughters were born or had birthdays, during the years I served as Director of the Bennington Writing Workshops, at ceremonies in his honor, or when in failing health Bern needed a hand with a suitcase or car—we saw each other often. At his death on March 18, 1986, it seemed to me and to my wife and children that we had lost a relative. The loss endures.

So I can't and won't pretend to critical distance; this is an author I loved and admire. At his best he strikes me as an enduring master of this ending century, and his best consists of the early novels (*The Natural, The Assistant, A New Life*) and a baker's dozen of short stories. Though lumped—to his disgruntlement—with that of other "Jewish" writers from Singer to Bellow to Roth, the prose was nonpareil. And the terms of appreciation feel oxymoronic as soon as applied: his is a magical realism, a simple complexity, a practiced naturalness. My guess is that, when the dust settles and those critics to whom we look forward look back, the work will loom large within our art's terrain—in the forest a tall tree. For his concerns are timeless not timebound, his preoccupations lasting and diction not likely to date.

At Bennington, in 1984, Bernard Malamud delivered a lecture titled "Long Work, Short Life." Its closing assertions are characteristic in diction and stance: self-assured yet modest, a high priest of aesthetics who's wearing a business suit.

> I have written almost all my life. My writing has drawn, out of a reluctant soul, a measure of astonishment at the nature of life. And the more I wrote well, the better I felt I had to write.
>
> In writing I had to say what had happened to me, yet present it as though it had been magically revealed. I began to write seriously when I had taught myself the discipline necessary to achieve what I wanted. When I touched that time, my words announced themselves to me. I have given my life to writing without regret, except when I consider what in my work I might have done better. I wanted my writing to be as good as it must be, and on the whole I think it is. I would write a book, or a short story, at least three times—once to understand it, the second time to improve the prose, and a third to compel it to say what it still must say.
>
> Somewhere I put it this way: first drafts are for learning what one's fiction wants him to say. Revision works with that knowledge to enlarge and enhance an idea, to reform it. Revision is one of the exquisite pleasures of writing: "The men and things of today are wont to lie fairer and truer in tomorrow's meadow," Henry Thoreau said.

I don't regret the years I put into my work. Perhaps I regret the fact that I was not two men, one who could live a full life apart from writing: and one who lived in art, exploring all he had to experience and know how to make his work right; yet not regretting that he had put his life into the art of perfecting the work.

Story after story and chapter after chapter represent this process of revision, a series of stages—sometimes as many as eighteen drafts—from holograph to galley proofs wherein the prose gets reworked. Malamud hand-wrote the *third* draft of *The Assistant*, for example, after his wife had typed a second draft from the handwritten first. Outline after outline and query after query provide a kind of "lesson plan," as though the habits of the high school teacher stayed deeply ingrained in the famous professional author; he became his own instructor in the subject and the discipline of art.

Henry James went out to dinner three hundred times a season and kept his notebooks assiduously; why should a chance remark at table have engendered *Portrait of a Lady*, and the next remark be merely gossip to his ear? Tolstoy read the paper each morning; why should an article about a woman and a train have engendered *Anna Karenina*, and the adjacent article about a man and carriage, say, have caused him, yawning, to turn the page? The world is full of instances, of stimuli; the question for the writer is more properly perhaps: what causes our response? How may one recognize a subject or, in Malamud's phrase, learn "what one's fiction wants him to say."

For once he *did* respond to or recognize a subject he left very little to chance. He filled notebook and journal with citations and quotations and articles and buttressing data; if his character went walking, he listed the flowers by season; if he read about the Nez Percés, he listed—for possible use in his character's sojourn in the region—authentic tribal names. He was not some sort of muse-blessed athlete of the pen, a Roy Hobbs write-alike with no hitch in swing or stride. Rather, his notebooks, letters, and his ruminations on art attest to a thoroughly self-conscious and disciplined writer—a picture at important odds with the widespread public notion of this artist as a "natural."

"There's no one way," as he remarked. "There's so much drivel about this subject . . ." Yet in little and large ways over the years he addressed himself unstintingly to problems both of character and craft. He was scrupulous as to procedure, systematic in his methodology, and retentive of his "by-blows"; in the age of the computer and the daily discard of revision it's improbable we'll find again so comprehensive a roadmap of one mind's terrain.

～

In 1997 his publishers produced an omnibus collection of short stories, with a jacket photo of a well-dressed Malamud in the New York streets. They are right to call attention to the body of the work, the bulk of it, and to remind forgetful readers of how long and much he wrote. But I prefer the rigorous triage he himself performed in 1983, choosing *The Stories of Bernard Malamud*. It's a telling title: reticent yet declarative, not "collected" or "selected," just *the stories*. No small thing.

In that book "The Magic Barrel" is of course included; it was the title tale of his first short story collection, the National Book Award recipient for 1958. The piece itself feels quintessential, and he wrote a useful lecture on its composition. That lecture—also called "The Magic Barrel"—has been published in its entirety in *Talking Horse: Bernard Malamud on Life and Work* (eds. Alan Cheuse and Nicholas Delbanco [New York: Columbia University Press, 1996]). Were there space enough and time, I would reproduce his notes verbatim; instead I urge the interested reader to consult the essay; it records his painstaking progress from first idea to final draft— from a vague notion that Chagallean imagery should enter into his prose to a discussion with his wife as to his ability to love. "First there is a note in my journal, dated March 8, 1954: It reads: 'Go back to the poetic, evocative, singing—often symbolic short story . . .'" Then entries span the period from August 21, 1954, to September 14, 1954, a relatively rapid time span, since once he did compose the tale he did so at some speed. The very first notation provides the dénouement:

> The young man somehow gets the girl. Not sure what the miracle is but he's got to do something that satisfies everyone but the m.b. He (the m.b.) has to be disappointed yet resigned. Once I work out the meaning of the piece I'll have the ending. Season with Chagall?

What Malamud would later call his "sad and comic tales" assume their definition in this template-text. First conceived of as "The Marriage Broker," it engages many of his oft-recurring motifs: beauty and morality, romance and realistic aspiration, paternal love and disappointment, two men at odd odds with each other. This agon between paired protagonists would be repeated again and again; such stories as "The Jew-Bird" and such novels as *The Tenants* are, in this regard, variations on a theme. The tone is vintage Malamud: rueful yet humorous, fast-paced yet meditative, an Old World circumstance translated to this Brave New World, yet with the bite and flash of inflected speech.

It might be worth repeating that our author was *not* an immigrant and *not* native to or fully fluent in Yiddish; the locale of *The Assistant* remained his native ground. As his notebook indicates, he reached back into Yiddish folklore and literature for a kind of collective memory, but the fashioning of that material was both highly conscious and wholly wrought.

> The idea for the story itself, the donnée, came about through Irving Howe's invitation to me to translate a story from the Yiddish for inclusion in his and Eliezer Greenberg's anthology called *A Treasury of Yiddish Stories.*
> My reading in Royte Pomerantzen provided the six marriage anecdotes—two of which were very important.

From literature, then, and collective researched experience stems the particular case. As Malamud observed, "I have never made a study of the main sources of literary material but I imagine they can be divided into two obvious categories: that of autobiography and sources other than oneself." Leo Finkle the rabbinical student and Pinye Salzman, who "smelled frankly of fish," manage somehow to be at one and the same time stock characters and, in their behavior, original. The *luftmensch* Salzman is a familiar type, a weightless man who lives on air, "though I had never met a marriage broker." And Finkle too carries somewhere about him the whiff of personal history—a lonely, romantic, and studious person in a rooming house. What matters here, however, is invention. The fierce and vivid circumstance, the colloquial austerity of language, the unexpected plot twists that, in retrospect, feel foreordained: all these signal mastery.

As does the wit. Much of "The Magic Barrel" is humorous—the reeking Salzman, the vaudeville series of slammed doors, appearances and disappearances, the comic disjunction between the advertised and actual truth about the hopeful ladies in the marriage broker's file. There is a series of missed signals that verge on the burlesque. But, as is always the case with this author, the laughter shades to grief: "my sad and comic tales" entail both penury and poverty; when a figure in Malamud's fiction weeps, the tears are real not feigned.

Which brings me to the story's close, its problematic final line: "Around the corner, Salzman, leaning against a wall, chanted prayers for the dead." Is Salzman's daughter dead to him, or has he somehow also died, or is the mourning general and Kaddish all-inclusive? Is Salzman deluded; is Leo; is the girl irredeemably whorish or about to be redeemed? Years later, in his final finished book, *God's Grace*, the author would complete his fable of all-leveling catastrophe in a markedly similar vein. George the gorilla has been taught both religion and language by Calvin Cohn, the lone survivor of thermonuclear war. When the paleologist also dies, his disciple dons "a mud-stained white yarmulke he had one day found in the woods. . . . In his throaty, gruff voice he began a long Kaddish for Calvin Cohn."

Yet there's salvation in the lovers' story, surely. "Violins and lit candles revolved in the sky. Leo ran forward with flowers outthrust." Here we see Chagall translated from the canvas to the page, and to the young couple at least the story's end looks happy. Malamud himself announced, "Don't worry about the ending. If you think about it it will come to you," but the "desperate innocence" of Salzman's daughter is at least in part offset by her corrupted worldliness. That star-struck creature, Leo, may be embracing ruination when he offers "Stella" a bouquet.

And there's a grace note, too, of the suspicion that the marriage broker has orchestrated all of this, even at the risk of his own forfeited commission; perhaps he sees in Finkle his daughter's last best hope. Nothing in the scene is simple; nothing means only one thing. "Stella stood by the lamppost, smoking. She wore white with red shoes, which fitted his expectations, although in a troubled moment he had imagined the dress red, and only the shoes white." When Leo "pictured, in her, his own redemption" is that picture accurate or wishful merely; is their happiness provisional or lasting; what wall does Pinye lean against, and why?

This, from *Pictures of Fidelman: an Exhibition.* Here we have the same self-deprecating intensity of effort as that which bedevils Leo Finkle; the locus has shifted from rabbinical studies to painting, but the harsh imperatives of work remain the same:

> The copyist throws himself into his work with passion. He has swallowed lightning and hopes it will strike whatever he touches. Yet he has nagging doubts he can do the job right and fears he will never escape alive from the Hotel du Ville. He tries at once to paint the Titian directly on canvas but hurriedly scrapes it clean when he sees what a garish mess he has made. The Venus is insanely disproportionate and the maids in the background foreshortened into dwarfs. He then takes Angelo's advice and makes several drawings on paper to master the composition before committing it again to canvas.
>
> Angelo and Scarpio come up every night and shake their heads over the drawings.
>
> "Not even close," says the padrone.
>
> "Far from it," says Scarpio.
>
> "I'm trying," Fidelman says, anguished.
>
> "Try harder," Angelo answers grimly.

Were there a motto for Malamud's performance as author-teacher, and a single instruction he gave to his students, it resides in the exchange above. *"I'm trying,"* says the anguished apprentice; *"Try harder,"* the master insists. From the "passion" of one who "has swallowed lightning" to the artist plagued by "nagging doubts . . . and fears" we may limn this writer's terrain. The imagination is allegorical and the plot lines have the force of parable; there's an insistent linkage of morality and art.

One hallmark of the work, of course, is this seeming-seamless blend of fact and fantasy—a magic realism that obtains in ballpark and island and tenement equally. Therefore in "The Magic Barrel" a photograph proves talismanic; for both the rabbinical student and the marriage broker, the snapshot of Salzman's errant daughter conjures blood-and-flesh. It's no small surprise to recognize that the story was composed more than forty years ago; if Cyril Connolly's definition of a masterpiece—a work that lasts a decade—be applied, then Malamud has managed to trick time.

His essay includes these final assertions as to the tale's origin; they are both wholly clear and opaque:

> Some other autobiographical elements are:
> 1. the rooming house.
> 2. in a sense, the time of year: between end of winter and spring is to me a very dramatic time.
> 3. the tomato, a detail from childhood

And here it's not inapposite to include two notes on *Dubin's Lives:* "One must transcend the autobiographical detail by inventing it after it is remembered. . . . If it is winter in the book spring surprises me when I look up."

To watch Bernard Malamud play poker was to observe him write. For years we shared a poker game in our little town. In the game there were faculty members from Bennington College, musicians, painters, sculptors; there was the local millionaire and the man who ran the gas station; we took turns playing host. Bern came properly dressed to table, arriving on the hour and departing when he'd said he would; well organized and solemn on those Thursday nights, he pursed his lips in concentration and adjusted his eyeglasses often and joked and chattered sparingly and allowed himself only one beer. The writer was serious rather than sportive; poker relaxed him, he said. But you couldn't tell that, really, from the way he played the game or how hard he studied the hand he was dealt and how he bet, bluffed, pondered, folded, raised. He kept his cards close to his chest.

It's simple truth to say he wasn't a good player, and that he had trouble figuring the odds. But night after night and week after month he defied those poker odds and came up with a perfect low or high full house or aces: he was patient, purposive, and went home a winner. So too with the great gamble of his imaginative word-work, though it was achieved in privacy: he sat at the table, studying, arranging, and discarding language until it grew unbeatable, then bet. . . .

For years before his death the Malamuds left Bennington during the harsh, grim winter and went south to their home in New York. Often Bern would call or write me asking for a favor—a note or draft or book or letter had been left behind and now was needed and would I mind collecting it and sending it on down? I had the house-key; I did not mind; I'd let myself in and find the needed passage and mail it to Manhattan. What was astonishing, always, was the precision of his files: if he told me where a book resided (which corner of which shelf) or a document could be located (which drawer of which cabinet), it came always precisely to hand.

In the case of "The Magic Barrel," clearly, the document itself has not been misplaced. One of the most celebrated stories in our literature, it need not be retrieved. But it comforts me to return, as it were, to his library shelf and find the necessary lines and be by them inspirited and send them on again. In the concluding passage of his own introduction to *The Stories of Bernard Malamud,* the author declares, "I've lived long among those I've invented." And Pinye Salzman, conjured back to life upon the page, has the last word. The Marriage Broker offers his "Professor" a fresh bride and, when his creator demurs, saying he already has one but is "hard at work on a new story," the old invented character withdraws. " 'So enjoy,' said Salzman."

An instruction to applaud, a sentence to repeat. "So enjoy," Delbanco says.

Note

Nicholas Delbanco is the co-editor, with Alan Cheuse, of *Talking Horse: Bernard Malamud on Life and Work* (New York: Columbia University Press, 1996) His own most recent novel is *Old Scores* (New York: Warner Books, 1997).

Chapter 6

THE RHYTHMS OF FRIENDSHIP IN THE LIFE OF ART
The Correspondence of Bernard Malamud and Rosemarie Beck

Joel Salzberg

> Your friendship and regard are the dearest things I have. . . .
>
> —RB to BM, March 19, 1961

> All joys are not retrospective; friendship is a continuing joy.
>
> —BM to RB, July 9, 1962

Friendship is not a word that Bernard Malamud took lightly. In particular, epistolary friendship with other writers and artists offered him momentary release from the uncompromising discipline he demanded of himself on behalf of his fiction. For Malamud, such friendship, especially early in his career, became a form of communion with those who shared his

Reprinted from *Salmugund: Journal* 47 (Fall–Winter 1977): 61–75.

commitment to the life of art. Although his correspondence was often spo-
radic, even with those he most admired, and lacked the extended ex-
changes that one usually finds in collections of published letters, there is
one notable exception: an epistolary friendship with Rosemarie Beck, a little-known, New York-based painter who still exhibits and gives lectures
on painting.[1] In a phone conversation with me, Ann Malamud, the author's widow, observed that the Malamud-Beck correspondence was the
most sustained and the most interesting of any in her late husband's files.
Accordingly, in 1990 she gave both sets of letters to the Berg Collection of
the New York Public Library.

Malamud wrote sixty-seven autographed letters signed to Beck, four
autographed letters not signed, ninety-three typed letters signed, one
typed letter not signed, and thirty-two postcards between September 23,
1958, and July 23, 1985. Beck wrote sixty-four autographed letters signed,
eighty-nine typed letters signed, and nine postcards to Malamud between
February 6, 1961, and August 26, 1985. Her letters to Malamud prior to
February 6, 1960, are lost, although Beck found copies of several of those
earlier letters, which she sent directly to me.

If there is one leitmotif that resonates throughout the approximately
three hundred letters that comprise the Malamud-Beck correspondence,
it is that deceptively simple but complex word *friend,* along with the cor-
relative word *friendship.*[2] For the more demonstrative Beck, addresses
such as "Dear friend" or "Caro Mio" were often substituted for "Dear
Bernie." For the more restrained Malamud, the brooding self-revelations
in some of his letters to Beck concerning his artistic direction, progress,
and frustrations—or simply sharing intimate family news—were in
themselves sufficient confirmations of his commitment to their friendship. But even Malamud on occasion could sign off a letter with a "multo
affetto" or, in later years, with "love." Despite fundamental differences
in temperament, and the occasional clash of their artistic perceptions,
each valued the respect and affection of the other and thus let pass moments of irritation from well-intentioned but unwelcome criticism of
each other's work.

Rosemarie Beck was an obscure figure among such notable corre-
spondents in Malamud's files, which include Saul Bellow, Philip Roth,
Alfred Kazin, I. B. Singer, Lionel Trilling, and John Updike. However,
the intimate confidences, both personal and artistic, exchanged in the
Malamud-Beck correspondence suggest that this friendship was perhaps the most complex that Malamud ever had. Moving in the same trajectory in their respective careers, each discovered in the other a
nurturing fellow artist along the way. When Malamud met Beck at the

Yaddo art colony in 1958, he was forty-four and she was thirty-five, and both had well-established marriages for over a decade. Bernard Malamud and Ann de Chiara were married in 1945 and had two children, Paul (1947) and Janna (1952). Rosemarie Beck was married to Robert Phelps in 1945, had one child Roger (1949), and remained married to him until his death in 1989.[3]

With the critical success of *The Natural* (1952) and *The Assistant* (1957) behind him and his first collection of stories, *The Magic Barrel* (1958), just out, Malamud appeared to Beck as wise, accomplished, and humane. Always an admirer of the art of painting, Malamud in turn found Beck a highly talented painter as devoted to her craft as he was to writing. Prior to their first meeting at Yaddo, Beck's work had been on exhibition at various New York galleries and had been favorably reviewed in several newspapers. A multitalented woman, Beck was often the recipient of Malamud's compliments: "You speak beautifully in three languages: words, music, and paint" (BM, July 2, 1960). Not only was Beck a gifted painter and an eloquent speaker but also she was a talented violinist who, for a time, played for the Woodstock String Quartet. Although she was chronically afflicted with self-doubt over the quality of her work, it should be no surprise that Malamud found in Beck a kindred spirit, whose personality complemented his own. While Malamud momentarily escaped his inherent formality and reserve through the emotional energy radiated by Beck's language and style, as well as her person, Beck found in Malamud a wise friend, a caring mentor, and a talented writer who was enthusiastic about her own potential as an artist. Often unsparing in her criticism of the work of other artists and writers, Beck's letters praising Malamud's fiction occasionally bordered on idolatry, but her language of adulation was, among other things, the glue that cemented this friendship over the years.

There were other sides to Beck—or, rather, rhetorical selves—variously expressed in her letters to Malamud. If Beck sometimes sounds like the worshipping apprentice or, at times, a knowledgeable critic, her voice could also sound maternal in its language and tone of nurturance. Surely these were qualities not to be lost on a Malamud who was deprived of his own mother at the age of fifteen, and who periodically alluded to her early death in interview, memoir, and, obliquely, his own fiction. Beck expressed concerns about Malamud's general well-being and also his literary future. This maternal tone, along with its more recognizably feminine counterpart, is characteristically one of the signatures of her letters.

Malamud was, first and foremost, a disciplined writer, who consulted his critical intelligence and not the stars when he crafted his stories. While part of him enjoyed Beck's feminine ministrations, and was both flattered and amused by her astrological speculations, he was not averse to censuring her when she used astrology, instead of her own artistic judgment, as a rationalization for her failures or successes:

> I am enormously conscious of form, the right place for the right idea, and it is form that I breed my ideas for; it is form, in a sense, that gives birth to them.
>
> So it was your bad aspects that "accounted for the failure" of your show? That makes it very easy. Why not never paint unless the aspects are good—then the show can't possibly fail, even when it hasn't [?] I sometimes wonder—please pardon me, I speak kindly—how you can tolerate seriously astrological "reasoning." It may be comforting in an escapist sort of way, and when used as Polly does in explaining your show, is certainly a form of rationalization. But what bothers me most about it is your need for it. I suppose it doesn't do any real harm to your art—Yeats had his theosophy, but it may to your knowledge of what the world is and what we can reasonably expect from life and the star-filled universe we are dust in. Unless you secretly use astrological predictions to shore yourself up when you need shoring, a sort of soft lying to the self, but in your heart know that it is you, and not your astrological houses, that is ultimately your power. Heraclitus cannot be denied: "A man's character is his fate." (BM, June 5, 1959)

As their friendship progressed, Malamud gradually overlooked Beck's astrological leanings, at least on his behalf as an artist, and even went so far as to put her hobby to use in the creation of his character Arthur Fidelman for the Fidelman stories, as we will subsequently see. But where does such collaboration often lead?

Seldom are friendships between men and women free of sexual stresses. If there is any implied romantic tension or suggestion of crisis in the Malamud-Beck relationship, it is introduced in one of Beck's letters to Malamud just after she used the language of astrology as a code for addressing their shared critical moment: "My dear, if we've really weathered last week's planetary barrage—to your Mars and Neptune, and to my Mars, from Jupiter, Saturn and Venus; besides, a waning moon—why we will be friends for life, better friends." In the same letter, Beck confided to Malamud her sense of inadequacy as a woman, and followed that declaration with an impassioned statement of how invaluable his friendship is to her: "Your friendship and regard are the dearest things I have, and the only things I have to give. . . . Do you know that I worked for 30 months under your blessed, unfaltering moral beacon with a firmer conviction than I'd ever before possessed, and it made me feel less greedy to believe that I served you a little bit this way too? It was my secret support; we were conspirators in the tiresome, dangerous, obsessive, sometimes gallant adventures of our separate crafts" (RB, March 19, 1961). In his reply to her letter, Malamud expressed amazement at Beck's self-abasement and regarded himself as being the beneficiary of her friendship: "I'd be crazy to give you up as a friend. Where do these fantastic doubts come from? Must I for the millionth time tell you your richness as a person, and my good fortune to have you as a friend? You say I've helped you; well know that you have helped me. I've never met anyone like you and I consider it a gift that I did. I do take pride in you as a woman and an artist. Frame this and put it somewhere to look at when you grow doubts" (BM, April 1, 1961).

What are we to make of words of admiration and praise that are delivered in a tone of affectionate irritation? Were they Malamud's way of maintaining the relationship but identifying its boundaries? While Malamud declared his appreciation for Beck both as an artist and as a woman, he maintained a degree of emotional reserve in his correspondence with her, yet he was capable of celebrating in the abstract the erotic glories of women in general: "One can get along without the opposite sex if he has to but I am far richer when I am with women. I love their beauty and read to their fruitfulness. My brain needs plenty of womb" (BM, August 14, 1959).

We do not know what Beck's response was to Malamud's apostrophe to women since her letters for this period are missing from the Berg Collection. However, Beck and Malamud's subsequent letters from 1960, and later, suggest that the critical episode was either buried or resolved, at least on Malamud's part. Eventually, Malamud moved beyond this awkward moment to celebrate his "Platonic" friendship with Beck in the style of an Emersonian epigram in the very first line of a subsequent letter three years later: "All joys are not retrospective; friendship is a continuing joy." Although in this instance, Malamud's euphoric praise of friendship was directed to Beck, and represents him in a moment of light-heartedness, there are occasions in his correspondence with others in which the value he placed on friendship caused him to speak of it with an almost forbidding moral earnestness. In one of his letters to John Hawkes, with whom he briefly corresponded, and whose work he held in esteem, Malamud suggested that both meet when Hawkes comes East, and concludes somewhat testily: "We can if we try; otherwise friendship's no more than talk" (BM, April 10, 1968). For Malamud, authentic friendship among fellow artists required a commerce of mind and spirit that involved face-to-face meetings, as he occasionally had with Beck.

The motives for friendship are usually various, sometimes complex, and often changing. It is clear that in Beck's case, her letters were written not only out of genuine esteem and affection but also in the belief that Malamud shared a similar distaste for the extremes of modernism that had begun to dominate contemporary art. Feeling isolated from her peers, the second and third generation followers of what was called the New York School, Beck felt that the success of someone such as Helen Frankenthaler, or even the later work of Robert Motherwell, had been achieved partly out of talent and partly out of modishness. These painters had embraced "risk" as an aesthetic principle and its corollary, the act of painting, as an end in itself, which Harold Rosenberg had labeled "action painting." Unlike her contemporaries, Beck felt that for herself "risk" was a matter of remaining committed to a largely representational art. In a lecture at Wesleyan University, delivered in May 1960, Beck observed: "We don't think in abstraction but in clotted materiality. . . . I have heard painters say they want to avoid the common inventory of things; they want the real subject of painting—its essence, its pure structure. They proceed directly out of the general (whereas painters of the past have begun almost always with the particular) from the *found* rather than the made; they are concerned with the wholes rather than the parts. The Means becomes Content and/or Subject."[4] Thus, apart from her exhibitions, her teaching of painting, and occasional lectures, Beck's letters to Malamud became for her a forum for asserting unfashionable ideological positions and a covert form of self-justification and self-empowerment.

While Beck received advice and support from Malamud on her painting, she in turn came to Malamud's aid when he was at low ebb. At a point at which he was having grave doubts about his ability to fuse historical issues with topical issues in the book that was to become *The Fixer*, Beck urged Malamud on as though his unfashionable enterprise—for so Malamud perceived it to be—of writing another novel about Jewish suffering was analogous to her own continuing painterly celebration of the human in art: "Perhaps you ought to make a secret rule that you cultivate and exceedingly nurture the side of your art that most disconcerts your admiring public (even your dearest friends) because it is, no doubt, the source of your genuine quality, your timelessness. And if I could wish anything away, it would be your fear of failure. . . . If you failed even badly, it would be more beautiful, more interesting than practically anyone else's success" (RB, November 9, 1963). In the context of her own self-assessments elsewhere in her correspondence, these remarks read as unintentionally self-directed.

No doubt with the purest of motives in mind, Beck regarded Malamud, despite his increasing success in the early 1960s, as another version of herself—that is, as a marginalized and not altogether appreciated artist.

At the same time, however, Beck also very subtly attempted to put her stamp on Malamud's approach to writing, a liberty, as we will later see, Malamud took with her painting. She observed: "Of the two Malamuds— the realist and the fantasist . . . I prefer the realist of *A New Life* and 'The Maid's Shoes'—that is my favorite story" (RB, October 10, 1963). In other letters to Malamud, she also reaffirmed her endorsement of Malamud the realist, as she encouraged him to develop the old man-young woman theme that was to be embodied much later in *Dubin's Lives* (1979). To be sure, it was Malamud who ultimately set the course for his literary direction, but he was not averse to using Beck's knowledge of astrology as a resource to invent the character of Arthur Fidelman, despite his earlier annoyance at Beck's dependency on her hobby for predicting her own success or failure:

> Can you get me Fidelman's horoscope[?] Lets say he was born Dec. 1, 1930, at 3:07 AM. I'm writing about him in June 1962. From about June 3 to June 16 he has been having a miserable painter's block—can't get the Venus right. What do you see in *his* Venus from June 16 to 30. When is a more propitious time for him? Why is he having trouble. Where is his Uranus, etc. Give me the business.
>
> All best
> Bern (BM, July 2, 1962)

After receiving the details of Fidelman's horoscope, Malamud responded with unusual exuberance: "The information is priceless and so are you" (BM, July 7, 1962). Following Malamud's expression of gratitude, Beck was quick to observe "that Fidelman's block might reside in his knowledge of Titian's process, his wishing to be true to it. His problem, poor nut, is insoluble, given time and conditions" (RB, July 11, 1962). Such collaboration between Malamud and Beck represents one of the mutually gratifying moments in their relationship.

The ongoing epistolary friendship between Malamud and Beck was not always, however, as Malamud had previously suggested, "a continuing joy." Instead, it sometimes resembled the onstage acerbic banter of Hume Cronyn and Jessica Tandy, as writer and painter engaged in well-meaning but perhaps tactless criticism of each other's work. In one instance, Malamud was annoyed by Beck's remark that he was "undressing in public" when, in one of his Bennington lectures, he discussed the origins of his story, "Idiots First" (BM, March 10, 1963). Beck, in turn, while acknowledging that she treasured Malamud's friendship, responded to his critical comments on a recent exhibition of her paintings at the Peridot Gallery in New York with a frank: "I'm *not grateful* for your *aesthetic evaluations*. . . . Happily,

I disagree with you, and that's all I'm going to say on the subject for now" (February 13, 1965). Beck's unusually tart reply was prompted by Malamud's well-intentioned critical judgments:

> There are some beautiful pictures, especially the smaller, simpler ones. The large paintings—please pardon my saying so—disappointed me somewhat, partly because they were too much like those in your previous show. Your strengths are forms and colors. You are magnificent in any object you paint; but I had the feeling this time of too many objects in the large pictures; the unity, the final composition was disturbed, hindered. And you are not finding new ways for your iconography. You have too much affection for everything you put down. In sum, there is a necessity for simplification and a new point of view. (BM, January 25, 1965)

Characteristically, Beck's enthusiasms or annoyances were never veiled, and her emotional candor often bordered on excess. In contrast, her response to Malamud's frank appraisal of her work is surely marked by restraint. For his part, Malamud was perilously balanced between his impulse to offer a reasoned critique of Beck's work and a desire to nurture her self-esteem. After reading Beck's response to his observations and suggestions, Malamud wrote again, but this time to apologize and explain himself. "My letter was badly done. I can imagine how I would have felt to have had something of the same sort from you. Part of my difficulty was in not wanting to say what I felt I had to say. . . . What bothers me now is, whether I am right or wrong, that I did not say it better, gently, with all the affection I feel for you" (BM, February 11, 1965).

At subsequent exhibitions, when Beck asked Malamud for his judgments, he also gave many of her paintings his approval and respect, reactions that were, for those who knew him, as scrupulous and honest as his criticisms of her earlier work. Addressing several of her paintings on exhibition in 1972, Malamud wrote: "I've never seen such an effective use of light and space, especially in landscape in your work. The composition is vivid, striking; the work is solid, lyrical, classic. I especially admire the Orpheus portrait, one of your very best. . . . The mythology nowadays is dangerous—it won't endear you to the critics" (BM, May 11, 1972).

Malamud and Beck did not always see eye to eye about each other's work, but they were often united in their condemnation of what they regarded as the wasteland of contemporary art. In 1965 Beck wrote: "There is nothing nourishing in the world of art now. Nothing even disreputable or idea-provoking. We've had 10 years of a jungle, and now it's the desert:

science or whatever you call this eye-punishing optical stuff. I adhere in my private disquisitions & in my classrooms to art as repository, hieratic truths, and to whatever feelings are still molten, anarchic, unformalized" (RB, March 8, 1965). Although Malamud indicated in his letters to Beck, as well as in interviews, an attraction to nonrepresentational and experimental art, in this instance he excelled Beck in his amusingly hyperbolic response to their offending excesses:

> The op-art shows are hard to take. I take little pleasure from them above the simplest, and trickiest esthetic satisfaction. I can't even call it satisfaction: it is that my eyes follow the command. To prove it they hurt and I come to the edge of nausea. Can I predict the next step in painting: more epater le viewer—the picture itself opens in the center, a mallet comes out and strikes the observer on the head. He sees stars, suns, asteroids, a double reaction. Where else can they possibly go from pop and op and electronic art? (This is what happens when one tries to fabricate what he must first see in a dream.) Another possibility of the new novelty is that the picture dispenses a capsule of LSD or a marijuana cigarette, and one imbibes or inhales for a better view of what is not there. (BM, March 28, 1965)

What gives this correspondence some of its more interesting rhetorical rhythms? If autobiography is a narrative of one's personal history, then correspondence as dialogue is the stuff of drama, particularly when writer and painter address each other's work, or the accomplishments of other artists and writers. The most graphic illustrations of the give and take with which Beck freely engages Malamud on questions about art are to be found in some of their earliest letters. Here, Malamud and Beck play out certain roles toward one and other, which are then turned around. For example, in what appears to be Malamud's first letter to Beck, he wrote to her as literary friend, mentor, and cultural critic, identities that she cultivated for him through the questions she raised in her own letters. In one moment, Beck is the eager and devoted friend and acolyte, and in the very next letter she may appear fiercely judgmental about matters of art, as well as proprietary and maternal, especially in rendering advice about his health.

In Malamud's first letter to Beck, he attempted to satisfy her curiosity about the source of the story "The Lady of the Lake." Addressing her with a touch of unconscious condescension, as "Rosemarie Dear," Malamud explained in some detail the origins of his story and followed his account of its genesis with an abbreviated lecture in the next paragraph on the dehumanization of man in modern writing. In the same letter he asked, "What questions have I not answered, Rosie?" (BM, May 1, 1959). The somewhat patronizing tone will largely disappear in the correspondence as Malamud, still young in his own professional career, recognized in Beck a confidante on whom he could comfortably unburden his own insecurities as an artist. The authority of the earlier Malamudian voice is soon displaced by one less secure, as he contemplated his potential beyond the euphoria of recent accomplishments.

Just after he had won the National Book Award for *The Magic Barrel* in 1959, Malamud was simultaneously buoyant and sobered by his very success. He confided to Beck his desire to penetrate the mysteries of his future in art: "I . . . want to know the secret of great strength. I never thought I would be a great writer, but I think it is possible to be a better one than I presently am. A very good friend, after reading *The Magic Barrel*, said he had the feeling that I hadn't used all my strength, that there is more in reserve. I'd like to prove that" (BM, April 3, 1959). Although Beck in other letters often sounded like a worshipful reader, as she did in her later rhapsodic praise of *A New Life* (not quoted), she could also be gently chastising and humorous in her attempt to have Malamud recognize the excesses in his own personality.

Referring in her 1959 letter to the recent success of *The Magic Barrel*, Beck suggested that Malamud now find leisure to enjoy life and his family, and she gently chided him for his preoccupation with the mystery of artistic greatness and the transformative power of art: "Do you know you are not a great writer? You say to me 'I hope you want to paint like a master.' What you should say to me is I should paint like myself (and that believe me is no small matter) and I should tell you the same. . . . Once we have gotten rid of all the mannerisms of a time and a style, the fear of losing face in the world of fashion; . . . then maybe we can shake hands with the masters or, at least, understand their humanity" (RB, ?, 1959). Beck was not receptive to Malamud's well-intended pleasantry that she paint like a master, and she responded as though he had touched a raw artistic nerve. In 1959 Beck's paintings were often semi-abstract and nonobjective, and when she distanced herself from such modernist conventions, Beck felt that she had sacrificed a wider acceptance of her work from her more avant-garde peers for the sake of her own authenticity—that is, as an artist whose true calling was to render recognizable human images.

In the same letter to Beck, Malamud had expressed his distrust "for this marvelous bit of magic" that in otherwise questionable men produces great art and, unlike them, he resolved to "use some of the talent to improve the person" (BM, April 3, 1959). Although Malamud admitted that such reflections sound like egotism, Beck was once again ready to give her own "lessons" to the master. On a satirical note, she asked him a series of hyperbolic rhetorical questions that eventually forced him to reconsider his own remarks. "Now, my dear," asked Beck, "what on earth do you mean by improving the person? . . . What is your theory of the person as 'stuff'? Will you practice moral exercises like ballet bars? Or will you practice patience like the saint; or loneliness like a hermit, or thrift like a defeated country[?]" (RB, ?, 1959). Beck went on to suggest that Malamud was already too good and that a little helpless folly would improve him. But then Malamud reestablished a renewed sense of purpose and authority at the end of this particular dialogue. He wrote to Beck a week later avoiding any reference to the irritating phrase of Beck's "painting like a master." Instead, he returned to a subject much closer to home: his position on "improving" the self. At the risk of having unintentionally trivialized one of the perennial themes of his fiction—the transformation of the self—he now explained to Beck, with greater elaboration than before, his philosophy of the "good" artist:

> What I wrote about "improving" the self perhaps came out a little pretentious. . . . We may not know what good means ultimately, but we know what it means to some extent. The good we embody is not all; there is more; an ideal is practical even when it is not realized, so long as it is there for the sake of those who may awaken to its beauty. When I say I want to be good, it is partly because good is beautiful; only thus may I become my own work of art. Many of us do too little with the self, starving it for art; but I think the art would be richer if the self were. The more the self comprises, in the sense of containing as well as understanding; in the sense of being able to "respond" to others, to their need for food of various kinds, as well as beauty, the richer the self is for life, for freedom, for the flight imagination takes from it, for the art it creates. Life, humanity, is more important than art. (BM, April 10, 1959)

Comparable paragraphs from Malamud to Beck verging on the informal or expository essay are interwoven throughout his letters and establish one of the dominant rhythms of the friendship. Despite her barbed wit and fierce independence, Beck made it clear from the very beginning of their letters that her friendship was unconditional, and thus Malamud's letters to her afforded him an almost unqualified freedom to ponder those moral and artistic concerns so native to his character and his fiction with less constraint than might have been possible in letters to other friends or in formal interviews. But it is the self-revelations that each writer shares with the other that compel the attention of the reader, as writer and painter grapple with the demons that drive their creativity. In Beck's case, however, more personal issues in her revelations occasionally surface, and are carried in a voice of muted longing.

In at least two instances, Beck's letters hover over an "unspeakable" issue that calls to mind Joyce's story "A Painful Case" or, perhaps, James's "The Beast in the Jungle." Malamud's pointed silences in the face of Beck's oblique references to their relationship propel the reader to fill the gaps. Occasionally, however, Beck edged beyond the tacitly accepted boundaries of their chaste discourse to fill in the gaps herself. In a moment of reminiscence, as she recalled the autumn of 1964 spent at Yaddo, Beck suddenly turned her attention to her relationship with Malamud, barely masking the romantic allusiveness of her language:

> How are you dear, and your dear ones, and your work in progress? You ask me this as I do you perennially. I can never answer properly, find a simple way of telling you. Maybe its just untellable, not in the way a finished work is, so we're together I guess for the moment in silence. But trustingly! I'm most of the time nervous, eager, doubtful, hopeful, questioning; and I'm making an effort to be honorable too. Can this be learned late in life? Even with practice it's an unnatural mode for me. (Is it unnatural for most women?) (RB, November 4, 1965)

Just as abruptly, she returned to the more neutral topics of friends and literature in the very next paragraph (not quoted).

Beck's cryptic confession to Malamud pivots on the word *honorable*. There are times, however, when Beck used a surrogate subject as a vehicle for unburdening herself of unspoken passion. In a letter written two years earlier, she reminded Malamud of a theme that he had brought up at their last meeting: "Your questions about love between the young and the old have set my mind spinning. Like the Jews it seems to me to be the very stuff of drama" (RB, October 19, 1963). Winding up her end of the exchange, Beck was nothing short of ecstatic over the "literary topic" Malamud had previously broached in conversation: "It's a glory of a subject! Bless you. It's all sexual too; Thank heavens" (RB, October 19, 1963).

When we consider Beck's dedication to their friendship, her romance with words, her repressed "romance" with Malamud, and the exuberance of her personality, it is not surprising to find that her letters are more numerous and more prolix than Malamud's to her. On one occasion, sounding guilty that his commitment to the correspondence did not equal Beck's, Malamud wrote: "When I think of the time I give to correspondence that means nothing to me, I wonder where my values lie" (BM, November 3, 1963). Previously, Beck's had expressed her concern over the increasing gaps in their correspondence: "These hiatuses between letters are getting longer and longer. I worry about it, but I know I shouldn't. We are good friends" (RB, November 13, 1962). Beck's apprehension of a growing distance from Malamud becomes almost a refrain in her letters and is sounded again with increasing insistence several years later: "I enjoyed being with you. We seem to pick up easily where we leave off even though the spaces in between are getting longer and the encounters briefer. But you are in my thoughts" (RB, March 23, 1968). Increasingly, the distance between letters grows longer, and Malamud's observations to Beck or Beck's to Malamud made in one letter do not necessarily elicit a direct response in another. As their careers and lives move in different direction in the 1970s, and as illness begins to take its toll on Malamud in the 1980s, the conspiratorial quality and comradeship of the late 1950s and early 1960s become the shadow of what they were, although there are moments of renewal for each party. After one of the long interruptions in their correspondence, Beck wrote to Malamud, citing an illegible postcard as his last communication to her, and nostalgically alluded to his letters of past years: "Did I tell you . . . I took down your letters from the earlier years, 1959–62, and reread them admiringly? Did ever any struggling, complaining, doubting creature have so much thoughtful rooting for [her] as I had in those needful years?" (RB, October 14, 1967). And there is a reciprocity of appreciation. In a meeting between Malamud and Beck in 1970, after a long period without communication, Beck observed in a follow-up letter that he had been "discrete and quiet" (RB, March 3, 1970), and his reply is reminiscent of a letter written nearly a decade earlier also notable for similar gallantries: "I tend to be silent while you talk because you talk so well. And your expressiveness—eyes, mouth, every muscle. There's so much to watch" (BM, March 11, 1970). As Malamud watched Beck, readers of this correspondence will find themselves equally caught up in the rhythms of this friendship, as it undergoes with time its inevitable changes.

Notes

1. Rosemarie Beck was born on July 8, 1923, in New York City. The family moved to Westchester (New Rochelle) shortly thereafter. Beck attended public schools and was graduated from Oberlin College in 1944. Initially, she went there to study music, but subsequently studied Art History. Beck also pursued graduate work in Art History at Columbia University and The Institute of Fine Arts at New York University.

2. Victor Luftig's book *Seeing Together,* a literary study of friendship between men and women in the late Victorian and early Modernist periods, offers a useful

perspective on the Malamud-Beck relationship, especially in its underlying romantic tensions.

3. In a letter to Beck (May 13, 1960), Malamud informs her that her husband's novel, which deals with homosexual love, was favorably referred to by Leslie Fiedler in *Love and Death in the American Novel*.

4. Beck's lecture was published in *Arts Annual*, 1961. See p. 64.

Part Two

INDIVIDUAL WORKS

Chapter 7

AMERICA AND THE HISTORY OF THE JEWS
IN BERNARD MALAMUD'S "THE LAST MOHICAN"

Karen L. Polster

"The Last Mohican" is part of Bernard Malamud's well -known short story collection, *The Magic Barrel*[1] that forms an extended examination of the primary values of human life and love in a world that Malamud views as becoming increasingly impersonalized and commercialized. "The Last Mohican" follows the pattern of these stories of broken lives imperfectly redeemed through restorative suffering and the acceptance of membership within a flawed human community. It differs from most Malamud stories, however, in its setting. Along with "Behold the Key," and "Lady of the Lake," it is one of his few stories set in Italy, not the Lower East Side. Although Malamud's wife was Italian and they visited Italy, Malamud takes his protagonist outside of America to examine the construction of his identity from the point of view of worldwide Jewish history. It is notable as well that, unlike Malamud's most common protagonists, Arthur Fidelman is not just any failure, but a failed artist. He has decided to forsake his unsuccessful painting career for something he assumes anyone, even he, can do: academia. He endeavors to remake himself as an art critic and arrives in Rome with the first chapter of a planned book on Giotto in hand. Malamud proved to be fascinated with this character and used the short story as the first chapter of the 1969 novel *Pictures of Fidelman*, which

59

follows Arthur through his entire sojourn in Italy.[2] Not only does "The Last Mohican" allow Malamud to examine the personal responsibility of the artist within society, Fidelman's attempts to remake himself in a new country form an interesting reexamination of the role of history and identity within the Jewish American community after 1945. This community had, after generations of striving, managed to assimilate within American life to an unprecedented degree, only to have its "ethnic" heritage brought to high consciousness again through the Holocaust. Malamud's "The Last Mohican" is part of this postwar reexamination of history and Jewish identity in America.

While Fidelman is an artistic failure, it is really his skill in self-absorption and his inability to reciprocally connect with anyone else that form his greatest failings. He has remained isolated and unmarried. When his artistic career does not succeed, he takes money from his sister Bessie to follow his latest experiment in employment. Bessie is trying to raise five children, yet manages to help him out financially and send him encouraging notes during his stay in Rome—notes he never bothers to answer. He is equally insensitive to the begger Shimon Susskind who, upon his arrival in Italy, immediately accosts Fidelman, pegs him as a fellow Jew, and hounds him for money, clothing, and even participation in a feeble business partnership. Susskind is Malamud's last Jewish Mohican, a refugee from both the Holocaust and the newborn state of Israel who demands recognition from the assimilated Fidelman. Since Fidelman does not see this, he labels Susskind "a real schnorrer," and desperately tries to disassociate himself as quickly as possible from the refugee. "I am not responsible for you," he insists as the beggar continues to follow him throughout Rome. "You are responsible," Susskind insists. "Because you are a man. Because you are a Jew, aren't you?" "I refuse the obligation," Fidelman returns. "I am a single individual and can't take on everybody's personal burden. I have the weight of my own to contend with." He gives Susskind five dollars and says "take it and after this please leave me alone. I have made my contribution" (165–166). Through the denial of Jewish history, and indeed, the history of human suffering at large, Fidelman reveals that he has denied the nature of his own existence and hence has been unable to communicate with others through his art.

Another reason Fidelman's identity remains incomplete is the result of his efforts to deny his Jewish identity and assimilate into a culture that is not truly his own. His arrival into Italy is reminiscent of the memoirs of Ellis Island immigrants at the turn of the century and their struggle to accommodate their often Orthodox upbringing to this new American culture. "The very clothes I wore and the very food I ate," David Levinsky remembers in Abraham Cahan's 1917 novel, *The Rise of David Levinsky*, "had a fatal effect on my religious habits."[3] The clothing of Fidelman's new chosen identity as an art critic is carefully described when we meet him: a tweed suit, gum soled oxblood shoes, and a pigskin leather briefcase. He is embarrassed by the old suitcase he has borrowed from Bessie that marks him as poor to the judgmental eyes of the Italian porters, and he vows to get a new one before he moves on to Florence. However, the past is not so easily eluded. It is difficult for him to eat spaghetti, and Susskind rebukes him saying, "We are not Italians, professor." In pursuing the culture of the Italian Renaissance, he has rejected his own. It is this lack of awareness of the importance of his own history to his identity that is responsible for Fidelman's failure both in life and in art.

Fidelman's attempts to remake himself in a new country form an interesting examination of the effect of assimilation on Jewish Americans after World War II. Traditionally, the widespread history of persecution and the memory of a common culture identified Jews as Jews, even without any strict religious observances. "*Yiddishkeit*," as Bonnie Lyons has described it, is "the sense of a people, a cohesive group bound together by ties of memory . . . Jewish tradition and Jewish history, especially centuries of dispersion, exile, precariousness, homelessness, and powerlessness, [which] gave rise to a distinct historical attitude towards humanity."[4] However, with the unprecedented economic success in America, this sense of ethnic identity had been weakened, and the American model of assimilation actually became desired. As Lewis Fried explains:

> The American inclination to conceive of the future as open and the past as "a bucket of ashes" encouraged a number of American Jewish writers to see their diaspora heritage as simply irrelevant to their circumstances . . . they would devour Emerson and Thoreau . . . Yiddish and Hebrew literatures were not taken as nourishing traditions . . . [a]fter 1945 that Jewish writers could subsist outside the traditions of their people was a point hardly raised.[5]

The "turning point" Fried refers to, of course, was the Holocaust, which forced an "ethnic" consciousness upon many members of a Jewish community who would have just as soon ignored diaspora history as provincial and obsolete. Philip Roth, among others, memorably recorded this condition in the families of "Goodbye, Columbus."[6] The Patimkins' Anglicized middle-class lives and Roth's stereotyped depiction of the more plebian Klugman's, could be summed up in a passage by Adrienne Rich in *Your Native Land, Your Life*. She pointedly quotes a naysayer who claims of American Jews, "*There's nothing left now but the food and the humor*."[7] But "there is something more," Rich insists, and so does Malamud.

Although it is clear that Judaism has undergone significant transformation in its immigration to America, the idea that Jews have abandoned Judaism has always been oversimplistic. Generations had struggled to escape what they considered the provinciality of immigrant life, but did survive the assimilation process as Jews. Practices may have changed, but the commitment to *yiddishkeit* has survived, including faith in the fundamental pursuit of justice and morality, a belief that the observation of ethical rules of behavior are more important than an unwavering belief in God, the conviction that it is within the capacity of human beings to create good or ill in the world, and an identification with the historical experience of the Jewish people. This ideology has remained very much in evidence, and "to dismiss second generation attachment to these ideas in deference to a conservative definition of Jewish identity based on religious observance," as Nancy Haggard-Gilson notes, "is not only wrong but unsympathetic to the culture of Judaism itself."[8] It is to this historical and ethical ideology that Fidelman, despite his name, is unfaithful.

With American assimilation, two versions of history collided. For Jews, *yiddishkeit* dictated that the diverse, pluralistic histories of all Jews of the Diaspora unite in a common narrative of cultural tradition prevailing over relentless persecution. As Irving Howe has noted, "[I]n speaking here of the line of Jewish sensibility which can still be found in the work of these [Jewish American] writers, it should be clear that we are speaking about historical fragments, bits and pieces of memory."[9] These diverse fragments of history were preserved within Jewish memory as essential to Jewish identity. But what happened in America? What was assimilation for any so-called "ethnic" group to this country, after all, but the effort to ignore the various pluralistic histories of the past for one culturally Anglicized narrative of the future? Assimilationists embraced the American belief that identity could be chosen and changed at will, and that achievement could mask born identities. Fidelman tries again and again to subsume the pluralistic history Susskind represents by violently attempting to rewrite his own history and therefore avoiding who he is. He refuses the responsibility to help another human being in need, but will be ultimately unable to escape the history Susskind represents.

Malamud uses Rome's colloquial reputation as "The Eternal City" literally in "The Last Mohican." In running from the past, Fidelman ironically journeys to this cultural cliché for history in Western thought. The past continually impinges on the present city within the fragments of ruined buildings and the traces of former cultures. With its layers of ruined civilizations, all ages seem to be simultaneously present here. Fidelman uses this adopted history in an attempt to escape his own. "Imagine," Fidelman exclaims while walking through the remains of the Baths of Diocletian. "Imagine all that history," while ignoring his own culture's past, which is much older. While ostensibly immersing himself in the past, he pointedly avoids any identification with it. "History was mysterious," Fidelman muses. "The remembrance of things unknown, in a way burdensome, in a way a sensuous experience. It uplifted and depressed." But he abruptly stops himself from these musings. I "am a critic now and shouldn't be excited like this," he scolds himself. But the more he avoids identification with what he is seeing, the more it moves him. "I've got to stop using my eyes so much," he lamely concludes. He has come to rewrite his own past using a culture that is not his own. Susskind, however, has the clearer vision. Despite the pains Fidelman has taken with his new appearance, "I knew you were Jewish," Susskind tells him, "the minute my eyes saw you" (157).

Fidelman continues to assume that he can consider Susskind the last of a vanished breed, just as James Fenimore Cooper described the character of the Mohawk Uncas in his novel *The Last of the Mohicans*. By the time Cooper's novel was published in 1826, the Native American culture had effectively been destroyed, and could now be nostalgically and romantically mourned by a country hungry for historical justification for its successful invasion and plans for expansion in the nineteenth century. Susskind is The Wandering Jew of ancient times, the shtetl Jew of medieval Europe, the ghetto Jew that was rounded up in concentration camps. "I'm always running," Susskind tells him, from "Germany, Hungary, Poland." "Ah," Fidelman replies, trying to reassure himself, "that's so long ago." The character of Susskind is a collection of the fragments of the history of the Jewish people. The beggar's gaunt, starved frame, his shabby brown knickers, black woolen socks, and above all, his eyes that reflected poverty or "want" as Fidelman describes them, illustrate the poverty and eccentric foreignness associated with Jewish history in the minds of American Jews. Assimilation was an attempt to replace the experience Susskind represents and remake Jewish culture within an American context.

History, however, is not on a certain linear trajectory in "The Last Mohican," in which an ancient culture's history can be simply replaced with a newer one. By the way the contemporary Italians live with and among the ruins of ancient Rome, Malamud is reminding us that every generation interprets the remaining fragments of history for its own purposes. In fact, he subtly chides the Italians for attempting to avoid certain aspects of their own history, as well. The first ruins Fidelman sees are the Baths of Diocletian, the second-century emperor who presided over the last great Roman persecution of the Christians. He notes that ironically, Michelangelo had been commissioned during the Renaissance to transform the Baths into a Christian church and convent. Rather than being the last of a race's historical line, in the world of "The Last Mohican," there will not be a shortage of Jewish refugees even after the establishment of Israel. Never a Zionist, Malamud makes Susskind a refugee from both Europe and Israel. Susskind is neither a noble savage nor an admirable pioneer revolutionary as he explains that he left Israel because life there required "too much heavy labor . . . the desert air makes me constipated . . . [and] I couldn't stand the suspense" (157–158). I would be better off stateless, he concludes, for then it would not matter that I lost my passport, I wouldn't be confined to work for Israeli companies even here in Italy, or be under the constant threat of being sent back to Israel." There is no simple cause and effect to history in "The Last Mohican."

Postmodern theories of history corroborate Malamud's acknowledgment of the fragmented nature of history and its place in the formation of identity. History is recreated by each generation into a coherent narrative from the fragments that survive. This construction reflects the interests of the present day. There is no "natural" narrative that can be recovered or developed. Jean-Francois Lyotard considers this "crisis of narratives" as the primary characteristic of postmodernism.[10] This construction of historical narrative is defined by Linda Hutcheon in the *Politics of Postmodernism* as "totalizing": "to point to the process . . . by which writers of history, fiction, or even theory render their materials coherent, continuous, unified." In postmodern discourse, this process has a rather sinister cast; as it unifies the fragments "with an eye to the control and mastery of those materials, even at the risk of doing violence to them."[11] Postmodernism is characterized by the distrust of narratives that attempt to deny the violent past of America in Cooper's *The Last of the Mohicans* and supercede the diaspora past of the Jews in Malamud's version. Roland Barthes notes his dissatisfaction against this totalizing in *Mythologies* when he writes about his "feeling of impatience at the sight of the 'naturalness' with which newspapers, art and common sense constantly dress up a reality which, even though it is the one we live in, is undoubtedly determined by history . . . [and] the ideological abuse which, in my view is hidden there."[12]

As Linda Hutcheon further notes, history is now used in a much more self-conscious sense. The effect of irony is used to highlight the fact that one is retelling history while at the same time acknowledging that the conventions of narrative themselves assure the events can never be "innocently" recalled (1–2). In both "The Last Mohican" and "Lady of the Lake" (another *Magic Barrel* story), Malamud's titles ironically invoke Western historical literary works to describe their protagonists' attempts to deny their own history. In "Lady of the Lake," Henry Levin, travels from New York to Italy and pretends he is not Jewish to seduce a woman on a small islet in Lake Maggiore.

While Malamud's use of history can be defined as ironic, there is a difference in attitude toward his material. Again, as Hutcheon notes, there is a smug kind of "knowingness" about the duplicity or doubleness of some postmodern writers as they use history. This knowledge has not given postmodern writers an intellectual advantage over those who would believe they had unearthed historical data. Malamud certainly does not romanticize Susskind, but the text does not belittle him, either, or appear to denigrate his experiences simply because they cannot be known in their entirety.

"The Last Mohican" also indicates that history must be remembered rather than replaced as Fidelman has attempted to do. "The postmodern reply to the modern consists of recognizing that the past, since it cannot really be destroyed, because its destruction leads to silence, must be revisited," Umberto Eco writes, "but with irony, not innocently."[13] Historical events cannot be ignored, since they are necessary elements in the construction of personal identity.

Since Malamud does not privilege a linear trajectory of history in "The Last Mohican," the fragments of both the Italian and Jewish past remain in discontinuous layers that constantly intrude and interact with the present. "History exists in fragments," Foucault notes in *Nietzsche, Genealogy, History*, "it opposes itself to the search for 'origins.' "[14] Jewish history does not follow a schedule from Exodus to Israel, but eternally repeats within the history of the life of Susskind. Fidelman tries to establish power over this history, however, Susskind is able to take away the only evidence of his flimsy self-constructed identity when he breaks into Fidelman's room and steals the first chapter he has written on Giotto.

With this one act, Susskind destroys Fidelman's attempts at self-redefining, and it is now the refugee who has the power over the narrative of both their histories and futures. Fidelman is devastated and can no longer work. The loss of his first chapter was like a spell cast over him. He tries vainly to recreate the chapter but whole pages would 'go blank' in his mind" (171). We read he "needed something solid behind him before he could advance. And that his inspiration had deserted him." He is powerless to move on to Florence and spends the days searching for Susskind and the missing chapter. "He was lost without a beginning," the text tells us (172).

Without the missing chapter of his history, Fidelman cannot construct an identity. While the work indicates Fidelman's attempt to remake himself, his crisis of identity is the result of failing to see Susskind as the missing half of his own yet to be realized identity. Susskind is introduced in the story as Fidelman's twin. Upon arriving in Rome, he has the eerie feeling of seeing himself in another person's eyes. "Fidelman became aware that there was an exterior source to the strange . . . reflection of himself he had felt," as he looks up to see himself mirrored in the eyes of what he first believes to be a skeleton. Instead of a ghost, it is the still living Susskind, contemplating Fidelman from the base of the famous bronze statue of the Etruscan wolf suckling the infant twins Romulus and Remus. The half of himself that American assimilation was to have eliminated, finds him in Rome and greets Fidelman with the Hebrew "shalom." "Shalom," Fidelman hesitantly answers, using the word for the first time in his life.

Fidelman dreams of pursuing Susskind through the Jewish catacombs and threatens to strike him with a menorah (170). He searches through the Jewish ghetto seeing the poor "oppressed by history" and is sent to look in a Jewish cemetery filled with victims of World War II, before he finally spots Susskind selling black and white rosaries and a few gilded medallions to Christian pilgrims on the steps of a cathedral. Fidelman offers him money for the return of the papers, but now it is Susskind who ignores the American. Now Fidelman must sneak around, following him home to the ghetto and then ransacking the pathetically dingy closet where Susskind lives; but he fails to find the chapter.

Susskind is not only the history of the Jews, but the history of all human suffering and yearning for a moral existence. While Fidelman and Susskind follow different historical impulses, their futures join in a humanistic identity responsible for the sufferings of others. While there may not be an authoritative historical narrative, Malamud does provide a unified identity for his characters, if not exclusively a Jewish one. Susskind craves to be treated as a human being, not as someone who can be dismissed with a handout. He calls attention to the rags he is wearing and begs for the second suit Fidelman is carrying in his suitcase. He is actually begging for acknowledgment from Fidelman that he is the other half of his identity or skin; but Fidelman will not concede this history or responsibility for other's suffering. It is this disassociation from others, Malamud suggests, that allows the centuries of persecution Susskind represents to continue.

Susskind appears in Fidelman's final dream as the poet Virgil leading him through the nature of evil as Dante was led in *Paradise Lost*. Is evil a Christian personification of the Devil, a cossack, or even a Hitler? In Dante's poem, by the time Virgil leads Dante to the character of Satan, the scene is anticlimactic. He has already displayed the corruptions of humans that have allowed them to lead themselves astray, such as lust, gluttony, greed, and inhumanity. Malamud invokes this same concept in "The Last Mohican." One cannot simply blame the Nazis as aberrant villains. It is the inhumanity, the uncaring of lack of association with other human beings that allows these "agents of evil," if you will, to do their work.

Portraying Susskind as Virgil continues the mix of philosophies and religions that Malamud consistently uses within "The Last Mohican" to universalize the nature of evil he is examining. Why is there evil in the world, and what is our responsibility to others, are eternal questions. "All men are Jews," Malamud has famously stated. "Have you read Tolstoy," Virgil asks Fidelman in his dream. "Why doesn't God help when the innocent suffer?" As the ancient rabbis have spoken: "I do, God replies, I send you," whether Jew or Gentile.

If the recognition of the fragments of history is a necessary element in the construction of personal identity, the knowledge of one's own identity is required in order to effectively communicate with others through art. Malamud's humanistic assumptions dictate that art and history must commit to the acknowledgment of our responsibility for the welfare of each other. In a later chapter in *Pictures of Fidelman*, Fidelman has attempted an artistic comeback by constructing a collection of carefully placed holes in the ground. A ghost reminiscent of Susskind ridicules this seemingly meaningless homage to form by throwing Fidelman into one of his holes. "So now we got form," the ghost sardonically notes, "but we also got content." As Christof Wegelin has noted, in this act "life and art are inextricably fused."[15]

"Why is art?" Susskind as the voice of Virgil continues, as he leads Fidelman and then leaves him in a synagogue that had formerly been a Catholic Church. As Fidelman absently looks up at the ceiling, he sees Giotto's fresco of St. Francis of Assisi handing his cloak to a beggar. Giotto's fresco brings home the point that technical virtuosity pales in recognition of the history of human suffering. Fidelman stuffs his suit into a bag and rushes to Susskind's closet to find the refugee burning the pages of the Giotto chapter for warmth. "Have mercy," Susskind says, "I did you a favor . . . The words were there but the spirit was missing." Fidelman leaves the suit with the words "all is forgiven" as "the ghetto Jews" stared, "framed in amazement in their medieval windows." Fidelman's epiphany has allowed Malamud to link history and art through the humanism of *yiddishkeit*.

Linda Hutcheon has noted that postmodern works "contest art's right to claim to inscribe timeless universal values" (*Poetics* 90). But Malamud in "The Last Mohican" insists on this privilege for art: not to tyrannically impose an historical narrative, but to posit an explanation for the crisis of assimilation in the American Jewish community of the 1950s. In referring to the historical justifications for American involvement in the Vietnam War, Richard Slotkin in "Myth and the Production of History" claims that there is often no logical connection between the history of a culture and their present actions. Efforts to create a single narrative are simply part of a powerful cultural mythology.[16] In "The Last Mohican," however, Malamud seems to suggest that the history of the different cultures of the Jews culminates in the history of humanity's constant rediscovery of our responsibility for each other. Malamud turns the attempt of totalizing a culture through assimilation into a pluralistic, humanistic effort of acculturation. He uses the various forms of the Jewish past to look toward a common future for all people. Historical retrieval systems may not be absolute, but certain value systems are in Malamud's world, and art has the responsibility and privilege to reveal them. One person has two suits, another has none. Malamud insists there is a "natural" response to this situation.

Notes

1. Bernard Malamud, "The Last Mohican," in *The Magic Barrel* (New York: Farrar Straus, 1958).

2. Bernard Malamud, *Pictures of Fidelman: An Exhibition* (New York: Farrar Straus. 1969).

3. Abrham Cahan, *The Rise of David Levinsky,* 1917 (New York: Harper Row, 1960, 110).

4. "The Price of Success," *Studies in American Jewish Literature* 12 (1993), 119.

5. "American-Jewish Fiction, 1930–1945," in *Handbook of American Jewish Literature*. ed. Lewis Fried, et al. (New York: Greenwood, 1988).

6. *Goodbye, Columbus and Five Short Stories* (Boston: Houghton, 1959).

7. "Sources" (New York: Norton, 1986, 19).

8. "The Construction of Jewish American Identity in Novels of the Second Generation," in *Studies in American Jewish Literature* 11:1 (1992).

9. *Jewish American Stories* (New York: New American Library, 1977, 12). Quoted in Victoria Aarons, *A Measure of Memory* (Athens: University of Georgia Press, 1996, 7).

10. *The Postmodern Condition: A Report on Knowledge.* 1979. Translated by Geoff Bennington and Brian Massumi (Minneapolis: University of Minnesota Press, 1993, xxiii).

11. 1989 (New York: Routledge, 1993, 62).

12. Translated by Annette Lavers, 1957 (New York: Hill Wang, 1995, 11).

13. *Postscript to The Name of The Rose.* Translated by William Weaver (New York: Harcourt Brace, 1983, 67). Quoted in Linda Hutcheon, *A Poetics of Postmodernism,* 1988 (New York: Routledge, 1992, 90).

14. Paul Rabinau, ed., *The Foucault Reader* (New York: Pantheon, 1984, 77).

15. "The American Schlemiel Abroad: Malamud's Italian Stories and the End of American Innocence," in *Critical Essays on Bernard Malamud,* ed. Joel Salzberg (Boston: GK Hall, 1987, 149).

16. *Ideology and Classic American Literature,* ed. by Myra Jehren and Sacvan Bercovitch (New York: Cambridge University Press, 1986, 84).

Chapter 8

ZEN BUDDHISM AND *THE ASSISTANT*
A Grocery as a Training Monastery

Edward A. Abramson

> Why bother with the world?
> Let others go grey, bustling east, west.
> In this mountain temple, lying half-in,
> Half-out, I'm removed from joy and sorrow.
>
> —Ryushu, 1308–1388[1]

In writings about the works of Bernard Malamud, the traditions that have been seen as most relevant to understanding his themes and the development of his characters have been Western ones: Judaism, Christianity, liberal humanism. Clearly, these are very important, but they are not the only traditions that throw light upon his fiction. He stated in an interview: "I don't know whether there is a 'correct' interpretation of my work. I hope not."[2] In *The Assistant*, Malamud has created an impoverished grocery store that can be seen as a training monastery in the tradition of the Soto Zen school of Buddhism. Individuals attempting to follow the teachings of the Buddha are referred to in Zen writings as "trainees"; in *The Assistant* the characters' levels of human development parallel the "Way," with some in training and some not.

Buddhism is not a theistic religion in the way that Judaism and Christianity are, but is nonetheless highly spiritual. The Buddha chose not to comment specifically on the existence of God, although there are statements of what God is not, as well as remarks that may be interpreted as pointing toward the existence of a supreme being. The Buddha preferred to comment on those matters that could be known and were of immediate concern to human beings having to cope with the inevitability of the suffering and dissatisfactions of life. Buddhism developed ways of training its adherents, meditation amongst them, which are stressed much less in Western religions. Master Hakuun Yasutani stated: "Enlightenment means seeing through to your own essential nature and this at the same time means seeing through to the essential nature of the cosmos and of all things. . . . One may call essential nature truth if one wants to."[3] Words present a problem, as the inner world beyond the ego-self, one's "essential nature," can be described only inadequately. However, the basic concepts can be discussed, though not experienced, through words.

The trainee looks inward to his or her "mind," attempting to reach through stillness the "Buddha Nature," "Unborn," or "ground of one's being"—to hear the "Lord of the House." These terms refer to an area that contains a basic well of compassion and relation to the "Eternal" that all possess. To the Buddhist, the terms *Lord of the House* and *Eternal* do not refer to God as such, although a Jew or Christian might see the enlightenment experience, one definition of which is a certainty of the nature of the "eternal," as synonomous with reaching God. In *Zen Meditation for Christians*, Hugo Enomiya-Lasalle, a Jesuit, missionary, and Zen Master, has written that

> it is therefore easily understandable that a Christian, when granted enlightenment, feels it to be a direct experience of God. . . . To remind ourselves again, *satori* [sudden understanding] itself is a direct perception of the True Self. Now this in no way contradicts what has just been said, because from here there is also a way to God. For the True Self is of a spiritual nature and lies deeply rooted in the original ground, which in fact is God. . . . It has been verified again and again, that when man arrives at this deepest Self, he finds God. At this point the Self is then dissolved and consequently the Buddhist experiences a complete at-one-ness or non-duality.[4]

Christian concepts of God such as that of the Trinity and of Unitarianism do not negate this insight, as the experience Enomiya-Lasalle describes underlies them.

Judaism sees God as pure spirit having no human form. God is personal, involved in the world He created, and indivisibly One. The Hebrew Bible begins with the words, "In the beginning God created . . . ," thus stating the belief that God's existence is to be taken for granted without discussion. In Judaism, one strives to know God through His teachings and commandments in the Hebrew Bible and the commentaries of sages in the Talmud. Both Judaism and Zen Buddhism stress the importance of living with a form of mindfulness, of not separating "religious" awareness from everyday activities. However, unlike Buddhism, Judaism does not stress what can best be called the mystical, except in study of Kabbalah, which, unlike meditation in Buddhism, is outside the mainstream of religious practice.

Suffering, its nature and what to do with it, is a major theme in *The Assistant*, as well as in Malamud's work as a whole. The following exchange is both humorous and telling:

> **Interviewer** What about suffering? It's a subject much in your early work.
>
> **Malamud** "I'm against it but when it occurs why waste the experience.[5]

Although Malamud does not like suffering, he believes that human beings may develop morally through a correct understanding and use of it. Judaism parallels this view, not only in trying to see something positive in the often somber centuries of post-exilic Jewish history, but from its very beginnings:

> Malamud thus follows in the ancient Jewish tradition of
> the prophets, Amos, Jeremiah, the Second Isaiah, who an-
> nounce suffering to be the Jew's special destiny, evidence
> of his unique covenant with God, proof of God's concern
> in that only those who are loved are chastised, and the
> means of the Jew's peculiar awareness of his identity.[6]

Despite his wish for an easier life, Morris uses suffering within the Jewish understanding of its purpose: to act as a representative of the Law, and to make himself a better person. It seems to have been responsible for sensitizing him to the plight of others, such as the neighborhood's poor, Podolsky, and Frank. The Orthodox rabbi and theologian Joseph B. Soloveitchik has written: "Suffering comes to ennoble man, to purge his thoughts of pride and superficiality, to expand his horizons. In sum, the purpose of suffering is to repair that which is faulty in a man's personality."[7] While suffering can make individuals bitter, both Morris and Frank become better men through their responses to it.

Suffering in Buddhism is the base from which religious training flows and is an essential source for human growth as one tries to come to terms with it. Unlike the linking in Judaism of the suffering of the Jewish people and God's covenant, Buddhism speaks of suffering in relation to the human condition, that of all sentient beings. The two faiths share the insight that suffering is not to be avoided but used as a training device.

Coming to grips with suffering also lies at the center of Christian belief. From the concept of original sin through Adam's fall, to the agonizing death of its founder on the cross, Christianity has been centered in suffering, although, like Judaism, believing that God is good. Also, the crucifixion may be understood as showing that suffering can be both evil and good: evil in that the son of God was killed; good in that for believers his death on earth was actually life-giving: his sacrifice providing a means of salvation for human beings who should not try to avoid all suffering, which is impossible, but use it for their spiritual growth. For Frank, Morris's suffering becomes something to be emulated, Christ-like in its compassion, paralleling the life of Frank's hero, St. Francis.

Thus, an important aspect of suffering in the three religious traditions is as a training device for the development of the spiritual life, and to bring forth compassion. Each of the three religions may fruitfully be used as a base for understanding *The Assistant*. However, because Buddhism places the nature of suffering at the center of its concern, it has evolved a specific set of doctrines and methods for coping with suffering's inevitability. This renders Buddhist ideas very useful in interpreting the novel, since suffering is so much at the center of *The Assistant*. Although suffering is an important problem in both Judaism and Christianity, it is through the insights of Buddhism, as manifested in Morris's teachings, that one can arrive at a particularly clear understanding of Frank's journey to move beyond fruitless attempts at explanation and evasion of suffering.

The grocery store may be viewed as a monastic training ground in which four basic Buddhist concepts are applied to the characters who enter it: *anatta* (no separate self or soul); *anicca* (impermanence, transience); *karma* (the law of cause and effect); and the Four Noble Truths (suffering exists, suffering's cause, suffering's end, the eightfold path). The various characters are at different stages of the "Way": there are those who are close to enlightenment (Morris, Breitbart); a trainee "monk" (Frank); one attracted to training but not fully committed (Helen); and those left in samsara (this world of life and death: Ida, Nat, Louis, Karp, Sobeloff, the

"Macher"). While focusing upon Morris and Frank, as fulfilling most clearly the Master-pupil role, I shall also note the reactions of other characters to illustrate what a lack of commitment to training can lead to.

The concept of *anatta* is central to Buddhist thought, and an issue that has raised more controversy than any other in Buddhism. It seems most probable that the Buddha wished to put an end to ego, in his belief that there is nothing permanent about a human personality that survives death or is permanent in life. The ego-self is like a series of stills in a film: it gives the appearance of wholeness but is, in fact constantly changing from moment to moment, substance and continuity being an illusion. In *The Assistant*, we see Frank developing toward an understanding of the lack of importance of the ego-self, a focus upon which causes detachment from others and life itself. Malamud characterizes him as someone who is obsessed with the ego-self and must transcend it in order to realize what he already posesses—his essential nature, which connects him to all other sentient beings. Great Master Eihei Dogen (1200–1253), the founder of Japanese Soto Zen, observed in a talk to his monks: "The main point is that, whatever the situation, you must discard attachments to fame and the Self."[8] Early in the novel, Frank states that "when I need it most something is missing in me, in me or on account me. . . . I don't understand myself. I don't really know what I'm saying to you or why I am saying it."[9] Buddhism stresses that all humans possess the Buddha Nature and are complete in themselves; the problem is recognizing this and being able to re-establish contact with one's basic nature, which is "void, unstained and pure."[10]

Frank must learn that there is nothing missing in him; as he says, he simply does not understand his true nature, but is being pushed in particular directions by the ego-self, with its limitless cravings and desires. It is this aspect of the self that the Buddha felt should be subdued. Frank will learn which path to take through being taught by Morris, who has largely relinquished his ego-self in favor of direct responses to humanity, his customers, and others. Referring to the self-centered self, Malamud has commented: " 'I conceive this as the major battle in life, to transcend the self—extend one's realm of freedom.' "[11]

It is important to stress the discipline of the store, which has brought Morris to where he now is and which will bring Frank to the same stage of development. Ida is worried about Morris after his return from hospital and convalescence. However, she is incapable of recognizing the store's importance. When Morris leaves his bed to see what is happening in it, Ida remonstrates:

> "What are you doing, Morris—a sick man?"
> "I must go down."
> "Who needs you? There is nothing there." (*T.A.*, 173)

In fact, Ida is both wrong and right, although she would not understand
this. There is "nothing" in the store, but that is the very situation that Morris, and Frank, require. Due to its lack of customers—unfortunate for business, fortunate for growth of awareness—the store is *still*, the way both men
must be: "The store was fixed, a cave, motionless. He had all his life been on
the move, no matter where he was; here he somehow couldn't be. Here he
could stand at the window and watch the world go by, content to be here"
(*T.A.*, 55). At times, the store induces a state of meditation in both men as
they are engulfed by its emptiness: the outer state affecting the inner. Here
Frank will learn to be content to *be*, and his developing awareness of his essential nature shows signs of overcoming his grasping self, which must be
subdued if he is to move forward in his training: "He was afraid to look into
the mirror for fear it would split apart and drop into the sink. . . . The rage he
felt disappeared like a windstorm that quietly pooped out, and he felt a sort
of gentleness creeping in. . . . He felt gentle to the people who came into the
store. . . . He was gentle to Morris, and the Jew was gentle to him. And he
was filled with a quiet gentleness for Helen . . ." (*T.A.*, 78–79).

Recognizing that his salvation lies here, he will do anything to stay. In
fact, it may not be overstating the case to say that Frank loves the store:
"Yet when the clerk got back to the grocery he was glad to go in" (*T.A.*, 75);
and he recognizes its centrality to his training. If he is asked to leave, "he
would try in some way to stay longer. That was his only hope left, if there
was any" (*T.A.*, 160). "If the store blows away some dark night I might as
well be dead, Frank thought" (*T.A.*, 166). Sidney Richman thinks this attraction the store holds for both Morris and Frank abnormal: "Such refine-
ment of masochism—and there is no other word for it—is in many ways
unprecedented in American literature."[12]

Of course, the store is no paradise. Despite endless hours behind the
counter, price cuts, and attempts at improvement of its appearance, all to
attract new customers, the store barely supports the family, let alone
Frank. However, though both characters rail against it, despite themselves,
they recognize the grocery's value, which to them compensates for the inadequate livelihood it provides: it is the place wherein they may realize
the essence of their natures; the Buddha nature, which all possess, being
the essence of compassion. Frank stays for love of his teacher, repeatedly
justifying his decision by saying that he owes Morris something. Ostensibly, he also stays for Helen, but his true reason, as he admits to himself, is
"For love . . ." (*T.A.*, 167). Given the compassion that Morris draws out of
Frank and which both exercise toward the customers (at 6:00 A.M. serving
the "Polisheh" her roll; granting credit to the family of the impoverished
house painter, Karl; etc.), "love" must be viewed in a wider perspective.
Frank does have a sense of what he needs, insisting on being accepted as
Morris's "pupil," a novice serving under a master. He forces himself into

the grocery after Morris collapses, while stating, "I need the experience" (*T.A.*, 52). Malamud tells us that "[i]n the store he was quits with the outside world . . ."(*T.A.*, 55); here he can concentrate on more important things so that, in time, he can interact with the outside world from a new center.

Morris and Breitbart come together in the store and extend themselves beyond the ego-self, both recognizing that to separate themselves from others is a falsehood. Buddhism teaches that people are different, but not separate; their Buddha Nature, or the Unborn, is an area shared by all. Despite his brother's having destroyed his business and run away with his wife, Breitbart "never complained." He takes care of his dullish son and trudges the city's stores offering light in the form of bulbs. He is the essence of compassion; as Morris says, "The world suffers. *He* felt every schmerz" (*T.A.*, 10). We are not told whether anyone accepts his light, but Morris offers him tea and a sympathetic ear. Breitbart attends Morris's funeral, and he appears in the store on the last page, taking up with Frank the position he had with Morris. It is as though Frank and Breitbart recognize in the other someone who has relinquished the ego-self in favor of that essential nature that relates one to all.

Malamud tells us that Helen thinks: "If you had lived so long in one place, all but two years of your life, you didn't move out overnight" (*T.A.*, 21). She has lived in the ego-self, and in both the store and hope for the future; she has been unable to live in the moment, a basic Zen concept. Both the past and future do not exist—they are abstractions. Only the present is real, and is where we live our lives: "For there is never anything but the present, and if one cannot live there, one cannot live anywhere."[13] Malamud's characters frequently carry burdens from the past which they must slough off if they are to be able to live full lives. Frank works at this, as can be seen in his initial remark below, and moves steadily toward success; Helen's reply shows that it is different for her:

> "Time don't mean anything to me."
> "It does to me." (*T.A.*, 90)

Frank has moved toward a position of being able to remove time as a factor in his life. While he longs for Helen, he is still able to live in the present. Helen is far less advanced, and does not realize what she must do to lead a full life. Completely absorbed in *self*, she lives for her future, colored by the past, the present being the least important time for her. Her lack of development is due not alone to her wanting the contradictory worlds of literature, with its humanistic values, and of being attracted to that of Nat Pearl, with its materialistic, social status orientation. It is her inability to let go of her idealized version of the future, to live in the present and be fully engaged in the moment, that makes her life so inadequate. Because of her grasping at ideals in order to fulfil a needful self, she is incapable of understanding a basic Zen teaching that although various events occur, in a real sense it is pointless to speak of bad weather—there is only weather. The external world is there and is always changing. What is important is how an individual perceives it. She is incapable of appreciating what is available to her without the barn:

> Barn's burnt down—
> now
> I can see the moon. (Masahide, 1657–1723) (Z.P., 127)

If the separate self, the ego-self, is placed in a central position, all events will be judged only in relation to how they affect it. This prevents a true relationship with other people and with events. It explains, in part, why for much of the time Helen is incapable of fully appreciating either Frank or, at his death, her father's "holiness." In fairness to her, the numerous instances I have cited of Frank's ego-self assertions must be recalled. Her problem is that she has not kept up with his development, and this has occurred because of what I have described as her own much more limited progress. The situation in relation to her father is more complex. Morris has failed to provide well for his family materially, and suffers guilt feelings because of this: " 'My child,' he sighed, 'for myself I don't care, for you I want the best but what did I give you?' " (T.A., 23). Helen, while loving him and recognizing his honesty, cannot quite forgive him for his incompetence: "[W]ho can admire a man passing his life in such a store. He buried himself in it; he didn't have the imagination to know what he was missing. He made himself a victim. He could, with a little more courage, have been more than he was" (T.A., 204).

In Malamud's terms, Morris could not have been any more than he was. A *schlimazl* in America, Morris is Malamud's holy fool. Helen responds too strongly to the foolish and not sufficiently to the holy aspects of her father. While one can understand some of her disenchantment with her lot, her inability to attain more peace through her father's "holiness" shows how far she lags behind Frank. Although it is true that a glass of water is both half full or half empty, there is a world of difference in the life lived by the person who takes each stance. Even in the negative, the positive exists:

> See the sun in the midst of the rain;
> Scoop clear water from the heart of the fire[14]

Helen is incapable of living fully in the present because she is obsessed with self and idealizes the future: "The difference between Frank and Helen is that Frank is able to escape his idealism by living his life as it comes."[15]

Except for Ida, the remaining characters in the novel are not even aware that they lack anything other than material goods, and even Ida veers in this direction at times. The others view people merely as extensions of themselves and their needs. Since Ida's financial insecurity had led her to pressure young Morris into rejecting a career as a pharmacist, he felt forced into what proved to be a dead-end grocery. Nonetheless, she does worry about Morris and Helen, and is concerned about people other than herself. Unfortunately, she is limited by fearfulness of her non-Jewish neighborhood, with the assault and robbery having made things even worse. She has no connection to other women in the area, and is also ignorant and anxious of America beyond the neighborhood. This combination of factors has made her appear carping and hard, but these traits emanate from fear and loneliness. The concept of *anatta* would not be entirely foreign to her, as she does possess a limited sense of selflessness. The other minor characters act as though the ego-self is all that matters which assures that they will not progress in understanding. When Morris works briefly for his former crooked partner Charlie Sobeloff, he must wear a jacket that sums up Charlie's attitude, but that is ironically unsuited for Morris's own level of understanding: "Morris saw himself putting on a white duck jacket with 'Sobeloff's Self-Service' stitched in red over the region of the heart" (*T.A.*, 184).

Julius Karp does not hesitate to give advice that is not wisdom but that of a Bellovian reality instructor. Interestingly, although ignorant and a materialist, Karp recognizes in Morris not a businessman but a man who is living from a different center than himself: "For some reason that was not clear to him Karp liked Morris to like him . . . (*T.A.*, 134). Regardless of whether they are of use to him, Morris shows compassion to people; and he sells them milk rather than the alcohol Karp dispenses. He gives credit, and some respond. The Polisheh leaves six cents for the rolls she took when Morris was ill; and after Morris's death, "One man said the grocer was the only storekeeper who had ever trusted him for anything. He paid Frank back eleven dollars that he owed Morris" (*T.A.*, 206). What the man owes to Morris is more, of course, than eleven dollars. These actions explain why Karp wants Morris to like him and illustrate some of what Frank is learning in his novitiate.

From a Jewish perspective, the store provides a place wherein Morris can live out the commandments of Judaism, a religion that has both universal and particularistic aspects. For Morris, however, it is Jewish Law, with a capital L, which he interprets in a wholly universalistic manner, believing that this contains the essence of Judaism:

> "This means to do what is right, to be honest, to be good.
> This means to other people. Our life is hard enough. Why

should we hurt somebody else? For everybody should
be the best, not only for you or me. We ain't animals. This
is why we need the Law. This is what a Jew believes."
(*T.A.*, 112–113)

Morris's definition of Judaism stresses its liberal humanistic aspects at the
expense of its particularity. He is not bothered by his lack of synagogue at-
tendance nor by his ignoring the dietary laws. Frank is correct in his response: " 'I think other religions have those ideas too . . .' " (*T.A.*, 113).
Even the rabbi at Morris's funeral praises him for his humanity and
largely exonerates him for his distance from the more formal demands of
Judaism. Of course, this follows on from Malamud's metaphorical definition of the Jew as a good man who suffers and extends compassion and
aid to his fellow human beings. Thus, Frank, even before his formal conversion to Judaism at the end of the novel, as well as, for example, George
the Gorilla in *God's Grace*, are both Jews to Malamud.[16] However, Judaism,
itself, would disappear as a distinct religion if Morris's definition of it were
all that it was.

Frank combines Christian (St. Francis) and Jewish (Morris) teachings
to develop into a moral individual. Frank's Roman Catholicism teaches
him the value of poverty, selflessness, and self-discipline, attributes that he
has been unable to live up to in his past but which, under Morris's influence, become a part of his life. While Frank embraces Judeo-Christian beliefs, Morris becomes a semitic St. Francis, and the store a Christian
monastic cell, which is both in the world and outside it. Both Buddhist and
Christian monastic traditions are relevant here, with the store providing
an appropriate setting either for training in order to grasp one's essential
nature or to try to emulate Christ.

The concept of *anicca* points to the impermanence of all things, particularly evident when individuals try to grasp, hold on to, something and
preserve it. It is not a pessimistic belief, as negative situations will inevitably change, tyrants fall, our lives move on. Suffering occurs when we
try to hold on to those feelings, situations, body appearances that we like,
rather than recognizing that impermanence is a basic law of the universe.
Anicca explains the basis for living in the present, as this moment is all we
possess with certainty.

Zen does not teach that one should avoid action or planning for the
future. Rather, it stresses that the present is too important to allow the future to highjack it: "This is not a philosophy of not looking where one is
going; it is a philosophy of not making where one is going so much more
important than where one is, that there will be no point in going."[17] Morris does not *go* anywhere, and suffers on account of his difficulty in coping with impermanence, the transience of experience, as can be seen in

his railings against Karp for renting to another grocer. However, his *moral* imperatives remain constant, as he does not engage in duality, seeing his own self as separate from and above that of others. He applies right action where he is. Thus, he refuses to cheat Podolsky, or take up the "macher's" offer. Julius Karp, Charlie Sobeloff, Nat Pearl and others are incapable of this, viewing others as separate and less important than themselves.

Using the analogy of climbing a mountain as a parallel to Buddhist training, Master Sheng Yen states that

> [s]ome encounter easy flattish areas while others come across exceedingly steep slopes. We are pleased with the easy slopes and feel the mountain climbing is going well. But on the flat area the climber is not getting any higher! Someone struggling with cliffs and boulders on the steep slope may be on the quicker path. The climber wandering along on the flat area may be going around the mountain rather than up it! This is especially likely if he is climbing in a cloud.[18]

In the store Frank must choose whether to take the easy, flattish, route or "struggle with cliffs and boulders on the steep slope. . . ." It is only on the latter that he can cleanse aspects of his *karma;* that is, actions or deeds, either good or bad, past or present. As the novel progresses he chooses this steeper, more difficult, path more and more. "It is not fate, but one's own doing which reacts on one's own egocentric self so it is possible for us to direct the course of our karma. . . . Our will, or ego, is itself the doer of karma, and feeling is itself the reaper of the karmic fruit. . . ."[19] Put another way, the law of *karma* means that as you sow, so shall you reap. "The Buddha taught that for an action to produce karma, it has to be accompanied by a conscious will, which presupposes a capacity of free choice."[20] Almost all of Frank's development involves his attempts to cleanse, almost redirect, the course of his *karma* through exercising choice before acting and renouncing the self. The doctrine of rebirth is based upon past *karma*. "Past karma conditions the present birth, and present karma, in combination with past karma, conditions the future birth" (*Z.E.L.,* 10). Since Frank is an orphan, some of the essential elements of his past are a mystery to him. What he knows is his present situation and enough of himself to relate it to certain patterns of past behavior.

He refers constantly to mistakes he has made and the negative effects these have had upon him. He explains to Morris that "[w]ith me one wrong thing leads to another and it ends in a trap" (*T.A.,* 36). Frank has to break the cycle of one wrong thing leading to another by changing his actions, so changing his karma. Only through the discipline imposed by the store is it possible for him to end the cycle. The Buddha said:

> Let no one think lightly of evil and say to himself, "Sorrow will not come to me." Little by little a person becomes evil, as a water pot is filled by drops of water. Let no one think lightly of good and say to himself, "Joy will not come to me." Little by little a person becomes good, as a water pot is filled by drops of water. (*Dham.*, 109)

The result of this change in attitude is that "Little by little, Frank learns to govern and then give up his appetites."[21] Because *karma* is, at base, cause and effect, Frank will have changed his future *karma* by controlling his passions.

Morris's *karma* is very different from Frank's, and helps explain both his acceptance of suffering and his understanding of its place in human existence. Morris's choices are always compassionate, and are based upon an exercise of will. Robert Ducharme was only partially correct when he wrote: "It is not true that Morris made himself a victim; he simply accepted what seemed to him his unavoidable destiny."[22] From a Buddhist viewpoint, Morris was born with certain predilections due to the *karma* that came to him from a past life. However, this did not prevent him making choices, in essence acting to shape his life. His actions assured that he would eliminate any bad *karma* for the future (only good effects can emanate from good causes), either in this or in another life, would create merit in this life, and provide a positive example for those around him who were able to appreciate what he was offering, as did Frank. Breitbart has also acted to create positive *karma* in future. He has chosen the more difficult, but more moral, path with his son, and faces life's hardships with equanimity. Moral and uncomplaining, he goes about trying to spread light through his example. While Morris equals him in morality, he can learn from Breitbart about acceptance of the impermanence of life; Frank can learn all things from Brietbart.

Helen tries to affect her *karma,* but is unable to move beyond attachments to worldly success. Her clinging makes it impossible for her to let go of the ego-self, cleanse her karma, and develop along the Way, as does Frank. Sidney Richman notes that "her personality is a shambles,"[23] and Robert Ducharme observes: "Furthermore, her selfishness prevents her from seeing the moral quality of Morris's life, the pathetic beauty of his soul."[24] Her personality is divided, dualistic in that she sees her own self as separate and more important than that of others. While she is certainly a less extreme example than Ward, she is not dissimilar to Nat. Her lack of insight into her own nature is illustrated by the fact that she rejects Nat in part because she sees him as too self-centered, unable to give or to relinquish his personal desires in order to understand those of another; however, she is blind to the fact that she suffers from a similar shortcoming. ("Do not give your attention to what others do or fail to do; give it to what you do or fail to do" [*Dham.*, 89]). Unable to change her *karma* through positive action born of an understanding of her situation, she cannot respond to the significance of Frank's change, of his development.

This negative *karma* may have come from a previous life, for Helen is described as perpetually unfulfilled: "But her expression was discontented, and her mouth a little drawn. She seemed to be thinking of something she had no hope of ever getting" (*T.A.*, 59). Philip Kapleau has written:

> For it is the mind that feels itself separated from life and nature, dominated by an omnipresent Ego-I that lashes out to destroy and kill, to satisfy its desire for more and more at whatever the cost. It is the unaware mind that breeds insensitivity to people and things, for it doesn't see and appreciate the value of things as they are, only seeing them as objects to be used in satiating one's own desires.[25]

The first sentence applies more to Ward than to Helen; the second is more appropriate in describing Helen's attitude, both to her father and to Frank. Helen's *karma* makes it difficult for her to perceive what she needs to, but Frank has overcome even more negativity and is proceeding on the Path. The remaining characters are not aware of the need to cleanse their *karma*, to attempt to change their futures by making different choices in the present. They are unaware, and suffer because of this.

The grocery store is a microcosm for the depiction of The Four Noble Truths. The first Truth is that suffering (*dukka*) exists. Everyone desires contentment, but most people find that life brings a great deal of frustration. Additional definitions of *dukka* include Christmas Humphreys's (*Buddhism*, 81):

> ... disharmony, discomfort, irritation or friction, or, in a philosophic sense, the awareness of incompleteness or insufficiency. It is dissatisfaction and discontent, the opposite of all that we mentally enbrace in the terms wellbeing, perfection, wholeness, bliss.

Morris understands this, stating: "'If you live, you suffer'" (*T.A.*, 113). Buddhism teaches that "[l]ife is change, and change can never satisfy desire. Therefore everything that changes brings suffering" (*Dham.*, 30). Everyone will experience sickness, old age, and death; also, everyone will have to find a way to live with the dissatisfactions and disappointments of life.

The Buddha's message was that there is a way to cope with the inevitability of suffering.

The second Noble Truth identifies the cause of suffering, which is the demands we make of life, our selfish desires, attachments, and cravings. Life is difficult because of the changes, the impermanence that is inherent in it; however, it is largely what we require of life that causes our suffering, our constant need for personal satisfaction and the belief that in order to be happy we must get our own way, must have what we desire. It is this self-centered craving that is at the root of despair.

Frank begins to learn about the nature of suffering:

> Suffering, he thought, is like a piece of goods. I bet the Jews could make a suit of clothes out of it. The other funny thing is that there are more of them around than anybody knows about. (*T.A.*, 204)

Frank's extension of suffering from the Jews alone to people in general shows his growing understanding of its rootedness in the nature of things, and leads to the growth of compassion that can be seen in his treatment of the customers. For example, he visits Carl the painter to collect seventy dollars owed to Morris, but is appalled by the family's poverty and the children's having to go to bed hungry. He leaves without a cent.

Morris is an expert on suffering and, while he does not like it, he recognizes that it would be increased if he were to give in to his own desires. Thus, he will not sell the dead-end store to the refugee Podolsky, nor will he demand payment of bills from people he knows are suffering great poverty.

The Third Noble Truth is that suffering can be cured by eliminating selfish desire. Breitbart appears to have reached this state; Morris has virtually reached it, as has Frank by the end of the novel. Helen is still beset by cravings that cause her unhappiness. None of the other characters understand that their own attitudes have anything to do with their state of happiness or despair.

The following exchange takes place between Morris and Frank:

> "What do you suffer for, Morris?" Frank said.
> "I suffer for you," Morris said calmly.
> Frank laid his knife on the table. His mouth ached.
> "What do you mean?"
> "I mean you suffer for me."
> The clerk let it go at that. (*T.A.*, 113)

For Frank, at this point in his training this is an incomprehensible idea. Toward the end of the novel, however, he will understand his teacher's words without further explanation; not due to an exercise of his reason, but through what he has realized in his own nonrational experiences in the store. Morris does not offer any real explanation of his words; he knows that Frank must experience the fact that suffering is not an aberration, not something to view as abnormal, but what much of life is. One must learn from it, and develop compassion for others, not seeing one's own self as more important than another's. The important aspect of this teaching is that Frank will realize its importance not through thinking about it but at a different level than thought: call it intuition or an awareness of the universality of the Buddha Nature.

Right speech, right action, and right livelihood are natural progressions from right thought, and have to do with speaking and acting with kindness, and considering the needs of others. One's occupation should be one that adds to life and does not diminish it. Early in the novel, Frank's potential for inner growth is highlighted by his hero worship of St. Francis, someone who lived up to the standards of right speech, action, and livelihood. Frank tells Sam that St. Francis " 'gave away everything he owned, every cent, all his clothes off his back. . . . He was born good, which is a talent if you have it' " (T.A., 31). As Buddhism teaches that all humans are born with the Buddha Nature, it follows that all are born good and are capable of being compassionate and living with the values of a St. Francis. Training does not add to what human beings already possess; it peels away the layers of obscuring habits and accretions so that what is already there may reemerge. At the end of the novel, Frank's actions are those of St. Francis, and his outer appearance matches his: "For himself he spent only for the barest necessities, though his clothes were falling apart. When he could no longer sew up the holes in his undershirts he threw them away and wore none" (T.A., 213). As Frank learns right speech and action, he perceives the store as providing him with right livelihood.

In Morris, not only do we see someone for whom right speech and action have become the natural outgrowth of an enlightened life, but whose livelihood also is right, as it could not be otherwise given that all flows from right understanding and purpose. Morris feeds the neighborhood, accepting credit from everyone, like Mr. Panessa, in "The Bill," "because after all what was credit but the fact that people were human beings, and if you were really a human being you gave credit to somebody else and he gave credit to you."[26] Although Morris has not trained his mind to the extent that would give him peace, he recognizes the power of thought. Schmitz opens a new grocery nearby: "Let him sell, thought Morris. He thought, let him die, then severely struck his chest" (T.A., 74). Striking his chest most likely reflects Morris's belief that a thought might affect reality directly. However, there is also a sense of awareness that holding such a thought is immoral, infecting, and affects one's attitude and actions toward others. Thoughts are the roots to the branches of action, preceding them. If thoughts can be kept pure, action will be, too.

Frank learns from Morris's actions that his thoughts either are pure or that he is working to make them so, and he begins to concentrate on his own. Although not particularly perceptive, Ida is so exercised by Frank's possible interest in Helen that whenever she is around him, she intuits his divided mind—one of his central problems: "He was like a man with two minds. With one he was here, with the other some place else" (*T.A.*, 110). Frank must unify his divided mind so that his actions will be affected positively. He must let go of thoughts of the past, because he is frequently living there instead of in the real present. The past does not exist; it is as ephemeral as a shadow, but can take on a delusive substance of reality in the mind. In speaking of the prison motif in his work, Malamud has described it as: "The personal prison of entrapment in past experience, guilt, obsession—the somewhat blind or blinded self, in other words. A man has to construct, invent, his freedom. Imagination helps."[27] To be free one must learn from, then let go, the past so as to be able to act effectively in the present—where one's life is.

Frank describes his memories of raping Helen as incapacitating him for moral action in the present since "it was done, beyond him to undo. It was where he could never lay hands on it any more—in his stinking mind. His thoughts would for ever suffocate him. . . . He had lived without will, betrayed every good intention" (*T.A.*,156). An important part of Frank's battle to become a moral person is to move beyond his imprisoning thoughts of the past and live a simple, moral, mindful life in the present. He has not been successful in eliminating craving, as he still longs for Helen. Also, he lapses at times into old habits: climbing up the airshaft to spy on her. Then he stops and Helen notices a change in him due to his developing discipline, his control of his thoughts, which leads to different actions: "[H]e had changed into somebody else, no longer what he had been" (*T.A.*, 215). He has not changed into somebody else; he has reestablished contact with his Buddha Nature, his true self.

As compared to a Jewish or Christian view, I would argue that interpreting the novel from a Buddhist perspective provides a useful vantage point from which to understand the conflicts at work within it. While not in basic conflict with a Judeo-Christian approach to the novel, Buddhism has its own highly developed way of understanding the nature of the human condition, and has developed particular methods of living and growing within it. This approach can only add to an understanding of a novel that, in its apparent simplicity, focuses upon some of life's essential elements: suffering, impermanence, and the nature of the self. In its depiction of Frank Alpine's growth toward morality under the tutelage of Morris Bober one can see a novice-master relationship such as has existed for centuries in Buddhist monasteries. Indeed, the conditions existing in the store itself, with its repetitious round of chores (the six A.M. rise for the Polisheh, sweeping, shelf stocking, salad making, etc.), along with its silence and stillness, mirrors a number of aspects of training monasteries in the Buddhist, and Christian, traditions. While everything can provide an opportunity for training, it is only a few who recognize the possibilities presented in daily life. Malamud is at pains to show what can be accomplished by a character whose eyes have been opened by failure and suffering so as to realize the importance of working on himself. Frank's goal, one that Morris is well advanced upon, is to remove those aspects of the ego-self that have been allowed to obscure the goodness of the true self. This is an area of particular concern to Buddhism, which, therefore, provides an excellent tool for its analysis.

In the penultimate paragraph, Frank imagines St. Francis stopping at the grocery. Like him, Frank is now poor and without desires for himself. His final state mirrors that not only of St. Francis but of Ryokan, the most beloved monk-poet in the Zen Buddhist tradition whose poem is a testament to all three trainees and describes the position Frank has reached:

> Without a jot of ambition left
> I let my nature flow where it will.
> There are ten days of rice in my bag
> And, by the hearth, a bundle of firewood.
> Who prattles of illusion or nirvana?
> Forgetting the equal dusts of name and fortune,
> Listening to the night rain on the roof of my hut,
> I sit at ease, both legs stretched out. (Ryokan, 1757–1831) (Z.P., 79)

Notes

1. Ryushu quote taken from Lucien Stryk, ed., *The Penguin Book of Zen Poetry* (London: Penguin Books Ltd., 1977), 68. Future references in text to *Z.P.*

2. Leslie and Joyce Field, "An Interview with Bernard Malamud," in *Bernard Malamud: A Collection of Critical Essays*, ed. Leslie and Joyce Field (Englewood Cliffs, N.J.: Prentice Hall, Inc., 1975), 12.

3. Quoted in David Scott and T. Doubleday, *The Elements of Zen* (Shaftsbury, U.K.: Element Books Ltd., 1993), 2.

4. Hugo M. Enomiya-Lassalle, quoted in *The Practice of Zen Meditation* (London and San Francisco: The Aquarian Press, 1992), 91–92.

5. Daniel Stern, "The Art of Fiction: Bernard Malamud," in *Conversations with Bernard Malamud*, ed. Lawrence M. Lasher (Jackson, Miss.: University Press of Mississippi, 1991), 63.

6. Sheldon Grebstein, "Bernard Malamud and the Jewish Movement," in *Bernard Malamud: A Collection of Critical Essays,* ed. Leslie and Joyce Field (Englewood Cliffs, N.J.: Prentice Hall, 1975), 21.

7. Quoted in Harold S. Kushner, *When Bad Things Happen to Good People* (New York: Avon Books, 1981), 20.

8. Eihei Dogen Zenji, *A Primer of Soto Zen* (the *Shobogenzo Zuimonki*), trans. Reiho Masunaga (London: Routledge & Kegan Paul, 1972), 23.

9. Bernard Malamud, *The Assistant* (Harmondsworth, U.K.: Penguin Books Ltd., 1967), 36–37. Future references in text to *T.A.*

10. "The Scripture of Great Wisdom," in *The Liturgy of the Order of Buddhist Contemplatives for the Laity,* ed. P. T. N. H. Jiyu-Kennett (Mt. Shasta, CA: Shasta Abbey Press, 1990), 73.

11. Daniel Stern, 62.

12. Sidney Richman, *Bernard Malamud* (New Haven: College and University Press, 1966), 51.

13. Alan W. Watts, *The Way of Zen* (London: Arkana, 1990), 144.

14. Ibid., 138.

15. Jeffrey Helterman, *Understanding Bernard Malamud* (Columbia, S.C.: University of South Carolina Press, 1985), 49.

16. For a fuller discussion of Malamud's definition of the term *Jew,* see my "Bernard Malamud and the Jews: An Ambiguous Relationship," in *The Yearbook of English Studies* (Modern Humanities Research Association), vol. 24 (London: W.S. Maney & Son Ltd., 1994), 146–156.

17. Alan W. Watts, 145.

18. Master Sheng Yen, *Catching a Feather on a Fan: A Zen Retreat with Master Sheng Yen,* ed. John Crook (Longmead, Shaftesbury, Dorset: Element Books Ltd., 1991), 67.

19. Reverend Master P. T. N. H. Jiyu-Kennet, *Zen is Eternal Life* (Mt. Shasta, CA: Shasta Abbey Press, 1987), 9. Future references in text to *Z.E.L.*

20. Eknath Easwaran, ed., *The Dhammapada* (London: Penguin Books Ltd., 1987), 106. Future references in text to *Dham.*

21. Jeffrey Helterman, 39.

22. Robert Ducharme, *Art and Idea in the Novels of Bernard Malamud: Toward The Fixer* (The Hague: Mouton, 1974), 84.

23. Sidney Richman, 58.

24. Robert Ducharme, 106.

25. Philip Kapleau, "Introduction," in Thich Nhat Hanh, *Zen Keys* (New York: Doubleday, 1995), 5.

26. Bernard Malamud, "The Bill," in *Selected Stories* (Harmondsworth: Penguin Books, 1983), 250–251.

27. Daniel Stern, 62.

Chapter 9

MALAMUD'S *NEW* [ACADEMIC] *LIFE* — AND OURS

Sanford Pinsker

Although I first encountered Malamud's *A New Life* in a college lit. course, it wasn't until I schlepped myself across the country to accept a graduate assistantship at the University of Washington that the novel began to read me rather than the other way around. Not only was I heading West for my own version of the new academic life, but there were other intimations that Malamud's novel might be singing my song. True enough, I was hardly cut from the same tsouris-burdened cloth as the antiheroic S. Levin, but certain correspondences made the novel warrant a close second read. After all, I, too, was a stranger amid the breathtaking Pacific Northwest Cascades, and like Levin, I often saw myself as a Jewish sad sack; but most of all, I carried the banner for liberal learning at a university that often seemed concerned with everything *but* the humanities.

By now some readers must be wondering why my opening paragraph reveals more about my personal history than it does about Malamud's novel. Think of it as an unintended irony, the sort that creeps up only years later to bonk you on the beezer, and you'll have some idea of why Malamud's novel continues to interest me. For as I did my academic stint in the Pacific Northwest, the seeds that would become my dissertation on the schlemiel began to be planted. *A New Life* fit the template, admittedly with a bit of pulling and tugging on my part. Malamud seemed to specialize in characters who are, roughly speaking, the architects of their misfortune. And the S. Levin who finds himself in the backwaters of Oregon is as good for laughs as was, say, Dr. Joel Fleishman, inveterate New Yorker and consummate whiner, among the oddballs of Ciceley, Alaska. The difference, of course, is that TV's *Northern Exposure* had its several seasons of fame while Malamud's novel still abides, and continues to interest.

Why so? Because *A New Life* not only transcends the quotidian details of its time and place, but also its status as an academic novel. Depending on how loosely one defines this subgenre, one might argue that the general form is as old as Aristophanes's *The Clouds*. There, Socrates was held up to ridicule as a man riding through the heavens in a basket; and the label of dreamy impracticality stuck not only to him, but also to all the befuddled academic types who have followed. Caricature is, after all, the great leveler, a way of pulling down the vanities of those we fear— whether it be the cackling scientist, the loony psychiatrist, or the absent-minded professor. Generally speaking, this is not a good formula for the richly nuanced characters we expect to meet in a first-rate novel; and if you tally up the sheer number of academic novels that have (rightly) slipped down the memory hole, it is hard to escape the feeling that such novels comprise a very minor, minor form. John O. Lyons's scholarly study of *The College Novel in America* (1962) confirms the suspicion by including a bibliography crowded with 215 titles, most of which nobody— with the exception of Lyons himself—has ever heard of.

By contrast, *A New Life* is longer on artist vision and the word-by-word, sentence-by-sentence choices than most cardboard fictions set in Eyesore U. In this sense Malamud's account of life among the burned-out and beaten-down joins classic novels such as Mary McCarthy's *Groves of Academe* (1952) or Randall Jarrell's *Pictures From an Institution* (1954) as the gold standard against which subsequent academic novels set in America must be measured.

It is, of course, quite another story across the pond, where British writers have put aspects of the academy to good use since the days of Chaucer. If his Canterbury pilgrims provided bawdiness and hypocrisy in abundant measure, the scholarly Clerk (a man who would "gladly lerne and gladly teche") is the notable exception. He earns Chaucer's sympathy as well as ours. But such admirable academics are rare, as are portraits of the university as a kinder, more gentle place. What, for example, would Hardy's Jude the Obscure be without his tragic dream of a university education? And what does his travail tell us about the caste system, then and now, known as Oxbridge? My point is that British higher education is rather like the rolled lawns on which the rich smack at croquet balls; it takes centuries for a tradition to take hold, and I suspect even longer for it to be dismantled.

In Britain, class differences—based on bloodlines, advantage, and not least of all, place-defining speech—are a story (perhaps *the* story) that has few counterparts in America. Kingsley Amis's *Lucky Jim* (1954) is perhaps the watershed example of what would become a changing landscape. The new "red brick" universities not only turned higher education into an analog of national health, but also offered up delicious possibilities for talented British novelists in search of a subject. David Lodge and Malcolm Bradbury are the names that most often pop to mind—whether one's favorite happens to be Lodge's *Changing Places* (1975) or Bradbury's *Rates of Exchange* (1983). Unlike many American novelists who feel that only a mighty swing for the fences is worth the effort, their British counterparts seem less driven by market pressures and the churning ambition to write their country's version of the Great American Novel. After all, with a crowded field of *genuine* greats looking over your shoulder—Austen and Elliott, Dickens and Conrad, Joyce and Lawrence—you can turn out a "jolly good read" without worrying too much about elbowing yourself into a latter-day version of F. R. Leavis's Great Tradition.

By comparison, American writers have fewer precursors to worry about. The earliest academic novel that American literary history can offer up is Nathaniel Hawthorne's *Fanshawe* (1828), a book that so romanticizes the Bowdoin of his college years that he (rightly) tried to suppress the few extant copies. Granted, F. Scott Fitzgerald's *This Side of Paradise* (1920) made a splash when its insider account of Princeton as the "pleasantest country club in America" divided the world between those who knew what "petting shirts" were and smug Victorian parents who didn't; but for all the snippets of Triangle Club productions and screamingly bad undergraduate poetry that Fitzgerald shoveled into his pages, there is precious little that one could, properly, call an academic novel. At least two-thirds of its action occurs elsewhere. Edmond Wilson, Fitzgerald's classmate and "intellectual conscience" (Fitzgerald's phrase), dutifully ticked off the misspellings and the solecisms, and then declared that it nonetheless had the essential ingredient of genuine fiction: an abiding sense of *life*.

Fitzgerald was clearly onto something, although that *something* would have to wait until *The Great Gatsby* for form and content to merge seamlessly into an aesthetic whole. And when the ingredients for one of our most evocative American novels fell into place, it was the secret sharing of Nick Carraway (late of Yale) with Gatsby (never at Oxford) that gave the work its tragic resonance. In this regard, Tom Buchanan, the boorish, perennially adolescent college boy, is reduced to a minor character—good for comic relief and a certain amount of social commentary, but decidedly not where the novel's real action was.

One can, I suppose, point toward Thomas Wolfe's pantingly romantic Eugene Gant or to others who move through college on their way to some special destiny, but the truth of the matter is that when we think of college novels we tend to think of their more permanent residents—faculty members who grumble and plot insurrections, deans (and, sometimes, presidents) who dream about signing their dismissal notices, and increasingly, flashy academic superstars who liven up a moribund campus with insider gossip and the latest trends in literary theory. In short, what makes the little wheels of plot invention turn in an academic novel is academic politics, a phenomenon usually described as being particularly nasty because the stakes are so low. I prefer to think of such outbursts of pique in Conradian terms—that is, as a "fascination of the abomination"—for nothing (not ideas, not library research, and certainly not correcting student themes) provides the same adrenaline rush as efforts to humiliate one's academic enemies or the fear that they might well return the favor.

In this sense, a novel set on a college or university campus is not unlike one that sets out to describe the day-to-day life of a professional writer. It may well be true that writers worth their salt spend an inordinate amount of time hunched over a writing desk, turning sentences around and around in an effort to get the overall rhythm and individual words down right; but this "truth" is likely to fare badly on the page and even worse on screen. Far better—and certainly more profitable—to dress the writer in a safari outfit and have him blast away at rhino (Hemingway springs to mind, but he is hardly the only example of a writer who never lets you see him sweat, much less struggle with a dangling participle) or to chronicle the drinks, drugs, and affairs that presumably come with the territory of being an American novelist.

The same argument can be applied to a novel in which professors are hardly ever seen preparing lectures, teaching classes, or grading papers. The merest hint of verisimilitude is quite enough. Why so? For much the same reason that movie audiences in the 1930s preferred escapist fare (gangster sagas or lavish musicals) to grimly realistic portrayals of the Great Depression's quotidian life. Even longtime professors will not turn pages of a novel that moves *too* realistically through the semester. Rather, they insist on excitement, be it infighting over a disputed tenure case or all-out warfare against a damnable dean, in ways that people addicted to pulp Westerns want to see shootouts. And that said, nothing makes the heart of an academic beat faster than the threat of some imminent, cataclysmic change: a new building, a new curriculum, a new chairperson. The operative word, of course, is *new*, something that even the most radical professors abhor, especially if it means altering one whit of *their* life (the lives of others, often large groups of others, is a very different matter). In this sense, most academics—and certainly most academic novels—are deeply conservative in temperament, no matter how many passionate denials are likely to pour in from those who think of themselves as world-shaking types, but who, in truth, simply want their assigned campus parking space to stay right where it is, thank you very much.

Having established (albeit in a thumbnail sketch) the tradition in which academic novels find themselves, let me return to *A New Life* and why it may finally tell us more about Malamud's complicated moral vision than it does about the dailiness of daily life among certain English professors.

On its most immediate level, *A New Life* is about a young, idealist English instructor from New York City who finds himself out West and surrounded by philistines of the first water. One succeeds in Cascadia's English department by not making waves and by doing one's best to introduce engineering students to the niceties of subject-verb agreement. As Professor Fairchild, department chairman and embodiment of its ethos, puts it:

> Our main function, as I always tells everyone we employ here, is to satisfy the needs of the professional schools on the campus with respect to written communication. In science and technology men must be taught to communicate with the strictest accuracy, therefore we teach more composition than anything else in this department. Our literature offerings aren't very diversified or extensive but they're adequate to our purpose.

The purpose, of course, is to be the consummate service department. In such a world, students get pretty much what they want—which is what they think they need—and the faculty is relieved of the pressures that come with the territory of English departments on the make: not only to publish, but also to read and think about the inextricable relationship between a literate public and a healthy democracy. Rather than a collection of individuals (who can be problematic or worse), the department Fairchild imagines in his mind's eye is low speed, placid, and most of all, conforming: "There are two kinds of people I deplore in the teaching profession. One is the misfit who sneaks in to escape his inadequacy elsewhere and who ought to be booted out—and isn't very often; and the other is the aggressive pest whose one purpose is to upset other people's applecarts, and the more apples the better." The pest he has in mind is Duffy, a disgrace of a teacher (so far as Fairchild is concerned) who increasingly turns out to be Levin's ghostly double.

Among the things that Levin and Duffy share are dreams of a richer, more intellectually attuned life than that which his colleagues dully live. Rather than becoming dead on the inside, Levin is filled with self-improving plans:

> He considered a philosophy project, to work toward a unity of Plato and Aristotle? Or maybe learn Russian and read Pushkin in the original? Or take up the guitar or recorder, Bach on both? Maybe paint weekends, not that he could weekdays. He had no heart for any of these things, then wondered if he could begin to collect material for a critical study of Melville's whale . . . but gave up the whale when he discovered it in too many critical hats. He wrote down possible other titles for a short critical essay: "The Forest as Battleground of the Spirit in Some American Novels." "Stranger as Fallen Angel in Western Fiction." "The American Ideal as Self-Created Tradition."

To be sure, Levin is a product of the age of criticism, and I was probably more right than wrong when some years ago I pointed out that "one has the sinking feeling one had encountered such titles before." But the intensity and persistence of these dreams makes him an appealing character, even as we also know that he is the comic antihero who spills his soup on the *schlimazel,* and often on himself. After all, Levin's imaginary work-in-progress is awash with speculations about American guilt and Edenic innocence. He means well, but nothing he has reveries about is likely to appear in print.

Why so? Because Malamud is interested in what happens to an essentially good man under extraordinary pressure; but unlike Hemingway, he has little belief in the theatrics of defying death—whether the challenge comes from the battlefield, the bull ring, or the charge of an African rhino. Even more important, Malamud was not afraid (as Hemingway sometimes was) to add a sense of humor to the scenario. For example, here is Levin waxing rhapsodic about nature in ways that simultaneously crack the heart and put a smile on one's face:

> As he drove aimlessly on, in sadness contemplating all the failures of his life, the multifarious wrong ways he had gone, the waste of his going, he sniffed the sea smell, Whirling down the window, he smelled again and let out a cry.
> The ocean! . . . . He beheld in the distance a golden lace of moonlight on the dark bosom of the vast sea.
> Ocean in view, oh the joy. "My God, the Pacific!"

For Levin, this "new life" offers him a chance to erase the wasted years of alcoholism and assorted disappointments, for here is a landscape as large as one's best dreams. Levin wants, above all else, to become a "new" person in this new, unspoiled landscape and this impulse is what places *A New Life* much more solidly within the major traditions of American literature than inside the limited orbit of most academic novels.

Granted, Levin is the small-r romantic tenderfoot writ both large and funny. Here, for example, is Levin as he tentatively approaches Lady Macbeth, a colleague's feisty, potentially dangerous, cow:

> He followed her directions—going around the back of the house and across the weedy pasture. He crossed a dirt road he wasn't sure was part of Dr. Fabrikant's property—trespassing made him uneasy—went through a stand of poplars and as they thinned out, found himself confronting a hefty, big-uddered white cow, Lady Macbeth, without doubt, and God help him if her lord were around. Horrified by the immensity of the beast, he retreated, his hat slapped off by a poplar branch. Levin stepped into a recently deposited cow pie. Cursing, he wiped his shoe on some dead leaves. Lady Macbeth approached, mooing. Levin grabbed up his hat and retreated through the trees. On the road he heard the sound of hoofbeats, and as he looked up, saw a horse galloping toward him. He jumped wildly aside. The startled rider managed to pull the animal to a halt; Levin knew at once he was Dr. Fabrikant.

Stand-up comics live or die in terms of three things: timing, timing, and timing. The same thing is true (albeit, much harder to pull off) for those who would crack their jokes in print. Levin's assorted misdirections and pratfalls mark him as the butt of jokes, but it is important to remember that Malamud is just behind the curtain, pulling the strings. During Levin's first days at Cascadia, for example, he joins the Gilleys for dinner and ends up with a "hot gob of tuna fish and potato" casserole spilled onto his lap. Such is the comic side of Levin's destiny. Moreover, as the gap between his innocent idealism ("The liberal arts . . . have affirmed our rights and liberties") and the pragmatism of most English department old-timers widens, the incongruity at the heart of humor takes a serious, even tragic turn. Why so? Partly because Levin allows the Good, True, and Beautiful to remain in the hands of those wedded to administrative accommodation (one colleague continually revises his perfunctory composition text book while another cuts out pictures from old *Life*

magazines for a "picture book" of American literature, and partly labors
fitfully on a Laurence Sterne dissertation that nobody will publish) and
partly because Levin reminds us of more typical Malamud characters
chained to failing grocery stores or desperately trying to make ends meet
among the vicissitudes of urban life. The most memorable of these characters make the heart crack, not only because they lay bare the soul of
weariness and lament, but also because, in an age of minimalist fiction
and the *uncertainties* of certainty, they remind us that the same corrosive
forces in life that bear down on one will sooner or later bear down on all.
I make these claims knowing full well that they run counter to our current fascination with "privileging" works of art that either call their own
foundations into question or that deconstruct long-held assumptions
about hegemony. Put even more baldly, I would argue that what continues to interest us in Malamud's fiction cannot be easily placed within
handy reach of the contemporary lit-crit seminar.

Malamud's typical protagonists are immigrants scraping by on the
city's meaner streets and their half-Yiddish, half-English speech suggests
the very dislocations that earlier Jewish American novels faithfully
recorded. But that said, let me hasten to add that Malamud's fiction resists
such comparisons at least as much as it seemingly invites them. For Malamud radically altered what is normally meant by terms such as "social realism," just as his sense of "cityscape" differed markedly from the detailed
descriptions of tenement squalor that had once been the benchmark of
American Jewish literature's peculiar regionalism. For what throbs just beneath a shared sense of external conditions is a sexuality at once palpable
and repressed, a force simultaneously tied to gnawing sacrifice and wedded to desperate abandon.

Granted, Levin brings his urban Jewish sensibility to the panorama of
big mountains and wide skies, usually in the form of bad memories about
the "old life" he is trying to escape. In a largely ahistorical West, Levin's
palpable sense of history—both collective and personal—comes to him as
naturally as does breath. He grieves for the broken man he once was, even
as Levin remembers the transcendent moment when the veil lifted and he
became a serious person:

> For two years I lived in self-hatred, willing to part
> with life. I won't tell you what I had come to. But one
> morning in somebody's filthy cellar, I awoke under
> burlap bags and saw my rotting shoes on a broken chair.
> They were lit in dim sunlight from a shaft or window. I
> stared at the chair, it looked like a painting, a thing with a
> value of its own. I squeezed what was left of my brain to
> understand why this should move me so deeply, why I

was crying. Then I thought, Levin, if you were dead there would be no light on your shoes in this cellar. I came to believe what I had often wanted to, that life is holy. I then became a man of principle.

That Levin makes this confession to Pauline Gilley, the woman he will eventually come to marry, is hardly coincidental, for her unhappy condition (mirroring in certain respects his own) is badly in need of saving. Here, one cannot help but think of Leo Finkle, the tormented seminary student in "The Magic Barrel," who rushes toward a date with a prostitute in the hope that he can save her, and, likewise, she can "save" him. Many early readers (and I count myself among them) were less sure about Finkle's moral arithmetic. At the time, a phrase of mine—"moral bungling"—was meant to indicate the comic incongruity between high purpose and disastrous consequences.

This same skepticism can, and has, been directed Levin's way, because the novel ends with him willingly giving up a teaching career as part of the human cost of rescuing Pauline. As Pauline's husband puts it, "An older woman than yourself and not dependable, plus two adopted kids, no choice of yours, no job or promise of one and assorted headaches. Why take that load on yourself?" As somebody pecking away on a dissertation, Gilley's eminently sensible words caught me up short. Could he be right—this character who had been set for cuckoldry from the novel's first chapter? Indeed, Gilley struck me as everything I hoped to avoid in the academic job I did not yet have. On the other hand, to chuck it all—as Levin is willing to do, and to do because, as he puts it, "I can"— seemed unfathomable. True enough, I kept saying to myself, Levin is a fictional character—nothing more, but also nothing less. Small wonder, then, that I emphasized the comic dimensions of his fateful choice, and that I did so at the expense of what makes *A New Life* not only distinctive, but also more than yet another saga of a dreamy professor who gets the sack. For Levin is a person who can finally love, and who can act upon that love. The disasters Gilley imagines as his car chugs fitfully on its way out of town may indeed happen (Malamud is, after all, just as much a fictional realist as he is a romantic fabulist), but even if one mounts up a bill of particulars against the foolish, self-deluding Levin, he is still more human, more *alive*, than is Gilley. If character is still destiny (those who deny that there is such a thing as "character" would surely pooh-pooh this equation), Levin, in the final paragraphs, is headed toward precisely this destiny.

In the decades since Malamud held Cascadia College up for satiric inspection, other academic novelists have tried their hand at similar ventures. Let three such examples stand for the many, as well as for the differences between Malamud's exploration of the human heart in conflict with itself and with academia, and lesser novels that more closely adhere to the essential formula of the academic novel: Jane Smiley's *Moo* (1995), John L'Heureux's *The Handmaid of Desire (1996)*, and Richard Russo's *Straight Man* (1997). Of the group, Smiley's is probably the weakest because it tries to pack too many disparate types between one set of hard covers, and because far too much of the plot revolves around a pig secretly being fattened up under the very noses of those going about the dailiness of their daily (academic) life. Smiley's point, of course, is that large Midwestern universities are now more akin to corporations than they are to institutions of higher learning, and that generating dollars is much more important than mulling over ideas. Power is what makes this world go around, and clout comes to those who can breed a gigantic pig or use their economic savvy to exploit foreign countries. Meanwhile, the others continue to stare at the walls of their particular caves, reasonably content in their deluded lot.

Smiley is best known for *A Thousand Acres*, her lyrical evocation of Iowa farm life as it recapitulates the rhythms—and often the plot line—of *King Lear*. *Moo* is decidedly slimmer goods, but its sense of how universities currently operate is a welcome addition to the pile of fiction narrowly focused on whether or not a sad sack can or should get tenure. Near the end of Smiley's doorstopper of a novel, a provost finds himself mulling over the very question that *Moo* has explored from every possible angle—namely, "What is a university?" No clear answer comes to mind. That's the good news, as it were, because we are thus spared pontifications on his (and Smiley's) part. The bad news, of course, is universities have come not only to resemble corporations, but in truth, to *become* them. Given shrinking budgets at the state legislature and the inertia of excess everywhere to be seen on campus, something will have to give. But what? Surely not the buildings already completed or those in the planning stage; surely not programs in place or promised, much less the professors who lobby for ever-larger budgets. And most assuredly not anything remotely connected to athletic programs that provide undergraduates with the "bread and circus" of big-time football games.

By setting her story in the 1989–1990 academic year, Smiley could hardly avoid the rich material that political correctness has served up. But like most of the faculty at Moo U., she gives the subject only a passing nod. Only Chairman X, a former sixties radical who continues to mourn the passing of communism, takes the infinite variety of campus-based ideology with any degree of seriousness: "It was well known among the citizens of the state," he tells us early on, "that the university had pots of money and that there were highly paid faculty members in every department who had once taught Marxism and now taught something called de-

construction which was only Marxism gone underground in preparation
for emergence at a time of national weakness." For better or worse, this
view quickly folds into the larger heap of superstitions that consign each
group to the isolation of its own unquestioned viewpoint (the very last
thing that happens at Moo U. is candid debate) and that makes Moo U. the
anti-university it most assuredly is.

From what William Gass calls "the heart of the heart of the country,"
we move to sunny California and the Stanford-like university where John
L'Heureux's *The Handmaid of Desire* is set. Here, we are in the belly of the
English department beast (as we were in Randall Jarrell's *Pictures of an Institutions*), with all its requisite egomania and vaulting ambition. This time,
however, what divides the good old boys (known as the Fools) from the in
crowd (the Turks) are not quarrels pitting the New Criticism against the
Old Scholarship, but whether there should be a literature department at
all. Why not simply come clean and admit that "theory" is much more in-
triguing—to say nothing of career-enhancing—than going over the same
old dreary texts written by dead white European males? The rub, of
course, is that deconstructing a department requires votes, and what they
have instead is a paralysis of the deeply divided.

Enter Olga Kominska, a visiting writer/cutting edge theorist, who
turns out to be as enigmatic as she is magically powerful. L'Heureux takes
a hard, satiric look at a handful of academic feminists, would-be fiction
writers, and those who think of departmental life as a chess game in which
taking somebody's pawn is part of a larger plan to knock off their king.
Kominska, to her credit, operates on quite other assumptions, manipulat-
ing her colleagues until something akin to rough poetic justice is meted
out and the lives she has touched take on the aura of aesthetic wholeness.
Mission accomplished, she flies off at the novel's end, just as she had descended from the clouds in the opening chapter. In between, of course, is
where the action—and the academic satire—bubbles. Here, for example, is
how Zachary Kurtz (his last name is hardly accidental) describes the department of his deepest dreams:

> It would include Comp. Lit, Mod Thought, and all the lit-
> tle language departments—French, Russian, Spanish,
> you name it. It would take on all written documents,
> equally and with absolute indifference to the author's
> reputation or the western canon or the nature of writing
> itself—whether it was Flaubert's Bovary or a 1950 tax
> form or the label on a Campbell's soup can . . . and sub-
> ject them all to the probing, thrusting, hard-breathing
> analysis of the latest developments in metaphilosophical
> trans-literary theory.

And what would this new disposition call itself? Easy . . . The Department of Theory and Discourse. The S. Levin who had such high hopes for English departments must now be spinning in his fictional grave.

If *The Handmaid of Desire* is a send-up of life at a hot academic center, Richard Russo's *Straight Man* is a saga of those who occupy a spot well down the intellectual food chain. On its best days, fictional West Central Pennsylvania University is mediocre, and perhaps not even that. As temporary chairperson of the English department, William Henry Devereaux Jr. (son of a one-time king of American literary theory) tells it as it is when he talks to his Dean: "Mediocrity is a reasonable goal for our institution." Small wonder that Devereaux has a long-standing reputation as a pain in the ass—among administrators and fellow department members alike. He is also one of the more memorable curmudgeons I have encountered in years. Here, for example, is his "take" on faculty meetings:

> Despite having endured endless faculty meetings, I can't remember the last time anyone changed his (or her!) mind as a result of reasoned discourse. Anyone who observed us would conclude the purpose of all academic discussion was to provide the grounds for being further entrenched in our original positions.

Wry musings of this sort dot Russo's landscape, but fortunately, they are forced to share floor space with some of the funniest, most outrageous plot developments this side of *Lucky Jim*. Devereaux begins the novel with the wounds caused when a feminist poet of dubious distinction took exception to a stray remark he made at a department meeting and smacked him on the nose with her spiral notebook. A loose wire puts an ugly gash on his nose and, thus, we get a picture of life among short, academic fuses. But even this ante goes up considerably when Devereaux threatens to kill one campus pond duck for every day that the administration fails to provide him with the English department's annual budget. Talk about "all hell breaking loose!" The reverberations (duly covered by the local TV station) more than make up for the long uneventful stretch he put in at West Central.

And that manufactured, fictional excitement is perhaps the nub of why novels about campus life continue to have such an intrinsic appeal. For what we get is not really academic life as it actually is, but rather, a heightened, highly patterned alternative. Professors devour such novels because they contain just enough to seem familiar, even as their pages move steadily into territories over the top. One way of describing the effect might be to call it comic relief; another possibility is the sense of superiority fostered as the distance between a loony "them" and an altogether worthy *us* steadily increases.

But in the best of the breed, what readers (academics and nonacademics alike) react to are the special pleasures that only a piece of well-wrought fiction can provide. In comic novels, timing counts for virtually everything—although it is hard to imagine a successful novel about academe that does not have its ear to the campus ground and its heart in roughly the right place. When all its cylinders are working, the result is, finally, a human drama filled with very fallible human beings. And because ideas are—or should be—as much a part of the geography as the student center or the football stadium, these novels provide rich entertainment for those able to get the allusions and then calculate how a given writer has used them. When, for example, a character in an Allison Lurie novel describes her teenaged children as "nasty, brutish, and tall," those in the know smile knowingly. It is one of the minor benefits of a college education, but one that helps us actively resist the steady, downward spiral of much that passes itself off as contemporary culture. There are, after all, many ways to deal with the shoddier aspects of mass entertainment: one is to actively take arms against it, rather as Don Quixote tilted against windmills; another is to rigorously tend one's rose garden.

What I had not bargained for, however, is the way that enemies of the humanistic spirit would erect their various tents *within* English departments—not, as was the case at Cascadia, because of the claims of science and technology, of engineering and agriculture, but because the news from the cutting edge is that literature no longer speaks to the individual heart. Indeed, when texts are properly understood, there are no authors, no readers in the old-fashioned sense of the term, no transcendent meanings. What we have instead, many literary theorists would insist, are social constructions of reality, slippery linguistic slopes, and most important of all, thinly disguised political agendas. Levin conducted his comic battle for literary value at a time when most English professors probably cheered him on from the sidelines of their respective institutions. One wonders if that would still be the case now. Not only do his projected articles seem time-locked and entirely retrograde, but his blathering on about the humanities is the stuff that fighting words are now made of. A Levin worthy of wide support would be cooking up articles such as "Otherizing the Other: Melville's Marginalized Sailors"; "Revolution and Hegemony in Hawthorne's Victimized Imagination"; and, of course, the all-purpose "Race, Class, and Gender in Damn Near Everything." In short, the age of theory can be at least as insidious to everything Levin once held dear as was the soul-shriveling atmosphere he encountered at Cascadia.

By contrast, *A New Life* is a much more inner-directed, humanly significant work. Levin feels the world's pain, and his own, in a heart—and this, I would argue, ultimately matters more than the squabbles that contemporary academic novels currently report: heavy-water theorists versus academic traditionalists, those who see the university-as-corporation versus those who see it as the proper arena for various social transformations. That Levin is able to act in accordance with the whole retinue of gestures and attitudes known as *Menschlichkeit* makes Malamud's novel simultaneously more distinctive and more important.

When Leslie Fiedler spoke publicly about Malamud, he often focused on what might be called the directional arrow view of American literature: North and South, East and West. In his view, *A New Life* was noteworthy because it served up the cultural clash between East and West, Jew and gentile. Malamud's posthumous novel, *The People*, suggests that he shared at least some of Fiedler's general inclination to merge *davening* with a rain dance. The difference, however, is that Fiedler's brand of dazzle has largely slipped down the memory hole. The f-critic most often cited these days is Foucault. Indeed, he has become something of a whipping boy for queer theorists who quarrel with his reading of the homoeroticism Jim and Huck presumably experienced on the raft and for feminists who spin-doctor his ideas about the male flight from domesticity, often without the bother of giving credit where it is surely due. By contrast, *A New Life* survives its rereadings, partly because it remains one of the better academic novels produced in America, partly because the essential struggle between the self and society remains an abiding American concern, but perhaps most of all, because the more the assault on liberal learning changes, the more it remains, alas, the same.

Chapter 10

THE LIVES OF DUBIN

Walter Shear

It's an old American ethical dilemma: Are you as good as you could be? And if you could be, would that be good? For Bernard Malamud the impulse toward goodness in his characters provides a central impetus in many of his novels, but always with big complications. William Dubin, the central intelligence of *Dubin's Lives*, has several predecessors—Frank Alpine in *The Assistant*, S. Levin in *A New Life*, Harry Lesser in *The Tenants*, Yakov Bok in *The Fixer*, each burdened with a conscience, each involved in a forbidden love, each attempting to live according to certain principles, each working on a code of ethics that will enable them to come to terms with their present situation. Thus, while an extramarital affair supplies a skeletal structure for *Dubin's Lives*, the text is heavy with ethics—two sets, one of which reminds Dubin that in chasing after a woman thirty-plus years younger he is betraying a wife, living a lie, and the other, inspired by D. H. Lawrence, the subject of the biography Dubin is writing, commends the passionate life as the highest form of living, hectoring the conscious self, "let life invade you." Like Alpine and Levin, Dubin, faced with the intensity of new possibilities, feels his past life as a drifting lack of inspired commitment, but how Lawrentian audacities blend with his liberal humanism is less clear.

In tracking the conscientious Dubin we see a man feeling his way though that unknown territory that is life, trying to balance love and marriage, work and family life, but one who also often gives off the discomforting and relentless feeling of a man in pursuit of himself. He disciplines himself, with diet, exercise, walking/running, and cold showers, but invariably these seem desperate attempts to control his mind rather than simple acts of will. For all its descriptions of nature, the book is at its essence subjective. Even when Dubin is lost in a snowstorm he is unwilling to accept the purely objective: "He had changed his black inner world for the white, outer, equally perilous—man's fate in varying degrees; though some were more fated than others. Those who were concerned with fate were fated" (149). However, his liberal impulse—"I'd regret it beyond bearability if I were not involved in the lives of others" (34)—and his writing of biographies where he imaginatively tries to identify with his subjects prevent him from being too self-absorbed. His summing himself up, "I'm an odd inward man held together by an ordered life" (326), is accurate enough, but what we as readers bear witness to is the enormous effort necessary to order his life.

Though Dubin has many guises in the novel, his dreams and difficulties throughout are structured by his struggles as the aging male. He describes himself as middle aged, but since he is fifty-six, one might more accurately say he is on the far side of middle age. Besides the trials and tribulations of writing his Lawrence biography, he is constantly afflicted by what he refers to as "the age of aging," where he fears "illness, immobility; the disgrace of death" (318). He is a man suffering from his time of life. Not only is he is stricken with impotence in his sexual relations with his wife, at one time, fearful of forgetting, he is plagued by an inability to remember what he reads and in his writing, he cannot seem to grasp the words and images his mind searches for. Physical reminders of aging crowd upon him:

> A shocking multitude of single hairs appeared in his comb. His chest hair was turning gray. A rotting tooth had to be pulled. He held a book two feet from his face to focus the words. His handwriting grew in size: he'd been avoiding glasses. His haggard face was slack, faded eyes furtively hiding. (317)

One of his early visions involves seeing himself in his grave. The book, in fact, develops a motif of death through both his thoughts and the repeated visits he and Kitty make to various graves. Even the discovery of his vocation is tied to this distant dread: "In biographies the dead become alive, or seem to" (98).

As the voice of death sings in his soul, Fanny Blick with her youth becomes to him a symbolic as well as an erotic being. At the beginning, he is half-joking when he imagines himself saying, "I want the experience before I'm too old to have it" (56), but eventually the idea becomes a basic truth about this stage of his life. He tells himself repeatedly that this pleasure is something he is entitled to. Lawrence, his biographical subject, seems to advise him to be daring before it is too late ("Dubin wrote listening to Lawrence's high-pitched insistent voice in his ear" [114]), and he may remember the urging of his other biographer, Thoreau, to "adventure upon life now." He recognizes only too clearly that Fanny makes him feel young, that the years have deepened his need for love, not extinguished it, and he begins to regard middle age as the time "when you pay for what you didn't have or couldn't do when you were young" (140). The text comments, almost pathetically that "he wanted time on his side" (345). So overtly is Dubin thus impelled in his affair with Fanny that she warns him resentfully, "I have got to be more to you than a substitute for your lost youth . . ." (267–268).

It is Fanny Blick's entrance into Dubin's life (and into Kitty's as well) that seems the basic triggering mechanism for much of the misery and desperation in his brooding on age. At first the moralist/humanist fends off her advances—including her panties tossed directly to him—with a definite negative. Yet soon, with a naivete not unlike that of Goodman Brown off for but a single night in the woods, Dubin is arrived in Venice with Fanny and dalliance on his mind. As his dream of a brief romantic interlude turns to nightmarish farce and Fanny humiliates him by engaging in sexual encounters with much younger men, he finds himself slowly but firmly pushed into a subjective labyrinth, one manifestation of which is a severe case of writer's block over the Lawrence biography.

At this point he begins involuntarily to examine his own life, which unfolds before him as a series of discrete roles—father, son, husband, lover, biographer. In this postmodern analysis the previously unified self becomes a series of selves. And in this respect the lives of the title are not simply his biographies (written and unwritten), but those varied roles that his liberal sense of tolerant sympathy and humanistic responsibility has transformed into separate selves. He is different as he tries to relate to different people. Indeed, the book may be too successful in documenting this, for one of his critics, Malcolm O. Magraw, sees "a kind of mad choreography of dissociations from and attempted associations with the 'lives' of others, both dead and alive" (222). As a result, Magraw believes in a Dubin who never achieves psychological coherence.

Dubin's comment in a letter to Fanny, "There ought to be a way of having other selves to be with those we love" is not merely rationalization (though rationalization is undoubtedly involved) (233). Part of this mode of thinking may have resulted from his work with Thoreau, since we are told Dubin "wanted nature to teach him . . . perhaps to bring forth the self he sought" (10). The more he cultivates this protean version of himself (which seems based on a liberal sense of responsibility to each individual), the more basic actions and attitudes of other people begin to act as mirrors for examining his case. (At least two other critics, Chiara Briganti and Leon Edel, have as well remarked on Dubin's tendency to use his bio-graphical subjects and other characters as mirrors.) As Dubin explains to Kitty in regard to biography, "You see in others who you are" (130). And what he sees in other people is both who he is and who he is not. Eventually we see him, like many other Malamud protagonists, not only a man eminently earnest in his analysis of others but in the process of evaluation on his own road to judgment.

The analytical division of the self has some psychological advantages for him. For example, there is a disjuncture between Dubin the father and Dubin the lover in that peculiar incident in Venice when he believes he glimpses his daughter Maud in the company of an old man. There is a mystery about this episode that is never really clarified; was it she or wasn't it? (Bizarrely, Maud finally confesses to having been there with her lover, but at a different time.) Despite the similarities between himself and his daughter's lover—both are older, married men with minority back-grounds, and both are in a Venetian liaison with a twenty-year-old woman—despite this, Dubin never pushes the similarity to any conscious conclusion. The disjuncture remains—Dubin the father does not confront Dubin the lover (though James Mellard argues that something of the sort occurs on the unconscious level).

When he looks at himself as a father, Dubin feels he has worked hard to love both his children and to love them equally. Yet he recognizes how far their adult lives have separated them from both him and Kitty; he compares them to distant relatives. The liberal father has radical children. Foster son Gerry is a war protester, then a deserter, finally a communist and a member of the KGB. The fact that William accepts the Medal of Freedom award from Lyndon Johnson underlines the contrast with his protester son. His daughter, an eater of organic food, is for a time a member of a Zen commune and then an unmarried mother-to-be. Both the children seem extremely uncom-municative with him, very subjective, people prepared to act on and search for intensely personal beliefs. In short they show him his moralism and his subjectivity without its liberal, civic context. In turn he believes himself to be "little known" by his children and is frankly puzzled by their lives (168). All this serves to illuminate how much the novel's character groupings are structured by the idea of a generation gap, one that reflects the broader so-cial canvas and accents the typical Malamudian situation, the search for eq-uity within an intensifying social-political context.

Looking at his role as a son, Dubin imagines that much of his youthful life was in fact unlived. His parents are long dead and his current success as a writer seems to have distanced himself even more from their lives. Of his mother, he remembers mainly the mad helplessness. His father is presented as a waiter who thought his job responsibilities began and ended with doing well and whose job attitudes thus stubbornly reflected a suppression of his own personality, a tendency he evidently brought home as well. That he is a developed presence early in the book demonstrates that Dubin's early family life, while not exactly bleak, lacked vitality, an elan, a sense that life itself was fun. Thus, this side of Dubin is the man who feels deprived, that he wasted his youth, in some way was cheated or cheated himself. And as he feels such anxieties and confusions about his life, he feels a further loss, that his father is not present to accept and understand, to have pride in his achievements, and to convey approval for the life he has made. What he begins also to sense in a melancholy manner is that a part of everyone's biography is a past lost to time, a fact that it is the writer's task to remedy. Now at the moment when his mind and body both seem ready to fail him, he feels spun back into this lost past of his own: "Time ran in Dubin; he ran in time. . . . Time preached dying. . . . Lost self, selves. Dubin feared his mother's fate, saw her go mad in his looking glass" (318).

The major disjuncture and the crux of the moral dilemma in the novel is that of Dubin the husband and Dubin the lover. As the affair progresses (and it is not his first), he becomes not merely intensely conscious of the conflict but in effect a victim of it. Fanny's attractions are very clear and to his mind incredibly insistent. "Dubin loved her body, was conscious of her sensuality, aroused by the force of her sexual being" (218). Not only does she feel sex is "the most satisfying pleasure of life," she informs Dubin, "I think we're entitled to have sexual pleasure any way we want" (33). In her opinion she has become a better person because of her sexual experience. An instinctive, giving person, she seeks an uninhibited existence. When he says, "Some things you want to do you don't," she replies, "I wouldn't live that way" (243). While Dubin is properly appreciative of her spontaneity and Lawrentian instinctuality, he is more than once forced to confront their difference in values. In Venice, for example, when he wants to continue to expound on the art and culture of the place, she clearly has had enough and wants to go shopping. Still, Dubin senses that "the fountain of youth is the presence of youth" even as he feels the shame of lust at his age. He is in fact aware that his age is probably intensifying his experience, "love as a breakwater against age, loss of vital energy, the approach of death" (260). As the affair progresses, he feels he is changing because of Fanny and he wonders if his wife Kitty notices: "[D]oesn't an experience of love produce a newly experiencing self?" (241). In his case the answer is yes.

But the old self, the married self, does not disappear; it experiences new and alarming discomforts. As he analyzes it—while accusing himself and Kitty of too much analysis—their marriage from the beginning lacked spontaneity. He responded to her advertisement in the personals as she was in the act of withdrawing it. One could describe theirs as the modern counterpart of an old-country arranged marriage. Dubin views their deciding to marry as essentially an intellectual rather than an emotional decision. His attraction to her was based on the notion that she was "good people," "capable of a serious act of imagination: to be willing to love someone willing to love you" (47).

Like her husband, Kitty at fifty-one has periodic thoughts of death; he eventually concludes that her constant smelling the gas burners for leaks is in some way a ritual against death. He also believes that she has her former husband Nathaniel, long ago dead, too much on her mind, and there is plenty of evidence that this is the case.

The amount of thought Dubin devotes to Kitty in the course of the book is testimony to a bond beyond loyalty. He explains to Fanny that there are commitments in marriage, yet these have obviously become uncomfortable for both William and Kitty. But as Chiara Briganti argues, the typical Malamud protagonists find true freedom through commitment (151). Curiously, both Kitty and Dubin stray to other people in parallel fashion: While Dubin is in Venice, Kitty is drawn to Roger Foster. Eventually both are having affairs. Still, William suffers a guilt that affects not merely his work on D. H. Lawrence but his whole existence. He believes, as he puts it, that "loving Fanny he withheld love from his wife and daughter" (279). This formulation of his problem seems typical of the kind of guilt that can be experienced by the liberal conscience: no simple immorality but some deeply felt sense of an injustice being done, the principle of fairness being violated.

Still, Dubin's rational examination of his marriage's shortcomings is quite definite and basically convincing: They married each other's wounds, they try to define too much, and most significantly at the present, they take no joy in one another. True or not, such analyses afford him little peace of mind. He backs away when Kitty suggests divorce, but he also resists Fanny's increasing demands for firmer commitments. He articulates a fundamental insight into himself when he admits to a pressing Fanny, "I'm a family man" (362). This is, I believe, a basic truth about him. (I'm with those readers who believe that for all the ambiguity of the ending, he will eventually return on a permanent basis to his wife. Rita K. Gollin's "Malamud's Dubin and the Morality of Desire" makes the strongest case for a resolved ending to the book.)

Dubin tries to explain himself to Fanny—he loves her but he loves his wife's life. While this may be the biographer speaking, it as also the insight of a man who has begun to realize how much her life has been like his. To some extent they are sharing the same dilemma of life, one that demonstrates how much the book reflects the era in which it was written. Both of these people are reasoning humanists who have been suddenly confronted by the fact of passion in all its varied manifestations—a desire for love, for deep convictions, for more joy in living, for life itself. Further, in historical terms, both are liberal humanists who have been plunged into an era of political and social radicalism, become unwilling players in the field of cultural politics. One sign of their social heritage is the name of the town, Center Campobello, with its associations with the great twentieth-century liberal, Franklin Delano Roosevelt. Dubin's father also states in the imaginary dialogue that the Medal of Freedom award would have been better had it come from Roosevelt.

Gradually, William and Kitty are becoming aware that they are living in a time when people are instituting new searches for belief, trying new value systems, and through a natural implication, this contemporary history calls into question their own value systems. When Kitty says they had no religion in common, Dubin, referring to their shared humanism, says they have. Kitty answers that this is not enough for kids. While Dubin states, "God is for those who find him," Kitty replies, "No, he has to be taught" (104). In his belief that one is confined to this world, Dubin stresses his secularism, and Malamud is in fact careful to point out that Dubin's own humanism, while related to his Jewish background, is distinct from orthodox faith: "Once in a while Dubin prayed. It was a way of addressing the self; God had a tin ear" (210). Earlier, in a dispute with his father over his marrying out of the faith, Dubin asked, "How can a man be a Jew if he isn't a man?" (69). (Daniel Fuchs accuses Dubin of being an "ethical Jew, whose ethics include discarding what is identifiably Jewish when it matters" [208].) Although Dubin responds throughout to signs of Judaism (Fanny's wearing of a Star of David and the synagogue across the street from her apartment), the lack of an active religious element creates more strain on the humanistic value system the novel evokes and serves to throw Dubin more precariously on his own waning resources.

Dubin initially becomes aware of the social changes that are occurring in America through his relationship with Fanny. In one of their first conversations he feels obliged to admit, "I'm only recently a visitor to the new sexual freedom" (58), an admission that begins to define the historical context in which he will wander throughout the book. His buying into this new freedom may be more a matter of the psychology of aging than any conviction on his part, but, as his subsequent agonies dramatize, it unleashes on his vulnerable rationality the full irrational and ferocious forces of his sensual appetite and the surging social alterations of history. Finding himself suddenly separated from the younger generation by age, he struggles mightily to reestablish and maintain a connection, however it may challenge his being and threaten to inundate him. As his cynosure, he will place his faith, desperate at times, in reason.

A major frustration is that the humanistic emphasis that both Dubin and Kitty place on learning from experience requires for optimum efficacy the perspective of a life span, the kind of expanse one would get in the context created by a biography; otherwise they act constantly on the basis of partial knowledge, what can be figured out liable to be too dependent on a particular time. (So why not be more impulsive?) In this context the novel revisits a major formulation of Malamud's humanism. In a famous passage in *The Natural* Iris tells Roy: "We have two lives . . . the life we learn with and the life we live after that. Suffering is what brings us toward happiness" (*Two Novels*, 135). This is very close to the way Dubin has thought of his marriage: "Each . . . suffered. More or less, they educated one another experiencing their natures" (101). As he thinks of Fanny's experiences, he speculates, "It seemed to him a commentary on himself that he expected her to have learned something" (103) . Though some commentators on the novel have seen her as this learning figure (Briganti and Field, for example), a remark she makes to Dubin clearly sets out her priorities: "I'm not living my life to learn lessons. . . . Most of all I want to enjoy it" (247). Her emphasis on instant living or joy in the process of living itself, on spontaneity, challenges what he also has seen as a weakness of his humanism.

Furthermore, Dubin's increasing consciousness of death serves, by intensifying the time pressure, to call into question Iris's terms of measurement: "William Dubin's in his last life, no longer those one lives to learn with, if he learns" (299). Faced with running out of lives, at least lives of his own, Dubin, however, refuses to run out of meaning. As articulated in Dubin's warning to himself, he sees his crucial problem very specifically: "It's one thing for a man not to know, not to have learned; it's another not to be able to live by what one does know. That's sure danger" (275). At this stage the difficulty is making a dynamic out of what he has already learned and what he is learning, of knitting the long past with the current moment.

For all of Dubin's puzzlements and persistent questioning, the novel is in many respects a book about learning, though not a guidebook with definite answers to specific questions or even a bildungsroman. At the heart of virtually all Dubin's relationships is the idea of learning and the kind of disciplined hope it inspires; he studies nature, for example, making himself memorize the names of flowers and trees that he might be, in the manner of Thoreau, the careful observer, one who knew how to look. In Dubin's view Thoreau's main concern was learning how to live his life, an aim that Dubin apparently absorbed in the process of writing about him. As a biographer, he thinks, with a wistful sadness, "One learns where life goes" (12). But the experience with Fanny and the writing about

Lawrence make him more aware of the reciprocity between his life and his art: just as Fanny's early betrayal of him in Venice plunged him into a total writing block, so his later successful sexual experiences with her help him to understand Lawrence more fully, "his religion of sexuality; a belief in the blood, the flesh, as wiser than the intellect" (219). But it is exactly these ideas—almost anti-ideas—that challenge both Dubin the biographer and Dubin the man. As many people remind him, he and Lawrence are almost completely opposite: Dubin, the man of the mind; Lawrence, the poet of the body. Dubin's friend Oscar Greenfeld also reminds him, "Your friend Lawrence . . . insisted there's no knowing one's way through life" (325). Rather cryptically, Dubin replies, still opting for his own point of view, "I won't relinquish for myself what he failed to know about himself." Dubin's further mention of the mystery he sees in Lawrence's life really takes him full circle (just as his walks had), back to an earlier, very humanistic insight into the unavoidable limit of his work, having at the essential secret any human life refuses to divulge: "no one, certainly no biographer, has the final word. Knowing, as they say, is itself a mystery that weaves itself as one unweaves it" (20).

In one of the final episodes, Dubin—bizarrely treed by a dog and an angry racist farmer—calculates his fate, his faith, and his remaining strength and begins to assemble a final self—if not an identity. "I know who I am. . . . I learn best when struggling with the work—with the lives I write. . . . I must act my age" (23). The suffering inherent in the struggle of a writer is now integral with learning and both are, as the reference to aging suggests, basic and continuing parts of the total process of living itself. Frustratingly, however, the problem is the solution. Earlier, he had almost subconsciously remarked to Kitty, "[F]orgive who I am" (226). Recognition of weakness and the need to have the forgiveness of others is a vital part of the living process, but he now is ready to transcend the helplessness of this stage. The struggle with the inadequacies of the aging self now seems buoyed by an acceptance. In an important respect William Dubin does come back to a single, essential self with an awareness of what he has always been as a working artist: "Writing is a mode of being. If I write I live" (105). In realizing this, Dubin articulates what Sidney Richman refers to as "the soul-ordering powers Malamud attributes to language," for it is with language that William Dubin will struggle with and for his soul (210). That this is his essential passion is also attested to by the bibliography at the conclusion. For better or worse it is as a writer that he passes into his contemporary era as a man who does his own thing, his writing, like that of Frost, "a momentary stay against confusion."*

---

*Malamud cites this phrase in his introduction to his collected stories (*The Stories of Bernard Malamud*, xiii).

Works Cited

Briganti, Chiara. "Mirrors, Windows and Peeping Toms: Woman as the Object of Voyeuristic Scrutiny in Bernard Malamud's *A New Life* and *Dubin's Lives*," *Studies in American Jewish Literature* 3 (1983): 151–165.

Edel, Leon. "Narcissists Need Not Apply," *American Scholar* 49 (1979): 131.

Field, Leslie. "A Day in the Life of Charlie Dubin's Son," *Studies in American Jewish Literature* 7.2 (1988): 213–223.

Fuchs, Daniel. "Malamud's *Dubin's Lives*: A Jewish Writer and the Sexual Ethic," *Studies in American Jewish Literature* 7.2 (1988): 205–212.

Gollin, Rita K. "Malamud's Dubin and the Morality of Desire," *Papers on Language and Literature* 18.2 (1982): 189–207.

Magaw, Malcolm O. "Malamud's Dubious Dubin: The Biographer and His Square Walk in a Circle," *CLIO* 23.3 (Spring 1994): 219–233.

Malamud, Bernard. *Dubin's Lives*. New York: Farrar, Straus, Giroux, 1979. (Parenthical page references to the book are to this edition.)

———. *Two Novels*. New York: Modern Library, 1964.

Mellard, James M. "The 'Perverse Economy' of Malamud's Art: A Lacanian Reading of *Dubin's Lives*." In *Critical Essays on Bernard Malamud*, ed. Joel Salzberg. Boston: G. K. Hall, 1987, 186–202.

Richman, Sidney. "Malamud's Quarrel with God." In *Critical Essays on Bernard Malamud*, ed. Joel Salzberg. Boston: G. K. Hall, 1987, 203–221.

Chapter 11

GORILLA IN THE MYTH
Malamud's *God's Grace*

D. Mesher

> Oh God said to Abraham kill me a son
> Abe says man you must be puttin' me on
>
> —Bob Dylan, *Highway 61 Revisited*

In its references to classical sources and its use of traditional rituals, *God's Grace* (1982) is Bernard Malamud's most Jewish novel. And, in its vision of a thermonuclear destruction and Second Flood eradicating not only the human race (with one temporary exception) but almost the totality of creation, *God's Grace* is Malamud's most pessimistic. Yet Malamud himself argued for an affirmative reading of the ending of *God's Grace*. In an interview with Joel Salzberg, the author complained that "one of the misreadings of the novel, by the way, is that it ends in tragedy. Some reviewers have failed to recognize that a gorilla recites *Kaddish* for Calvin Cohn, and that is indeed a cause for optimism" (*Conversations* 127). The terms of that optimism are paradoxically suggested in a later interview with Salzberg, where Malamud explained that ending, which follows the death of the last man on earth, as "a way for man to have a possible future" (*Conversations* 142).

In effect, though humanity-the-species does not survive in the novel, humanity-the-quality does; or, to put it in more familiar Malamudian terms, though the last Jew is dead by the end, Malamud's mythic use of Jewishness continues in the form of a yarmulke-wearing, kaddish-reciting gorilla.

Malamud's Jewish metaphors are clearest in his early fiction, where Jewish characters—such as Morris Bober in *The Assistant* (1957)—are both individualized, with personal strengths and weaknesses, and universalized, as symbols of the inevitability of suffering and the possibility of redemption. When Morris talks about what he calls "the Jewish law," he means only "to do right, to be honest, to be good" (124). The rabbi at Morris's funeral says much the same thing, defending Morris as a "true Jew because he lived in the Jewish experience, which he remembered, and with the Jewish heart" (229). But even Frank Alpine, Morris's Italian assistant, recognizes that "other religions have those ideas, too" (124). What sets Morris apart, in fact, is not religion but empathy: "The world suffers," we are told at the beginning of *The Assistant*. "*He* felt every schmerz" (7).

If Morris is the measure of Malamud's mythic Jewishness, though, the Judaism of Calvin Cohn, the protagonist of *God's Grace*, is at once more traditional and less Jewish. Morris is, after all, indifferent to traditional Judaism. In reply to Frank's challenge that he routinely violates many Jewish laws, for example, Morris claims, "Nobody will tell me that I am not Jewish because I put in my mouth once in a while, when my tongue is dry, a piece ham" (124). In contrast, Calvin Cohn is the only character in Malamud's fiction who does worry about violating the laws of kashrut and the Sabbath, and who quotes not only from the Torah, but from the Talmud and Midrash, as well. Yet the reader should be wary of Cohn's promulgation of Jewish traditions from the first mention of his name—that is, long before we discover that Calvin has changed his name from Seymour. As with S. Levin, the protagonist of *A New Life* (1961), who uses the initial instead of Seymour, the name change partly suggests Cohn's unwillingness to "see more" deeply into himself. But the choice of "Calvin" also creates a religious admixture that is less fusion than confusion; Cohn himself imagines his father dismissing the name change as "a big naarishkeit" (135), or foolishness.

For someone who once sought to conjoin Christianity and Judaism in his own name (a *cohen* is a member of the hereditary priestly class among Jews), Calvin shows a surprising degree of intolerance toward the faith in which Buz, the chimpanzee, was raised by Dr. Bünder. (One is tempted here to recall that John Calvin was born Jean Chauvin—that is, with the same last name as Nicolas Chauvin, the Napoleanic soldier whose fanaticism gave us the word *chauvinism*.) When the chimp gives Calvin his crucifix to hold, for example, Cohn thinks, "One God is sufficient" (25), and considers throwing the crucifix into the water. Next, when Buz crosses himself as Cohn reads to him from Genesis, Calvin thinks that "if one of them was a Christian and the other a Jew, Cohn's island would never be Paradise" (54). Later, at the seder Cohn organizes to celebrate the miracle of the other chimps' speech, when Buz again crosses himself, Cohn tells him pointedly, "Do that later, Buz. . . . It's not part of this ceremony. It's another modality" (113).

For Cohn, there are two ineluctable modalities of the invisible: the duty of Judaism, and the love of Christianity. That this distinction has less to do with actual religions than with the novel's mythic use of them is suggested by Malamud's coupling, in his protagonist's name, of Cohn's Judaism with its stern Christian counterpart, Calvinism, in which election and salvation are strictly a matter of God's grace. Indeed, that Malamud employed a term from Christian theology for the title of the novel suggests just how unorthodox (in any sense of the word) Cohn's Judaism is when it suits his (or his author's) purpose. On one hand, the only scripture on the island is Cohn's "old Pentateuch" (40), and this is what "Cohn remembered: God was Torah. He was made of words" (92). When they arrive at the island, for example, Cohn accepts his salvation as a judgment. "The Lord, baruch Ha-shem, had moved from His Judgment to His Mercy seat. Cohn would fast. Today must be Yom Kippur" (27). Cohn's Judaism is a simple contract: God's rules are Law, or Torah, and you disobey them at your own peril. The commandments Cohn remembers tend to carry the death penalty for their violation, from keeping the Sabbath (129) to abjuring bestiality (161), and he even quotes Torah and Talmud to God himself, who has broken that contract with a Second Flood. On the other hand, Cohn himself uses "God's grace" as an affirmative interjection (43, 121), and his stern "God . . . made of words" seems at times much closer to the Gospel of John than Jewish sources, such as when Cohn tells Buz, "The word began the world . . . the God of Beginnings . . . said the word and the earth began" (68–70). Later, at the seder, in an attempt to communicate with George, the gorilla, Cohn relates the New Testament parable of the Prodigal Son, "and the gorilla listened with tears flowing as he consumed large pieces of damp matzo" (124).

Malamud has mixed Jewish and Christian imagery before, most notably in *The Assistant*, where Morris Bober's humanistic Judaism is balanced by Frank Alpine's devotion to Francis of Assisi. Cohn's Judaism, however, is a far cry from the suffering and compassion of Morris Bober. Though many of Malamud's protagonists begin their fictions as survivors—of a Harriet Bird bullet in the gut, of years entombed in a store, of alcoholism and other past-life mistakes, and so on—no one but Cohn can claim to have survived so much (the extermination of most of the living world, including the human race) while suffering so little (a few days of radiation sickness). Certainly, Cohn desires the best for his little community of primates. But even his seven Admonitions, baked in clay if not etched in stone, promote love as a utilitarian but not divine virtue. The third Admonition commands, "Love thy neighbor. If you can't love, serve—others, the community. Remember the willing obligation." This Admonition, however, is placed immediately after the second: "Note: God is not love, God is God. Remember Him" (171). Significantly, then, Cohn's apparent melding of Christianity and Judaism in himself and his name lacks precisely that quality, "love," that he finds intolerable in another's expression of faith.

The chief target of Cohn's anti-Christian dogma is Buz, the chimpanzee given the power of speech by Dr. Bünder. Buz frequently mentions "Jesus of Nozoroth" (66, 70), suggests "that maybe Jesus had invented language," and even claims that Jesus "preached to the chimps" (68). Cohn understands this as Buz's "metaphor. . . . 'The chimps as Christians'" (68), but Buz means it literally, and anyway it is Malamud's metaphor as well. Cohn is displeased by Buz's religious persuasion from the beginning. He thinks about offering the chimpanzee a yarmulke, but decides against it because "Jews did not proselytize" (54). Buz takes the yarmulke anyway and Cohn, who never sees it again, wonders if "perhaps in some future time, Deo volente, a snake might come slithering along wearing one" (54). The use of "God willing" in Latin, combined with the image of a yarmulke-wearing snake, makes clear Cohn's apprehensions about Christianity. No wonder that this "second son of a rabbi who was once a cantor" (55) continues to have "occasional hopes that Buz might ask to be bar mitzvah'd since he was already the equivalent age of thirteen" (148). Cohn imagines from the beginning a relationship with Buz "like brothers, if not father and son," and as soon as the chimp can talk, Cohn suggests Buz call him "Dad" (66).

One of the most telling instances of Cohn's intolerance toward Buz's Christianity is in his renaming of the chimp. Names and naming are always important in Malamud's fiction, and this is especially so in *God's Grace*, where Cohn, in one sense a second Adam, makes it his prerogative to name the island and everything on it. When Buz has the temerity to give recently arrived chimps mostly New Testament names, Cohn admits that "naming names was freedom of speech" (103), but then never allows Buz the chance to name anything else. As we have seen, Cohn had already renamed himself Calvin long before the Destruction. He renames Buz near the beginning of the novel, while they are still on board the *Rebekah Q* after the flood, rejecting the name Gottlob, which "Dr. Bünder had hung on the unsuspecting chimp" (21).

> Cohn got out his old Pentateuch, his Torah in Hebrew
> and English . . . flipped open a wrinkled page at random
> and put his finger on it. He then informed the little chimp

> that he now had a more fitting name, one that went har-
> moniously with the self he presented. In other words he
> was Buz.
>
> Cohn told him that Buz was one of the descendants of
> Nahor, the brother of Abraham the Patriarch, therefore a
> name of sterling worth and a more suitable one than the
> doctor had imposed on him.
>
> To his surprise the chimp seemed to disagree. He re-
> acted in anger, beat his chest, jumped up and down in
> breathy protest. (22)

Cohn's is a time-honored method of naming children, and Buz seems to have less to complain about than some characters in American fiction—such as Pilate and First Corinthians, two women whose family has also utilized this "blind selection of names from the bible" in Toni Morrison's *Song of Solomon* (18). Nevertheless, Buz's renaming (one might almost say "rechristening" here) is a clever Malamudian device. Gottlob, after all, is not only a name, but an idiomatic German interjection, literally meaning "God-praise," but used like "Thank God" in English. Though it sounds rather odd, Cohn himself uses "God's grace" twice in the novel (43, 121), as if it were an English equivalent for the interjection, *Gottlob*—a repeated anomaly perhaps designed to suggest a correspondence between "Gott-lob" and "God's grace." Though it is true that Buz was Abraham's nephew (Gen. 22:21), the name in Hebrew can mean "shame," "mockery," or "dis-grace." In effect, then, Cohn has changed the chimp's name from God's Grace to Disgrace, which explains the clever primate's angry reaction. Not until near the end of the novel does Buz manage to reclaim the name Gott-lob, along with a little of the accent he learned from Dr. Bünder, when he says, "I om not Buz, my name ist Gottlob" (215).

Cohn capitalizes on the "un-Bünder-ing" of Gottlob to help establish his fatherly dominion over chimp, but it is in Malamud's creative uses of the Akedah, the binding of Isaac—found, not coincidentally, in the same chapter of Genesis as the mention of Buz—that their father-and-son story achieves its ultimate form. The Akedah, of relatively little importance in Christianity, is a defining event in Judaism, and the subject of much commentary and legend. Cohn's sources are probably supposed to be the original Talmudic and Midrashic texts, but Malamud took almost all of the novel's Akedah-related materials from Shalom Spiegel's *The Last Trial* (1967), as noted in the novel's acknowledgments.

Spiegel bases his reading on several different traditions associated with the biblical text of the Akedah, some of which Malamud does not discuss, such as the possibility that the received version was originally a story of child-sacrifice as the ultimate devotion to God, a story that was imperfectly revised into one where God rejects human sacrifice and stays Abraham's hand. As Cohn explains to Buz about Abraham and Isaac, "The scriptures have them both going up the mountain to participate in the ceremony God had ordained, but only Abraham came down. So where was Isaac?" (74). Spiegel begins with precisely this query (2), and, as he shows, it is a question that has figured in rabbinical discussions at least since the first century, beginning with teachings of both Palestinian and Babylonian Amoraim, now preserved as midrashim (2–3). Spiegel himself, however, is more interested in surveying much later exegetical answers, which take Abraham's apparently solo return as indication that Isaac's fate is not fully recounted in the biblical text. Among these, Spiegel recounts teachings that Isaac's soul left his body—even though Abraham's knife never touched his throat—and he needed to be resuscitated by the angel Michael, and that Isaac was sacrificed and burnt to ashes, again to be brought back to life by divine intervention. Malamud incorporates into the novel yet another version, in which the wounded or dead Isaac is carried away by angels to the Garden of Eden, to be resurrected to this life after recuperating there for three years (*God's Grace*, 75–76; *Last Trial*, 3–7). Thus, Cohn's Akedah contains a son sacrificed at the hands of his father, and a resurrection anticipating that of Jesus because, Cohn tells Buz, "The New Testament scribes always set the Christian unfolding carefully in the Judaic past."

Unfortunately, Malamud (or at least Cohn) has the time-line wrong here. Even Spiegel himself, whose study was primarily intended to serve as background to the medieval Hebrew poem entitled "The Akedah," by Rabbi Ephraim ben Jacob of Bonn, can trace these midrashic tales of Isaac's death and resurrection no further back than "Isaac ben Asher la-Levi, one of the first Tosafists in medieval Germany" (6), who lived c. 1050–1130, or "perhaps the bloody events of the beginning of the Crusades" (134). Indeed, in citing "*a number of parallels* in the accounts by the two faiths of the happenings at Moriah and Golgotha" (103–104), Spiegel is defending the rabbinical legends against a reversed claim, that they were borrowed from "the redemption mythos of the Christians" (103). Malamud's apparent notion, then, that the Gospel writers had such Jewish teachings in mind when describing another resurrection, is highly improbable. This is only one of several examples in *God's Grace* of the author's shortcoming in traditional Jewish learning. At times, these are merely confusing, as when Cohn says "Talmudic sages" (74) and "Talmudists" (76), for example, in referring not to the Tanaim and Amoraim whose teachings are redacted in the Talmud, but to later commentators *on* the Talmud. At other times those errors become intrusive, as in Malamud's one tortured attempt in the book to transliterate a single line of Hebrew as basic as the Shema—in which he not only conflates Ashkenazic and Sephardic pronunciations, but twice leaves out a syllable in *adonai*, Hebrew for "Lord," all in the short space of six words (57).

Yet, his desire to use of the lore of the Akedah is all the more striking, just because Malamud's own background in Judaism was slight, based much more on popular Yiddishkeit than on traditional learning. This is one reason why there are so few specifically Judaic elements to be found in Malamud's art, other than *God's Grace*. And whatever the historical accuracy of its presentation, Malamud's artistic use of the Akedah is an artistic triumph. As we have seen, the Cohn's Akedah combines the conflicts between father and son, duty and love, Judaism and Christianity, salvation and extinction. Further, it exposes the failings of human perceptions of humanity: on hearing that, when Abraham is told to spare his son, he sacrifices a ram in Isaac's place, Buz asks pointedly, "Ond do you call murdering onimols a civilized act?" (73). The terminology here is doubly ironic, considering that the last act of civilization was to cause its own destruction.

According to Spiegel, incidentally, many of the same midrashic sources associate the blood Isaac lost when sacrificed with the blood of redemption at Pesach (54–59), perhaps explaining why the other major Jewish feature of the novel is a Passover seder, at which all the elements of the novel's climax are put in place: Cohn's inability to control the chimps, especially Esau; his worsening relationship with Buz; his sexual interest in Mary Madelyn, who is "an altogether interesting lady chimpanzee" and "would look lovely in a white dress" (119); and his emotional connection with the speechless gorilla, George. The climax then takes place in the novel's last chapter, entitled "God's Mercy" and specifically not "God's Grace." There the Akedah is reversed, and the son (again called Buz, to emphasize that relationship, even though the chimp reclaimed the name Gottlob in the previous chapter) sacrifices his father, Cohn.

If the amount of traditionally Jewish elements in the *God's Grace* is unusual for Malamud, much more of the novel should be quite familiar from his earlier work. The rivalry between males for an attractive female, for example, is a standard feature of all of Malamud's longer fictions, beginning with *The Natural*. And even sexual relations between Cohn and the female chimpanzee seem an almost "natural" progression from his earlier novels: in *The Assistant*, Helen Bober crosses religious lines for Frank Alpine; in *The Tenants*, Irene Bell (née Belinksy) crosses racial lines for Willie Spearmint; and in *God's Grace*, Mary Madelyn takes a lover from a different species, Cohn. Indeed, Malamud gives the chimp a speech defect— "whenever she pronounced an el it became doubleu. Buz giggled but Cohn liked the sound of it" (118)—just so she can become Cohn's "Juwiet" (158), and Cohn her Jew.

Another echo from *The Tenants* suggests that *God's Grace* also operates on a racial level. Lesser's last words to Willie are the insult, "Anti-Semitic Ape" (229), and Esau in *God's Grace* is, indeed, an antiSemitic ape who threatens Cohn with the taunt, "I will break every Jewbone in your head"

(201). Though there is certainly no hint in the novel of any equivocation of blacks and apes, and the echo from *The Tenants* seems more unfortunate than insightful, whiteness is an important theme in the novel. Cohn, after all, is first introduced not as a paleontologist but a "paleologist" (3), a word which, if it means anything, denotes an antiquarian (that is, not just ancient bones, but ancient lore as well), but which also might suggest someone who studies "pale" ones. This foreshadows Buz's description of his "dod" as a "white chimpanzee" (121), but as the novel progresses an albino ape becomes the object of fear for both Buz and Cohn. Cohn dreams of the white ape, and in what seems to be one of those dreams he is saved by George the gorilla (156). Before that, Buz warns him that "a white ape, they can be nasty people" (154), emphasizing the connection with humans like Cohn. As his island community is collapsing at the end of the novel, Cohn hunts and kills his pale bogey man, who turns out only to be an albino chimpanzee. "Not a god-like mysterious creature—simply a soiled white ape from the headlands, turning black in death; but Cohen felt as though he had murdered a man" (214). Perhaps he has done worse than that.

As depressing as so much of this seems, Malamud himself tried to find something affirmative about the ending of *God's Grace*. In an interview with Joel Salzberg, the author complained that "one of the misreadings of the novel, by the way, is that it ends in tragedy. Some reviewers have failed to recognize that a gorilla recites *Kaddish* for Calvin Cohn, and that is indeed a cause for optimism" (127). Perhaps. Certainly, Malamud's readers have heard a concluding kaddish before: first, at the end of "The Mourners," where Gruber, another landlord and prefigurement of Levenspiel, "became a mourner" for Kessler, his impoverished tenant, "having suffered unbearable remorse for the way he had treated the old man" (*Stories* 26); and then, on the final page of "The Magic Barrel," where a rabbinical student, Leo Finkle, picks for his bride the wanton daughter of his matchmaker, Pinye Salzman. "Around the corner, Salzman, leaning against a wall, chanted prayers for the dead" (*Stories* 215). Each of these recitations of the kaddish is ironic, and affirmative, in large part because no one has died in either case. When, however, Cohn is murdered at the end of *God's Grace*, the last survivor of humanity and the humanity of the last survivor are simultaneously extinguished, and the mantle of Malamud's metaphoric Jewishness devolves upon George, the kaddish-reciting gorilla. But it is as much the ability to recite as it is the meaning of the prayer recited that Malamud was commenting on in the interview; the optimism comes from George's apparently new ability to speak. Before, when only chimps and Cohn could speak, George was frustrated by being mute. At the seder, for example, when Cohn asks George to "say a good word to his friends-and-fellow-islanders," the gorilla is only frustrated.

> The giant ape . . . strove to speak. he coughed, strained,
> sighed. His throat bulged. Now he grunted as though re-
> sisting constipation. His heavy black form trembled as if
> he was feverish. In desperation, George rose from the
> chair and beat his booming chest. The cave resounded
> loudly with the drumming. With a roar of rage he lifted
> and overturned the teak table. (123)

Even from the start, however, George is different from the chimpanzees. It is George who nurses Cohn back from his illness, George who is most moved by the liturgical recordings of Cohn's father (even if he tries to eat one of them), George who responds emotionally to Cohn's telling of the parable of the Prodigal Son, George who "looked like himself plus something else he might be" (131), George who "kept his dignity" even when called a pariah by Buz (172). Human beings, in their mad vanity, had destroyed the world once, and Calvin Cohn, in his own vanity, had believed himself the proper candidate to create a new race, by mixing his genes with those of a chimpanzee. Cohn's plan only ends in greater losses: of his offspring, of his community, of the chimp's ability to speak, and finally of Cohen himself. But George's miraculous recitation of the kaddish after Cohen's death, while he is—"Deo volente"—wearing that lost yarmulke, is optimistic for Malamud because it affirms a divine plan far beyond the reckoning of Calvin Cohn, representative of humanity. This apparently religious affirmation, near the end of the career of a conspicuously secular-humanist author, may be the most surprising element of all.

Works Cited

Lasher, Lawrence, ed. *Conversations with Bernard Malamud*. Jackson: University Press of Mississippi, 1991.

Malamud, Bernard. *The Assistant*. New York: Farrar, Straus and Cudahy, 1957.

———. *God's Grace*. New York: Farrar Straus Giroux, 1982.

———. *The Stories of Bernard Malamud*. New York: Farrar Straus Giroux, 1983.

———. *The Tenants*. New York: Farrar, Straus and Giroux, 1971.

Morrison, Toni. *Song of Solomon*. New York: Knopf, 1977.

Spiegel, Shalom. *The Last Trial*. New York: Pantheon, 1967.

Part Three

THEMATIC THREADS:
PATTERNS IN MALAMUD'S FICTION

Chapter 12

REFLECTIONS ON TRANSMOGRIFIED YIDDISH ARCHETYPES IN FICTION BY BERNARD MALAMUD

S. Lillian Kremer

Folkloric characters of Yiddish literature have been successfully transmogrified by modern American writers who have transplanted treasures of the traditional canon to the American literary landscape.[1] Among the most successful of these contemporary translators is Bernard Malamud who has created a body of fiction incorporating stock figures from Yiddish literature and folklore—recasting them, reclothing them in modern dress, to explore themes of spiritual crisis. *T'shuvah,* turning to God or the right moral path, central to the Jewish principle of redemption, is a fundamental concept in Malamud's affirmative fictions. "The Magic Barrel" and two stories from *Pictures of Fidelman*, "The Last Mohican" and "Pictures of the Artist," evidence derivative Yiddish character constructs enacting Jewish themes. Although readers of twentieth-century American literature have passing acquaintance with the *shadchan* (matchmaker) and *schnorrer* (beggar) and have become conversant with the *schlemiel* (fool, simpleton) who has garnered substantial fictional treatment and critical analysis in Ruth Wisse's *The Schlemiel as Modern Hero* and Sanford Pinsker's *The Schlemiel as Metaphor*, the figure known as the *tzaddik* (righteous man) and the variant *lamed vov tzaddik* (one of thirty-six legendary saints) generally elude critical scrutiny in their nontraditional transformations and settings, and remain detached from their literary precursors in critical commentaries on Malamud's work.[2]

According to Jewish legend, as Philip Birnbaum explains, the *lamed vov tzaddikim*, thirty-six anonymous righteous men inhabiting the world in each generation, are described as being extremely modest, "concealing their identity behind a mask of ignorance and poverty and earning their livelihood by the sweat of their brow" (306). In the folk tales, these figures, also known as *nistarim* (concealed), emerge from their self-imposed obscurity to avert threatened disasters perpetrated against the Jewish people. As soon as their tasks are accomplished, they return to anonymity in the Jewish community. Each is unknown to, and independent of, the others, and when one dies another appears in his place.[3] While the persona has been used in twentieth-century prose in its traditional form of communal service, either warding off an enemy or giving solace to the suffering as for example in the prize-winning French novel, *The Last of the Just*, in Jewish American fiction the transformed character plays on an intimate stage of personal spiritual drama. Paralleling the traditional hidden saints, the American secularized incarnations are common men, boorish, yet verbally adept, materializing when needed, whether or not their presence is desired. Relentless until success is achieved, they then depart as mysteriously as they appeared.

Both Ita Sheres and Marcia Gealy argue persuasively that there are direct parallels, if not direct influences on Malamud's writing from biblical and talmudic texts. Analyzing Malamud's novels from the perspective of biblical and Jewish mystical thought, Sheres identifies three "keys" to understanding the Jewish nature of his work: the Akedah, Abraham's sacrifice; the legend of the *lamed vov tzaddikim,* and Isaac Luria's "mystical interpretation of Jewish exile" reading intense suffering for a purpose.[4] Sheres argues that "If the concept of change by individual righteousness and isolation [associated with the legend of the thirty-six hidden saints] is carried over to Malamud's novels one clearly realizes that the basic premise of the main protagonists is positive and that their decisions to attempt to transform their fates are closely related to a deep belief in the essential benevolence and grandeur of man."[5] Similarly, Marcia Gealy identifies some of Malamud's best short stories with the major teachings of Hasidism, isolating "the need to journey inward to achieve salvation, the importance of identification with a holy man or teacher, the primacy of love, . . . the reality of evil, . . . [and] the Hasidic belief in the sanctity of the tale, the notion that a story could have potency to effect change . . ."[6] Gealy enumerates characteristics Malamud shares with Hasidic storytellers—the same juxtaposition of sacred and profane, the same fusion of Jewish past and present—but judges that "in the best sense of the tradition, Malamud, . . . has broken away and found his own distinctive voice."[7]

Although Malamud read neither Hebrew nor Yiddish, he understood spoken Yiddish, attended Yiddish theater, and, in an interview with Curt Leviant, acknowledged that he had read classical Yiddish and Hebrew writers in translation, among them Mendele Mokher Seforim, Sholom Aleichem, I. L. Peretz, Sholem Asch, and I. B. Singer of the Yiddish writers and S. Y. Agnon, Amos Oz, Mati Meggid, Aharon Megged, and other Israeli moderns.[8] It is likely that Malamud would have encountered *lamed vov tzaddikim* in his readings and found them appealing and appropriate to his own tales of spiritual seeking and ethical exploration. The paradigm of the teacher-pupil relationship, one that recurs in Malamud's fiction, is central to these stories of quester and guide. During a period when much of American literature has been transfixed by self-absorption and self-reflexivity, Malamud's moral mentors, derived from the Jewish *tzaddikim*, transmit something of the rich store of ethical Jewish wisdom and collective historic memory. In their modern guise, they offer moral and aesthetic guidance to spiritually troubled or misguided novices or questers, cast as *schlemiels*—transplanted fools and bunglers of Yiddish folklore, comic figures who seem to be victims but, in fact, redefine their worlds and emerge as moral victors.

Contributing a veil of ambiguity to his modern morality dramas are Malamud's appropriation and fusion of the *tzaddik* figure with the more accessible *schnorrer*, the mendicant who often goads his benefactors to charitable action, and the *shadchan*, the marriage broker, who similarly perturbs his clients into action. Like many *schnorrers* of popular East European Yiddish literature, Malamud's provide the lapsed American Jew opportunity to fulfill charitable obligations while mercilessly lecturing him, for the *schnorrer* versed in Judaic thought knows he is regarded as a facilitator for the rich person's charitable deeds. The *shadchan*, initially and traditionally an important Jewish communal functionary performing his role for love of God and perpetuation of the Jewish family, has metamorphosed into a comic figure, the butt of satiric humor, guilty of embellishing the physical, intellectual, and social attributes of his clients. Both the *schnorrer* and *shadchan* are highly visible and agonizingly articulate when they choose to be, and vexingly evasive when it suits them to reverse the roles of pursuer and pursued. Had Malamud limited them to secular variants of the *schnorrer* and *shadchan*, Salzman of "The Magic Barrel" and Susskind of "The Last Mohican" would be no more than droll and amusing irritants to their fictional disciples and readers. They gain spiritual stature from their correspondence to the *tzaddik*.

One of Malamud's best loved stories, "The Magic Barrel," is a tale of spiritual turning. Its power is derived from the relationship of rabbinical student, Leo Finkle, and matchmaker, Pinye Salzman, cast as spiritual novice and hidden saint. Advised that marriage would enhance his chances for a rabbinical post, Leo enlists the services of a traditional marriage broker. Malamud draws this *shadchan* in broad comic strokes. A talkative humbug, with a genius for glossing over the physical and character defects of his clients, Salzman is conceived in the traditional satiric mode,[9] as lively, impudent, given to exaggeration and banter. Yet, he is also touched with comic pathos, characteristic of the long-suffering Jews who populate Malamud's fictional world. Undergirding Salzman's *shadchan* role, which has received ample treatment in the critical literature, is the motivation of the *lamed vov tzaddik*, a neglected aspect of his character. The originality of Malamud's treatment of the traditional character lies in his fusion of unlikely traits. Facilitating Salzman's role as hidden saint, Malamud casts him in the conventional mode: boorish, smelling of fish, impoverished; but he skillfully integrates the contemporary: comic, brash, aggressive, entrepreneur skilled at evasion and assertion.

A bridal candidate's misreading of Leo's spiritual ardor serves as catalyst for his identity crisis. Her error precipitates Leo's epiphanal discovery that aside from his parents, he has never loved anyone, that he did not choose his profession for love of God, and "that he did not love God so well as he might, because he had not loved man."[10] These realizations plunge the protagonist into emotional crisis. At his most vulnerable state he retrieves the photographs Salzman left him and is attracted to one woman whose eyes suggest that she "had lived . . . had somehow deeply suffered"(186). Despite Salzman's arguments designed to dissuade Leo from meeting this woman, whom he identifies as his errant daughter and claims is an inappropriate wife for a rabbi, Leo insists on meeting Stella, longing "to convert her to goodness, himself to God" (190). In a relationship with Stella, Leo hopes to attain the wisdom arising from love and pain. So transformed is Leo by this decision that he pursues Salzman until the reluctant matchmaker relents. The elder now perceives Finkle's eyes "weighted with wisdom" (190) and concludes: "If you can love her, then you can love anybody" (190).

Predictably, the final scene of "desperate innocence" coupled with implied corruption and Salzman's "prayers for the dead" (191), has generated much critical debate. One reading posits the view that the matchmaker is a manipulator who has consciously foisted his impure daughter on the naive rabbinical student, intending, from the outset, to trap him. A second argues that Salzman is truly chagrined at his blunder, that he regards Finkle as spiritually lost and that when he chants the prayer for the dead, it is meant for the suitor. Philip Rahv is among the critics who argue that Salzman "contrives to leave one picture in Finkle's room by which his imagination is caught as in a trap."[11] Sam Bluefarb perceives Salzman as "both cynic and innocent," he concludes that the marriage broker is unsympathetic to Leo's quest for love and that the tale's irony "is that the cynical, calloused marriage broker who deals in dreams isn't able to surmount, . . . his own level as a dealer, or better, a trafficker, in dreams."[12] In contrast, Sheldon Hershinow posits the view that "[t]he reader is left with the illogical vaguely unsettling but deeply moving impression that Pinye's mourning chant somehow captures the pain, suffering, and loneliness of life while also welcoming the possibility of spiritual growth."[13] Lawrence Dessner offers an engaging interpretation of Salzman's "metaphysical status" veering toward a supernatural element, citing textual passages tempting "us to imagine the matchmaker literally 'appearing,' . . . materializing out of spirit into the semblance of flesh."[14] Repeatedly, Salzman is said to "appear," "reappear," and "disappear" "as if on the wings of the wind" (185). Salzman's wife refers to him as a *luftmensch*, another suggestion of his supernatural status and an allusion to a figure in Yiddish folklore who, without an occupation to sustain him, "lives on air." Dessner asks the crucial question about Pinye Salzman, albeit misplacing him in a fairy-tale mode. Is he, "in keeping with the fairy-tale convention and with the suggestions of supernatural powers that often accompany him, . . . some sort of ministering angel or fairy godfather, chuckling to himself about his projected course of action, his strategy for redeeming the strayed man of God? Or is Salzman closer to the satanic model, leading Leo to destruction?"[15]

An alternative reading, consistent with Malamud's affirmative philosophy, suggests that the *tzaddik*/matchmaker knowingly introduces Leo to bridal candidates who will help bring him to self-recognition and spiritual redemption. The women function as diametrical opposites: Lily, the virtuous woman of good repute; Stella the fallen sister of ill repute. Just as Salzman is waiting and watching the Leo/Stella rendezvous from a distance, so Leo earlier suspected his presence in the vicinity of his meeting with Lily Hirshchorn. Lily's questions about Finkle's religious ardor delivered the spiritual initiate to the path of self-realization; now compassion and love for Stella will lead him to redemption. Stella appears in the stereotypical guise of the prostitute, standing beneath a lamppost and smoking. Yet, her image is enigmatic for she is clad in white dress and red shoes and she waits "uneasily and shyly . . . her eyes . . . filled with desperate innocence" (191). Contrary to the prevailing negative interpretation by critics who may be unfamiliar with Hebrew liturgy, Salzman's chanting of the *Kaddish* augurs an affirmative dénouement. Although this prayer has been appropriated by mourners, it is an integral element of the Sabbath liturgy. Referring neither to the dead nor limited to mourning, it is a hopeful prayer, one exalting the divine attributes of mercy and justice. Salzman has ample reason to praise God in thanksgiving for the redemption of two souls.

Given the red and white imagery of the concluding scene, allusion to the comforting and inspiring words of the *Kaddish*, and a celebratory Chagallian vision of "[v]iolins and lit candles revolv[ing] in the sky" (191), an optimistic interpretation of the meeting of Leo and Stella and the *tzaddik*/ matchmaker's response is apt and compatible with Malamud's recurring incorporation of the *t'shuvah* theme of spiritual return.

Leo's metamorphosis from ascetic student to compassionate wise man is achieved through Salzman's machinations. The matchmaker's manipulation leads directly to Leo's self-assessment that he will love God better through loving mankind better. As he approached Stella, "[h]e pictured in her, his own redemption" (191), sensing in Stella's eyes her father's sensitivity to suffering. However comic and crass Salzman's manner, we must remember the attention Malamud paid to his eyes, eyes that "revealed a depth of sadness"; melancholy eyes"; and "haunted eyes." These are eyes of the *tzaddik* who knows the pain and suffering of the human condition. Salzman's intentionality is congruous with the redemptive themes and character constructs in Malamud's early fiction. Reading Salzman as a derivative of the *lamed vov* tradition explains his boorish manner and accounts for his efforts to unite an intellectual, who needs to experience love, and his errant daughter, who needs love, as means for each to achieve spiritual return. Rather than viewing Salzman as a cynic, too calloused to believe in redemption, he should be recognized as redemption's facilitator. He acts honorably, if unconventionally, fulfilling the role of hidden saint. The comic *shadchan* guise allows Malamud to keep sentimentality at bay and permits Salzman to operate according to each subject's need.

Malamud continues to explore the redemptive theme through the spiritual seeker and *tzaddik* figure in the Fidelman stories with the additional theme of the artist's relation to his work. *Pictures of Fidelman: An Exhibition* is an episodic quest narrative uniting three previously published stories with three additions focused on the attempts of an American artist in Italy to come to terms with art and life. Iska Alter describes the work as "an inverted parody of the *Künstlerroman*,"as we follow the unmaking of an artist through his experiments with criticism, imitation, forgery, reproduction, and originality."[16] The text's subject is art and the questions posed are about art: What is the relation of art to life? Which is more important in the making of art, the artist's vision or talent? Or, in terms of the recurrent Malmudian subject of suffering, how is the artist's suffering transformed into art? The themes that unite the spiritual questor and guide are familiar to Malamud's readers: suffering and responsibility, the search for love and a meaningful life. The protagonist's literal and metaphoric journey takes him from Rome, to Milan, to Florence, to Venice, and home to America. Arthur Fidelman shares characteristics with other Malamud protagonists who travel in search of a new life, and true to the pattern Tony Tanner identifies in the novels, "[w]hen he arrives in the world where he is to search for his new satisfying life, despite his attempts to secure only his own interests and further his single development, . . . The search for a new freedom usually ends in an imprisoning tangle of relationships and commitments and responsibilities."[17]

Shimon Susskind, the comic guru of the first story, "The Last Mohican," which was originally published in *The Magic Barrel* collection, is an engaging, infuriating composite figure, alternately acting as *schnorrer* and *tzaddik*. He is Malamud's most improbable redemptive guide. "The last Mohican," Holocaust survivor, and refugee from many lands, who "seems to have stepped out of the caricature-filled world of Yiddish fiction,"[18] plays *schnorrer* on the tale's narrative level, and *lamed vov tzaddik* on its thematic level. He is spiritual guide to an American *schlemiel*, a "self-confessed failure as a painter,"[19] self-proclaimed art historian and critic engaged in a journey of self-discovery. Upon Fidelman's arrival in Italy to write a critical study of Giotto, he is excited by the architectural remains and ruins of ancient Rome, by "all that history" (138). Ignorant of, or unmoved by, his own people's ancient and recent history, he will, in the course of his *tzaddik*-designed education, become more familiar with that history and its ethical implications. A stranger who recognizes Fidelman as a Jew, and whom Fidelman recognizes as a fellow Jew, presents himself as a needy refugee and tour guide. Although Fidelman gives the beggar a modest donation in lieu of the suit he requests, he extends charity in a manner contrary to Jewish tradition, grudgingly, humiliating the recipient. Susskind therefore undertakes Fidelman's education, literally guiding him in the Maimonidean charitable code, Holocaust history, and coincidentally, teaches Fidelman something about art.

Modeled on the traditional *schnorrer* of Yiddish literature, a figure characterized by folklorist Nathan Ausubel, as having "[n]ext to his adroitness in fleecing the philanthropic sheep, . . . his *chutzpah*, his unmitigated impudence,"[20] Susskind appears, uninvited, at Fidelman's hotel and restaurant to engage the American in moral debate. He is, as Sidney Richman aptly notes, "one who fastens to the tormented [hero] like a spiritual cannibal and does not release his hold until the younger man submits to the terrors of rebirth."[21] To Fidelman's outraged questioning of his responsibility to the beggar, Susskind replies directly, citing a widely honored Jewish concept of communal responsibility: "Who else? . . . 'You are responsible because you are a man. Because you are a Jew, aren't you?'" (147).

To understand the meaning of Giotto, Sidney Richman contends, Fidelman must comprehend "that the way to the self is paradoxically through another."[22] Because Fidelman resists Susskind's instruction, the beggar adopts a radical teaching style leading to reversal of roles; the pursued becomes the pursuer. To that end, he steals Fidelman's briefcase containing the

manuscript on Giotto. Plagued by the loss of his work, Fidelman is para-
lyzed. He can neither rewrite the missing chapter nor create another. On the
night of the theft, he dreams of chasing the refugee in Jewish catacombs
under the ancient Appian Way and threatening to strike him with a seven-
flamed candelabrum. The dream reflects his anxiety and foreshadows his
pursuit of Susskind. The transgressing American's use of the religious arti-
fact as weapon signifies how far removed Fidelman is from spiritual health.

Malamud adds comic inversion to the self-discovery journey motif as
Fidelman now rushes around Rome in search of his "Virgil." His pursuit
courses through a series of real and imagined transformative encounters,
from the pathways of the art world to the labyrinthine maze of Jewish history—away from church, museum, and art library to synagogue, Jewish
ghetto, and cemetery. While most Jewish American writers were exploring
the possibilities of the movement of Jews out of the ghettos and into the
suburbs, Malamud, as Ezra Greenspan argues, "reversed the process by
sending Fidelman back to the ghetto—and one of the oldest ones, at that—
to discover the true nature of his identity."[23] As he tracks down his prey on
the banks of the Tiber, Fidelman enters a Sephardic synagogue and, untrue
to his surname, imitates the devotional form of the ritually purified wor-
shippers who "touched with loose fingers their brows, mouths, and
breasts as they bowed to the Ark" (155). Another Holocaust survivor, one
still mourning a son killed by the Nazis, directs Fidelman to the Jewish
cemetery where Susskind is occasionally employed to pray for the dead.
In the presence of headstones testifying to the Nazi slaughter of Italian
Jews, the art pilgrim, elated by Italian history, is brought into proximity
with Jewish history—a history from which he is still divorced as evi-
denced by his reflection that he is in the presence of memorials for "those
who, *for one reason or another* [italics added], had died in the late large war"
(157). The headstones accurately inscribe the deaths as Holocaust losses,
victims of a calculated plan to annihilate European Jewry and not as some
byproduct of a larger war. A stone carries the inscription "Betrayed by the
damned Fascists/Murdered at Auschwitz by the barbarous Nazis" (157).
The engraving removes the deaths from the sphere of warfare between
belligerent armies and places them in the Holocaust context, of a people
slaughtered solely because of their Jewish identity.

When he finally locates Susskind, Fidelman conducts a fruitless search
of his room, which inspires a second graveyard dream. In this revery, Fidelman, led by "Virgilio Susskind," finds himself lying beneath a Giotto
fresco of St. Francis giving his gold cloak to an old knight. Rising from an
empty grave to engage the critic in a dialogue on the meaning and purpose of art, the spiritual guide leads the novice to discovery of Giotto's
meaning in the context of Judaic ethics—Judaism's insistence on human
responsibility. The dream lesson, expressed in visual form, is the moral

lesson that the *schnorrer* had earlier sought to impart verbally. Signifying his spiritual metamorphosis, Fidelman voluntarily honors the commandments by giving his suit to Susskind, with the wish that the old man wear it in good health. He has learned that charity must come from the heart as well as the wallet. In the guise of a beggar, the redemptive agent has taught the American art critic what rabbis teach: Jews and all human beings, are responsible for each other. That is the essence of being human and at the heart of Judaic ethics and the charitable code that insists that compassion must be linked to social justice, and that *tzedakah* (charity) signifies "righteousness" and "justice," not mere alms-giving.

From the "last Mohican," a survivor of the near-extinct Eastern European Jews, a survivor of man's ultimate inhumanity to man, Fidelman learns the importance of the human bond and the connection between ethics and aesthetics. Only after he accepts the moral imperative of universal human responsibility can the art critic understand Giotto's interpretation of suffering humanity, and progress toward spiritual redemption and affinity with his name. As Fidelman laments the loss of his manuscript, the departing Susskind, "[l]ight as the wind in his marvelous knickers, his green coattails flying" (162), shouts back, "Have mercy, . . . I did you a favor" (162). Having traveled to Italy to study the work of a Christian painter, Fidelman has been introduced to Jewish ethics and become immersed in Jewish history, leading to his "triumphant insight," an epiphanal understanding in which he affirms the truth of the *tzaddik's* parting words, that he acted generously by destroying a chapter in which "[t]he words were there but the spirit was missing" (162). In Ruth Wisse's view, "Susskind has led Fidelman to a true understanding of his own schlemielhood, which is also the process whereby a man becomes a *mensh.*"[24] Having completed the task of directing the *schlemiel* to self-awareness and communal responsibility, Malamud's enigmatic spiritual guide, compound of the commonplace and mysterious, disappears, destined to keep on running, as the *lamed vov tzaddik* is to venture forth where he is needed.

"The Last Mohican" was published in *The Magic Barrel* before Malamud conceived of continuing the Fidelman stories in a collection of six tales, *Pictures of Fidelman: An Exhibition.* After the first tale, Susskind's role diminishes until the penultimate tale. Although his dramatic role ebbs, he remains a shadowy presence throughout the collection, becoming a permanent influence or irritant "both as a real character and as a moral image in Fidelman's imagination."[25] The man who advised the critic that his words lacked spirit in the first tale, appears symbolically in the second, "Still Life," when the painter rejects his own plans for creating a canvas in the traditional mode of the Madonna and Child as "[a]lmost in panic he [Fidelman] sketched in charcoal a coattailed 'Figure of a Jew Fleeing' and quickly hid it away."[26] Similarly, one of Fidelman's doodles in "Naked Nude," the third entry in the series, is that of Susskind in his long coat, "[l]oosely dangling from a gallows rope. . . . Who but Susskind, surely. A dim figure out of the past."[27] Sheldon Hershinow insightfully attests to Susskind's significance when he observes,

> It is as if Susskind's physical presence is necessary to focus and dramatize for the reader the deeply self-combative nature of Fidelman's internal conflict. . . . When Susskind later fades into the background . . . some of the substance of the reader's interest also disappears. Although the other characters . . . provide a narrative focus . . . only Susskind's interaction with Fidelman captures a sense of a primal— obsessive, reciprocal, irrational and mysterious, though ultimately beneficial—bond of intimacy.[28]

Susskind returns to his focal role through a most peculiar incarnation in "Pictures of the Artist." There, he assumes a series of surrealistic transformations while retaining his role as *tzaddik* and paves the way for Fidelman's regeneration in the concluding tale.

The "triumphant insight" Fidelman attained in "The Last Mohican" implies a reversal of spirit heralding a new life. That perception is entirely convincing for the self-contained story and, at the outset, "Still Life," confirms the change. Fidelman is looking for a studio, rather than a hotel or apartment; and he is now referred to as the art student rather than the art critic. Subsequent events in this and the later stories, however, reverse our expectations and reveal Fidelman in moral and aesthetic decline. He takes on the roles of painter, pimp, art forger, sculptor manqué. Far from moral regeneration, moral backsliding characterizes his dealings with others in most of the stories, especially with women in his adopted roles as abject lover and pimp. From artist as forger to artist as huckster and betrayer, Fidelman continues his moral downward plunge.

"Pictures of the Artist," the best of the post "Last Mohican" stories, is a surreal journey, a rich comic-tragic fusion recalling the mentor/disciple construct of the book's first story in which the mentor leads the *schlemiel* from callous disregard for human need to charitable conduct, from ethical blindness to moral insight. Malamud departs from the form of the intervening tales to structure "Picture of an Artist" as a series of surrealistic dreams filled with allusions to painters from other eras, other literary works, and to the other stories in the book. Paralleling the structural and thematic use of dream in the first tale, each dream in the fifth story explores the relation of art to life. The first two suggest that commitment to art may demand betrayal of one's humanity and the third offers the possibility of redemption on the condition that art be forsaken. In the initial dream, Fidelman has metamorphosed into a sculptor, digging holes in the ground which he passes off as modern art. These are "symbolic graves of his failure as an artist,"[29] or signs of the "death of expression."[30] The gravity of Fidelman's ethical decline is manifested in his callous rejection of any responsibility toward his audience. His disdain of their confusion is manifested in the meaningless theoretical jargon he spouts when called upon to explain his sculpture, and his refusal to return the fee of a poor Italian laborer who sees through Fidelman's sham and seeks return of the money he squandered on Fidelman's exhibit. When Fidelman responds to the polite and desperate pleas of his victim with a bogus art lecture followed by vulgar dismissal, a stranger appears, "wrapped in the folds of a heavy cloak" (158), but recognizable to the reader by his "short and bowed" nether limbs, clothed in black stockings as Susskind, who was described in "The Last Mohican" wearing "woolen socks drawn up over his slightly bowed, broomstick legs" (139). Speaking "in the accent of one from a foreign land" (158), using torturous English syntax and inflection evoking Yiddish speech patterns, the stranger asks for permission to view the sculpture and in response to Fidelman's empty jargon, calls his bluff: "To me, if you'll pardon me, is a hole nothing" (159). He emphasizes his point by tossing an apple core into the hole, noting, "If not for this could be empty the hole. If empty would be there nothing. . . . You have not yet learned the difference between something and nothing" (159–160). Malamud underscores the punitive role of the teacher in this scene rhetorically as well as dramatically in introducing the biblical phrase, "the stranger smote the horrified Fidelman." With a shovel blow to the head, he topples the artist into the hole and fills it with earth, creating a grave, "So now we got form but we also got content" (160).

The mentor's lesson reflects Malamud's attitude toward art and the Judaic principle of purposeful creative endeavor. Elevation of form to the exclusion of content "abuses Art and demeans the soul."[31] Accepting the National Book Award for *The Fixer* in 1967, Malamud forcefully advocated fiction of "signification," arguing, "To preserve itself [art] must, in a variety of subtle ways, conserve the artist through sanctifying human life."[32] Despite welcoming invention and experimentation with literary form, Malamud disavowed a theory that devalued the writer's personal and historical experience by limiting its presence in fiction. The lesson that Fidelman had yet to learn from the *tzaddik* is that life and art are inextricably bound.

At the nadir of Fidelman's aesthetic and ethical posture, Susskind emerges at first in the role of a Jewish Jesus and later in the shape of a voice emanating from a light bulb to reiterate the Judaic ethics he had taught Fidelman in "The Last Mohican." In a second dream, Susskind is Christ preaching from a mountaintop, a Jewish Jesus advocating love,

mercy, and charity. Susskind is now Susskind, once again, a moral and aesthetic savior, preaching the new gospel in the old Jewish format, from
whence it is derived:

> Tell the truth. Dont cheat. If it's easy it dont mean it's
> good. Be kind, specially to those that they got less than
> you. I want for everybody justice. If you feel good give
> charity. If you feel bad give charity. Must also be mercy. Be
> nice, dont fight. (162)

Echoing Jesus' words to the fishermen, he advises Fidelman "give up your
paints and your brushes and follow me where I go, and we will see what
we will see" (163). Susskind/Christ denies Fidelman's request to paint
him, citing the Judaic injunction prohibiting the production of graven images, the sin of idolatry, and the impossibility of capturing his identity in
any art form. He is aware, even as he articulates the prohibition, that the
artist will betray him as he follows another master whose demands often
dissent from his own. True to the prediction, Fidelman acts the role of
Judas, disobeys and betrays the master meaning to capture his essence on
canvas and "runneth out to buy paints, brushes, canvas" (166). Fidelman
paints a Crucifixion and Descent from the Cross, but he leaves the fresh
canvas intended for the Resurrection blank.

    The third fantasy, reiterating the themes of the others, begins with a
commitment to artistic creativity that displaces Fidelman's social/ethical
obligations. The final "picture" is of Fidelman as "the painter in the cave,"
located beneath his sister Bessie's house, trying to capture pure ideas in
abstract geometric designs while ignoring the needs of the dying woman
who has served as surrogate mother, object of his adolescent lust, and financial patron for his European sojourn. Susskind next reappears as a one-
hundred-watt talking light bulb—"the Hebraic light giving out its moral
message to the Hellenized painter."[33] The Yiddish accented and inflected
voice, representing the wisdom of Judaism as "a light to the nations,"
leads Fidelman away from art's domination into human community. The
parable of the speaking light bulb is delivered in syntax reminiscent of and
continues Susskind's Jewish sermon in "The Last Mohican." Abandon the
obsession with art to privilege human connection is the lesson. Directing
the brother to visit his dying sister, the voice urges generous behavior, loving connection, and compassion. The lesson Fidelman learned in the first
story: that one who fails to act charitably and humanely in personal relationships cannot appreciate great art, which has compassion as its theme,
must be relearned in the fifth, for the artist has descended, in the interim,
into a life of dissipation. What better source of instruction than the voice of
Judaic ethical wisdom, the voice of his earlier enlightenment. "Be my Vir-

gil" (174) signifies Fidelman's acceptance of the *tzaddik's* instruction, his wish to be led, like Dante, out of his self-designed psychic hell. Fidelman's deathbed visit to Bessie is a first step in his return to moral responsibility and departure from the selfish isolating drive that characterized his dedication to art.

Susskind existed in the first story "to test Fidelman's capacity for involvement, to renew his diminished emotional vitality, and to enlarge his limited humanity."[34] He follows a similar course in the fifth story, this time preparing the way for Fidelman's ultimate regeneration permitting him to step beyond the confines of his own consciousness and acknowledge the needs of another person. Fidelman now rejects "the despotism of art for the anarchy and unpredictability of life."[35] The unity between elements within the surrealistic fantasy and the links between the introductory and penultimate tales resides not only in Susskind's mentoring role and the dream/structure, but in the recurrent imagistic pattern of holes, grave, and cellar which recall the Jewish catacombs, cemetery, and Susskind's cold room in "The Last Mohican."

Susskind's absence from the final story is striking. His role as moral and aesthetic guide is assumed by a Venetian glassblower, an advisor who sounds and acts remarkably like Susskind. Reminiscent of the *tzaddik's* destruction of Fidelman's manuscript, which contained the words but lacked the spirit, Beppo recognizes that Fidelman's painting lacks authority and originality. Like Susskind, he argues, "Let me finish these off. . . . It's for your own sake. Show who's the master of your fate—bad art or you . . . Don't waste your life doing what you can't do" (197–198). As Samuel I. Bell observed, by "abandoning the pretenses of art for the honesty of craftsmanship,"[36] and overturning his typical selfishness by accepting love in the final story, Fidelman achieves the potential for moral decency implied in "The Last Mohican's" concluding reference to "triumphant insight." Fidelman's acceptance and return of love in the final story realizes the return to community heralded by his brotherly visit to Bessie in "Picture of an Artist." Susskind's absence in the last tale is entirely appropriate if we read him in the *tzaddik* mold. In accord with the disappearance of the legendary hidden saints when their salvational task is achieved, Malamud's *tzaddik* disappears, presumably to rematerialize when needed. Redemptive vision is confirmed in the final story when Fidelman acts unselfishly, denying himself the love he wants in order to benefit the relationship of those he loves. Robert Scholes considers this "allegory of the artistic and moral life . . . Malamud's finest comic work, [noting that while] Hogarth's Rake and Harlot progress downward to destruction, Fidelman progresses down and out—to salvation."[37]

"The Magic Barrel" and the first and fifth tales of *Pictures of Fidelman,* like much of Malamud's fiction is permeated by Jewish themes, characters,

and history, fiction that transmits Judaic concepts and Yiddish literary influences to American literature. David Zucker wisely reminds us that
Malamud writes as a *midrashic melamed*, composing biblical, historical, and
ethical *aggodot*.[38] Reminiscent of the great poets Harold Bloom cites in *Anxiety of Influence* (whose work evidences their adherence to and departure
from their precursors), Malamud engages in synchronous embrace and
departure from his Yiddish literary forbearers, and achieves artistic originality by "swerving" from precursors in ways that encompass and extend
the traditions of Yiddish literature and folklore in modern fiction.

Notes

1. Instances of the transplanted *schlemiel* in Jewish American writing are too
numerous to cite. See Cynthia Ozick's "Puttermesser and Xanthippe," in *Levitation:
Five Fictions* (Knopf, 1982); Marge Piercy's *He, She, and It* (New York: Knopf, 1991);
and Chaim Potok's *My Name is Asher Lev* (New York: Knopf, 1972) for incorporation and extension of the *golem* figure. Saul Bellow's Tamkin in *Seize the Day* (New
York: Viking, 1956) is a brilliant adaptation of the hidden saint.

2. I have recognized and written about the *lamed vov tzaddik* derivatives in
fiction by Saul Bellow and Bernard Malamud prior to my discovery of Ita Sheres's
article addressing Malamud's use of the figure in his novels and consequently do
not regard Sheres as influential in my position but as a scholar arguing for a similar interpretation of Malamud's characters.

3. Philip Birnbaum, *A Book of Jewish Concepts* rev. ed. (New York: Hebrew
Publishing Company, 1975), 306.

4. Ita Sheres, "The Alienated Sufferer: Malamud's Novel's from the Perspective of Old Testament and Jewish Mystical Thought," *Studies in American Jewish Literature* IV, 1(Spring 1978):68–69.

5. Sheres, 70.

6. Marci B. Gealy, "Malamud's Short Stories: A Reshaping of Hasidic Tradition," *Judaism* 28(1979):51.

7. Gealy, 61.

8. Malamud Interview with Curt Leviant in *Hadassah Magazine* 55 (June
1974): 18–19, excerpt rpt. in *Short Story Criticism*, Vol. 15, ed. Dan Siegel (Detroit:
Gale Research Inc., 1994), 188–190.

9. Matchmaking has a respected tradition in Jewish society. It had an honorable tradition for many generations and was originally regarded not as a business
enterprise, but as a pious calling devoted to the love of God and perpetuation of
the Jewish people. Folklorist Nathan Ausubel describes the figure as an "important
functionary in the Jewish community following the large scale massacres of the
Crusades and constant flights of persecuted Jewish communities that made nor-
mal social life impossible. In such circumstances, the *shadchan* became an important instrument preserving contact among scattered remnants of the population as

he traveled from town to town. In time, with the growth and permanency of Jewish settlements in ghetto towns, the traditional integrity of the *shadchan* began to waver. By the end of the sixteenth-century, there were already . . . moralistic writings critical of venal marriage brokers, for those who were guilty of greed and misrepresentation." Nathan Ausubel, *A Treasury of Jewish Folklore* (New York: Crown Publishers, 1948), 413.

10. Bernard Malamud, "The Magic Barrel," in *The Magic Barrel* (New York: Avon Books, 1980), 183.

11. Philip Rahv, "Introduction to *A Malamud Reader*," in *Literature of American Jews*, ed. Theodore L. Gross (New York: Free Press, 1973), 376.

12. Sam Bluefarb, "Bernard Malamud: The Scope of Caricature," *The English Journal* 53, 5 (May 1964): 325.

13. Sheldon Hershinow, *Bernard Malamud* (New York: Frederick Ungar Publishing Co., 1980), 131.

14. Lawrence Jay Dessner, "The Playfulness of Bernard Malamud's 'The Magic Barrel'," *Essays in Literature*, 15, 1 (Spring 1988): 87–101, rpt. in *Short Story Criticism*, Vol. 15, ed. Dan Siegel (Detroit: Gale Research Inc., 1994), 232.

15. Dessner, 232.

16. Iska Alter, "The Broader Canvas: Malamud, Art, and the Artist," in *The Good Man's Dilemma: Social Criticism in the Fiction of Bernard Malamud* (New York: AMS Press, 1981), 126.

17. Tony Tanner, "Bernard Malamud and the New Life," *Critical Quarterly* X(1968):160–161.

18. Irving I. Buchen, "Malamud's Italian Progress: Art and Bisexuality," *Modern Language Studies* XX:2 (Spring 1990):65.

19. Bernard Malamud, "The Last Mohican," in *The Magic Barrel* (New York: Avon Books, 1980), 138.

20. Ausubel, 267.

21. Sidney Richman, *Bernard Malamud* (New York: Twayne Publishers, 1966), 115.

22. Richman, 115.

23. Ezra Greenspan, *The Schlemiel Comes to America* (Metuchen, N.J.: Scarecrow Press 1983), 151.

24. Ruth R. Wisse, "Requiem in Several Voices," in *The Schlemiel as Modern Hero* (Chicago: University of Chicago Press, 1971), 108–124, rpt. in "Bernard Malamud," *Short Story Criticism*, Vol. 15, ed. Dan Siegel (Detroit: Gale Research Inc., 1994), 178.

25. Robert Ducharne, "Appendix: The Artist in Hell," in *Art and Idea in the Novels of Bernard Malamud: Toward the Fixer* (The Hague: Mouton & Co, 1974), 132.

26. Bernard Malamud, "Still Life," in *Pictures of Fidelman: An Exhibition* (New York: Farrar, Straus, and Giroux, 1969), 48.

27. Bernard Malamud, "Naked Nude," in *Pictures of Fidelman*, 70.

28. Sheldon J. Hershinow, *Bernard Malamud* (New York: Frederick Ungar Publishing Co, 1980), 88.

29. Ducharne, 138.

30. Ruth Wisse, 178.

31. Alter, 142.

32. Qtd. by Christopher Wegelin, "The American Schlemiel Abroad: Malamud's Italian Stories and the End of American Innocence," *Twentieth Century Literature* 19.2(April 1973):77–88, rpt. in "Bernard Malamud," *Short Story Criticism*, Vol. 15, ed. Dan Siegel (Detroit: Gale Research Inc., 1994), 185.

33. Ruth R. Wisse, "Requiem in Several Voices," in *The Schlemiel as Modern Hero* (Chicago: University of Chicago Press, 1971), rpt. in "Bernard Malamud," *Short Story Criticism,* Vol. 15, ed. Dan Siegel (Detroit: Gale Research Inc., 1994), 179.

34. Alter, 128.

35. Alter, 136.

36. Samuel I. Bellman, "Women, Children, and Idiots First: The Transformation Psychology of Bernard Malamud," *Critique* VII, ii(1965): 137.

37. Robert Scholes, "Portrait of an Artist as 'Escape-Goat,' " *Saturday Review* 152(10 May 1969):33.

38. David Zucker, "Malamud as Midrash," *Judaism* 43:2 (Spring 1994): 159–172.

Chapter 13

NOT TRUE ALTHOUGH TRUTH

The Holocaust's Legacy in Three Malamud Stories:
"The German Refugee," "Man in the Drawer,"
and "The Lady of the Lake"

Eileen H. Watts

In "Malamud's Jews and the Holocaust Experience" Lawrence Langer roundly criticizes Malamud for infusing his view of humanity into his novels and stories that evoke the Holocaust, either literally or figuratively. Jews in death camps, Langer argues, were not given "the gift of suffering" enjoyed by Morris Bober and Yakov Bok (145), and so are not realistic representations of the unspeakable powerlessness and hopelessness experienced by Holocaust victims, both the living and the dead. In contrast to the surreal grotesqueness of the Holocaust experience, Malamud's insistence on the intrinsic value and dignity of the individual would clearly offend Langer.

However, three years before his death, Malamud told Joel Salzberg: "I am compelled to think about [the Holocaust] as a man rather than a writer. Someone like Elie Wiesel who had first-hand knowledge of the experience is in a better position to write about it than I. He has become a voice for those people who could not communicate their personal experiences and emotions" (Lasher, 129). And ten years earlier, in a written interview with Leslie and Joyce Field, Malamud responded in the following way to a

139

question on the genesis of *The Fixer*: "Since I was interested in how some men grow as men in prison I turned to the Beilis case. . . . *The Fixer* is largely an invention . . . However, in it I was able to relate feelingfully to the situation of the Jews in Czarist Russia partly because of what I knew about the fate of the Jews in Hitler's Germany" (Lasher, 38).

It seems slightly disingenuous to criticize someone for not doing what he clearly did not set out to do. Malamud's stated intention is not to represent the Holocaust experience, but rather to gather its legacy into his work, and in a 1980 interview with Michiko Kakutani, he explained that his interest in Jews lay in their spiritual quality: "I was concerned with what Jews stood for. . . . I was concerned with their ethicality—how Jews felt they had to live in order to go on living" (Lasher, 94). Let me suggest that Malamud's concern is not only for what Jews must endure, but for how they must *transform* themselves to continue living in a world that orchestrated and tacitly condoned their attempted extinction. This current, I believe, underlies three of Malamud's Holocaust short stories, "The German Refugee," "Man in the Drawer," and "The Lady of the Lake." The first two are about Jewish writers, one living during the Holocaust, one in postwar Russia, who must go to great human and artistic lengths to continue living. Thus, in "The Lady of the Lake," The American-assimilated Levin, who is free to practice Judaism unfettered, changes his name, travels to Italy, poses as a Christian, and believes the love of his life to be Gentile. In reality, she is a Holocaust survivor, who has changed her name, presumably in order to live more peaceably in Italy. The stories dramatize the ways in which holocausts (whether physical or spiritual) reveal the extent to which language, survival, and Judaism are intertwined.

Consequently, in all three stories translation as a means of a Jew's survival figures prominently, if ironically, first in literary and then in increasingly figurative ways. In "The German Refugee" Oskar Gassner, a German immigrant in New York, has escaped the Nazis, but confronts another enemy within; as an immigrant, he himself needs to be translated as well as his language. Here, translation is revealed as a critical component of the immigrant's survival, for he must translate himself and his work into English in order to keep his job. In "Man in the Drawer," translation as a means of Judaism's survival takes on more figurative roles, as we are invited to translate or interpret a number of progressively embedded narratives.

To this end, Walter Benjamin's essay "The Task of the Translator" (in *Illuminations*) is enlightening. Benjamin suggests that a text's truth is located not *in* its lines, but *between* them and that truth is most visible in translations, that is, in between renderings of a text's original and secondary languages. Citing "the interlinear version of the Scriptures [a]s the prototype or ideal of all translation" (82), Benjamin posits a "language of truth: This language of truth is . . . the true language [and] is concealed in concentrated fashion in translations" (77). This is perhaps because the attempt to translate a given word from one language to another throws into relief its multiple connotations and associations, thus creating a richer contextual understanding of that word. When an entire work is translated this effect is multiplied such that the "soul" of the work is foregrounded, particularly for the translator. For his task is to capture that "soul" and communicate it in another language. This view of truth as almost a byproduct of translation suggests a useful lens through which to consider the ways in which translation functions vis à vis Jewish survival in "The German Refugee" and "Man in the Drawer."

Oskar Gassner, the newly arrived German Jewish refugee, is a famed critic and journalist to whom the narrator, Martin Goldberg, is teaching English. Having escaped Germany in 1939, Oskar must now write and deliver a lecture in English for a course he will give on "The Literature of the Weimar Republic" for the Institute of Public Studies in New York. In the process of his learning to speak English, we see the extent to which translation is emblematic of displaced people; their very selves must be translated, here from German and Germany into English and ultimately into American. (Assimilation is an obvious corollary, but is not at issue in this story.)

Oskar has escaped Hitler, but cannot escape language. The narrator tells us, "He would attempt to say something and then stop, as though it could not possibly be said" (Malamud, 94). The enormous effort expended to translate German thought into English words and get them said is a painfully common immigrant experience. As another of the story's refugees describes it: "I felt like a child, or worse, often like a moron. I am left with myself unexpressed. What I know, indeed, what I am, becomes to me a burden" (97). The immigrant is acutely aware of the extent to which identity is congruent with the ability to articulate one's thoughts and knowledge, such that what one is—one's soul—becomes only as valuable as the power of one's linguistic capacity to express it.

For the immigrant, the implications of identity or soul being commensurate with language are profound. Unable to write, Oskar explains:

> It is a paralyzis of my will. The whole legture is clear in
> my mind, but the minute I write down a single word—or
> in English or in German—I have a terrible fear I will not
> be able to write the negst. As though someone has thrown
> a stone at a window and the whole house—the whole
> idea smashes. (102)

Echoes of *Kristallnacht* serve as a metaphor for how Germany has destroyed his life. He even hates the German language and shouts that he "could not longer write in that filthy tongue. [He] cursed the German language" (99).

Oskar speaks in "handcuffed and tortured English" but loathes his mother tongue. This leaves the refugee, a writer, with no language—no self—no will—no faith—no "former value of myself" (103), and he announces that if he does not complete the lecture he will kill himself.

In an attempt to raise Oskar's spirits, Martin reads some German poets in translation and *Leaves of Grass*. He suggests to Oskar that the German poets had gotten from Whitman a "love of death," but Oskar corrects him. Not death, he says, "but . . . his feeling for Brudermensch, his humanity" (105). In other words, the truth of Whitman's poetry that has been successfully translated into German is brotherhood—a *feeling* of humanity—the truth that is tucked between the lines.

As Oskar finishes his lecture, Germany has invaded Poland. The lecture is a success, but two days later Oskar Gassner commits suicide by creating his own gas chamber via the kitchen stove. In Oskar's correspondence Martin finds a letter from the refugee's anti-Semitic mother-in-law, indicating that after Oskar had left for America, his wife had converted to Judaism, been transported to Poland and slaughtered in a mass grave along with "the naked Jewish men, their wives and children, some Polish soldiers and a handful of gypsies" (108). Thus ends the story. As Oskar had said, the humanity of Whitman's poetry "does not grow long on German earth" (105).

Oskar had tried to translate himself from a German- into an English-speaking writer; his wife tries to translate herself from a German Christian into a German Jew. Malamud's point seems to be that when there is no humanity between the lines, translations, whether in the form of emigrations or conversions, are doomed. In this case, Oskar, the German "text," could not survive translation into English because the truth, always for Malamud humanity, had been effaced from the original. Oskar had been too disillusioned and embittered by Germany. (One suspects that living amid and breathing the noxious fumes of Germany's anti-Semitism had substantially killed Oskar's spirit, (his humanity) long before he left Berlin. The kitchen stove affair was his way of announcing that Hitler's hand had reached across the Atlantic. Oskar Gassner, in New York City, was also a Holocaust victim. Similarly, his wife's conversion could not last because translations do not exist in a vacuum. They have readers, who, in Mrs. Gassner's case, were blind to any humanity between the lines. And of course, compounding the tragedy is Oskar's "survivor's" guilt, one of the more insidious legacies of the Holocaust. He did what he had to do to go on living, but could no longer live with himself. Both Oskar and his wife are, in an important sense, lost in translation; unlike history, however, for Martin must translate the German letter to learn of the Holocaust's reality.

∾

Like Oskar Gassner, Feliks Levitansky, the Russian writer of "Man in a Drawer," finds his soul inextricably bound to his writing. For the half-Jewish Feliks, however, the issue is not his ability to write, but his ability to get published in postwar Soviet Russia, which seems nothing less than a place of spiritual holocaust. There, anti-Semitism is not only institutionalized and government sanctioned, but is part of society's superstructure. Where in "The German Refugee" the Holocaust results in the death of Jews, in "Man in the Drawer" it results in assimilation (which, some would argue, is in effect, the death of Judaism). Feliks keeps his subversive manuscripts in a drawer (whence the title) and begs the narrator, Howard Harvitz, a visiting American writer whose poetry anthology, *Visible Secrets,* had been confiscated by the KGB, to smuggle the manuscripts into the United States and publish them—a dangerous enterprise. In the context of the assimilationist postwar decline of Jewish orthodoxy and practice, "Man in the Drawer" articulates an analogy between translation or metaphor and truth-telling (in the form of fairy tales), and how Jews must live to go on living.

Harvitz meets Levitansky in the Russian's taxi. The driver offers in English, "My profession is translator—English French" (194). Malamud's choice for Feliks's additional occupation, cabby, suggests another meaning of translate, "to transfer, to transport" (*OED*). Feliks, the writer-cabby-translator, takes people from place to place in space and in language. Howard Harvitz, we learn, has also dabbled in translations; he discloses that his last name had been Harris, but that he had recently changed it back to its original ethnic form. Howard's name began as Jewish, was translated into the Anglican Harris, then back again because, as Howard puts it, "I am closer to myself" (195). His soul seems intimately bound to his surname in its original language, a truth he was able to see only after Harvitz had been translated into Harris (another instance of Benjamin's truth emerging between translations). The immigrant desire to Americanize ethnic names suggests yet another version of translation—in language, custom, tradition, and belief. (Ironically, the Russian Jew must assimilate "to go on living," but the American Jew assimilates by choice.)

In "Man in the Drawer" Malamud uses translation to symbolize the multivalent dislocations that displaced Jews must negotiate. Actually, Jews of the diaspora are more accurately symbolized by the palimpsest, literally, "again rubbed smooth—a manuscript in which a later writing is superimposed on an effaced earlier writing . . . because of the cost of parchment," namely goat or sheep skin (*OED*). The Nazi practice of branding serial numbers on Jews in the camps is a grotesquely literal example of the Jew as palimpsest, as the lady of the lake, Isabella, proudly reveals the numbers burned into her breast, and refuses to marry the professed Gentile, Freeman. She values what she has suffered for; her serial number represents her identity. On the figurative level, the German refugee's translations of language and culture are also superimposed onto the human parchment of the psyche. On another metaphorical level, Freeman, Levitansky, and Harvitz, all assimilated Jews, have effectively effaced their earlier "script" (i.e., Yiddish, prayer, ritual, ethnicity) to some degree. Judaism, however, began with such "writing"; the circumcision scar is a mark of the covenant signed on human parchment. So, we recall that Jews and writing go back to the beginning.

In the course of the two writers' developing relationship, Harvitz assumes that Levitansky's stories are autobiographical. "Don't confuse my story of writer, which you have read, with life of author" (212), he scolds. To Harvitz's question of whether a particular experience described in the same story was true, Levitansky replies, "Not true although truth" (212). Here lies the way to Malamud's "language of truth." For the storyteller, what is *not true* is the observable content: metaphor, fiction, fable; what *is true* is the latent content, or that which metaphor attempts to describe, that is, nonfiction. By suggesting that *truth* is a component of the *not true*, the writer is arriving at Benjamin's language of truth from another direction— through fable. Indeed, Harvitz's advice to the frustrated Russian writer is, "Do what you can. It's amazing, for instance, what can be said in a fairy tale" (220). Fairy tales are patently not true, although they do reveal truth. The question then arises, can certain truths even be known or felt without one's thinking through the requisite translation from vehicle to tenor, which is what we do on an extended basis when we interpret fairy tales? As if to address this specific issue, "Man in a Drawer" ends with a tripartite allegory of Levitansky's translated stories.

Truth be told, "Man in a Drawer" ends twice. The first ending has Harvitz in a taxi to the Moscow airport with Levitansky's stories hidden in his luggage, fearing for the Russian's life should his stories be published in America. The second ending consists of three translated stories, which taken together, as I have suggested, function allegorically. The three stories concern stolen Passover matzos, a tallis, and a half-Jewish writer who burns his Jewish stories, respectively. As a trilogy the stories document the progressive "translation" in recent Jewish culture from orthodoxy to assimilation, and may be interpreted as representing a shift in religious practice through three generations of Jews in Russia, or America. Here is where the analogy between metaphor and the shrouded survival of Judaism is played out.

The first story paints a portrait of Jewish life in the Old Country. An old orthodox Russian Jew surreptitiously receives Passover matzos from an equally old rabbi. On his way home in a trolley, the matzos are stolen by another Jew, with whom the old man had spoken briefly in Yiddish. The old man is incredulous that a Jew could steal matzos from a Jew, but then says to himself, "If I could steal any, whether from Jew or from Russian, I would steal them . . . even from the old rabbi" (234). In this story having matzo for Passover is critical enough to steal for, whereas in the second story, a seventeen-year-old young man is trying to sell a beautiful white tallis so he can marry and volunteer with the communist youth organization, Komsomol. Outside a Moscow synagogue, the young man asks fifteen rubles for his late father's prayer shawl. The congregants suspect he is a government plant, for it is against the law to trade in religious articles. One man, the *gabbai* of the synagogue, agrees to buy the tallis, but insists that he needs to go home for more money. Instead, he calls the police. When the young man sees the encroaching authorities, he wraps himself with the tallis and prays "a passionate *kaddish*" (prayer for the dead). Levitansky writes,"No one imagined the youth could pray so fervently. What moved them was the tone, the wail and passion of a man truly praying" (236). The story ends with this Scheherazade-like scene of a man praying for his life, for as long as he prays, the police will not touch him.

In this story, Jew turns on Jew again, but not for matzo. The web-like politics of soviet life weave multiple ironies. Clearly, the young man with the tallis had come from a once-religious family; he knew how to pray. But his ambition was to volunteer with the soviet youth movement, whose mission no doubt included the extinction of Jews from the Soviet Union. When faced with the KGB, however, the young man has only G-d to turn to. The story's last line reads, "All that can be seen is the white shawl luminously praying." The tallis functions simultaneously as metonymy for and personification of Jewish prayer, keeping soviet authorities at bay, but running out of time. Perhaps the young man felt compelled to join Komsomol in order to survive in that country, but he ultimately turned to G-d to "go on living." Like the Passover matzos that are precious enough to break a commandment for, the praying tallis is a powerful symbol of the displaced Jew's dilemma: physical survival demands assimilation; spiritual survival (and in the case of the *davening* tallis, life itself) demands adherence to Jewish law and prayer.

The various translations of Jewish practice in the first story's orthodox sphere and the second story's political arena enter the realm of art in Levitansky's third story. This tale concerns Anatoly Borisovich, a half-Jewish writer who had been writing secretly for years. Like Levitansky, Anatoly "[h]ad gone into translation instead." Interesting phrase. Taken literally, the Russian Jewish writers had to go into "translation" themselves, into whatever Soviet Russia deemed acceptable, or risk silence—or death. Anatoly, like Levitansky, is tired of having to translate his stories into fairy tales, or write for the drawer, and submits for publication his stories about Jews caught between the "rock" of their religion and the "hard place" of Russian society. Victor, the editor, euphemistically refers to the stories as "unorthodox material" and questions why Anatoly writes about Jews at all. "What do you know about them?" he asks. "Your culture is not the

least Jewish, it's Soviet Russian." The exchange ends with the editor's accusing the writer of anti-Semitism and of having no sense of self-preserva-
tion. These accusations are somewhat paradoxical. Victor sees Anatoly's
ambivalence regarding Judaism. On one hand, portraying Jews as traitors
to their own religion is anti-Semitic; on the other hand, wishing to publish
stories about them for the purpose of exposing the mutually repellent
claims on the Russian Jew's identity is, indeed, suicidal. Victor finally
urges Anatoly to "destroy them (the stories) at once before they destroy
you" (238). The text concludes with Anatoly's burning his stories in the
kitchen sink, confessing to his nine-year-old son, "I'm burning my talent
. . . And my integrity, and my heritage" (239).

This story serves as a gloss on the other two. Here, the Jew is only *half*
Jewish, and, unlike the men in the other stories, he has a name, perhaps
signifying acceptance in his Gentile world. We are told that Anatoly knows
nothing about Judaism or Jews, and yet he writes about them. Thus, Anatoly meets Levitansky. Both insist that "stories are stories, they have not
nationality" (213). Both claim that there are no such things as Jewish stories, and of course, Levitansky too, is *half* Jewish. "I am atheist," he pro-
claims (213). Levitansky has translated himself into his stories, except for
the manuscript burning. Levitansky, like Malamud, wants his voice to be
heard, his stories read, while Anatoly succumbs to fear and burns his integrity and his heritage. Like Oskar Gassner, who surrendered his life to
futility and guilt, Anatoly surrenders his stories and burns his Judaism, in
a sense, reminiscent of the Holocaust's book burnings.

Even though Levitansky and Anatoly protest their atheism (too much,
one suspects), the original languages of Judaism—religious, cultural, ethnic—seem written into the writers' very souls. Here, the Jew-as-palimpsest
that I suggested above is borne out, even by Malamud himself, who, like
Harvitz and Levitansky and Anatoly, insisted that he wrote about Jews
only because he was comfortable with and knew about them. (Interview
with Curt Leviant, Lasher, 49–50.) As much as one believes one has effaced
the original scripture and written over it, the primary text remains—like
the name of Harvitz's anthology—as visible secrets. Thus, "Man in the
Drawer" begins (as Harvitz recalls entering Levitansky's cab), "A soft
Sholom I thought I heard. . . ." Malamud's *Brudermensch*; it cries out insistently from between his lines.

Perhaps Malamud sees language, particularly in the form of story, as
the currency of truth because of the way in which people learn truths. Biblical parables, Aesop's fables, fairy tales—all tell their truths indirectly. We
seem to require indirection to find direction out (as Polonius realized) either because of certain limitations inherent in language itself, because of
some chimerical quality of truth that renders it elusive to immediate expression in language, or because we need to arrive at truth ourselves in

order to actually believe it. In any case, metaphor, of course, allows us to know a hidden thing (the tenor) by means of invoking a revealed thing (the vehicle). "The German Refugee" and "Man in the Drawer" suggest that this dialectical nature of truth telling is analogous to the ways in which Jews (particularly in light of the Holocaust) must translate themselves in order to go on living. Malamud's Jews may appear German or Russian or American (the vehicle), but remain Jews (the tenor); that is, they feel their Jewishness most when they most try to hide or deny it. In one sense, "Not true although truth" is simply Malamud's translation of Polonius's instructions. Rephrased in the context of postwar assimilation, however, it might read: Not Jewish although Jew.

The theme of Jewish identity visà vis one's name is explored in a particularly poignant way in "The Lady of the Lake," but here it is woven into a love-story-cum-Akedah, implicitly linking the Sacrifice of the Six Million to Abraham's willingness to sacrifice Isaac. It is perhaps worth noting that romance in Malamud's fiction is usually characterized by brief entanglements that are defined and defeated by the lovers' differences—real or perceived—in race, religion, class, or age. (Willie Spearmint and Irene Bell, and Harry Lesser and Mary in *The Tenants*; Yakov Bok and Zinaida Lebedev in *The Fixer*; Frank Alpine and Helen Bober in *The Assistant*; Nathan and Ornita in "Black is My Favorite Color"; and Max and Miriam in "The First Seven Years," to name a few.) As a romantic and, at times, erotic story, "The Lady of the Lake" puts a biblical spin on the Malamudian theme of the thwarted romance; as a Holocaust story, however, it inverts the survival-in-translation paradigm explored in "The German Refugee" and "Man in the Drawer." Henry Freeman (born Levin) quits his job at Macy's and searches for romance in Italy. Wandering alone on the Island of del Dongo, he spies a beautiful woman swimming naked in a lake. Isabella del Dongo (born del Seta) is immediately attracted to Henry and he to her. However, both lie to one another about who they are. She pretends to be wealthy Italian aristocracy, while her family are only caretakers of an estate, including a statuary garden, and he pretends not to be Jewish, for fear of losing her. Unbeknownst to him, of course, is the fact that not only is Isabella Jewish, but a concentration camp survivor, who has asked him repeatedly "Are you Jewish?" and has given him every opportunity to admit that he is. His decision to lie to her, however, costs him his future with her, for by the time he can safely tell her the truth, she is gone, and he is left clasping a stone statue.

The perceived (but not actual) difference in religion here not only heightens the sense of needless tragedy, but allows Malamud to use romantic love as a sort of allegory of the Akedah, the binding of Isaac, in addition to four of the other ten trials of Abraham. (Henry Levin is no Abraham, thus he undergoes only five trials.) In Malamud's domesticated reworking of the Akedah, the binding, in which something else (a ram) is sacrificed in place of the beloved, the ram is nowhere to be found because Henry has no faith and is almost ashamed of his Judaism. His fear of rejection forces him to sacrifice his beloved, his future, his dreams, his happiness, and ultimately, himself.

In his way, Henry reenacts five of Abraham's ten trials. They are as follows: 1) Abraham realized that the stone and wood idols in his father's shop were mere statues and that there is only one G-d; he proceeded to destroy the idols. 2) Abraham was imprisoned in a dungeon for ten years. 3) He was commanded to leave his land and travel to an unknown destination, where he was told that four actions can change a heavenly decree, among which are being renamed and changing his residence. 4) Abraham was commanded to be circumcised. 5) He was commanded to bind and slaughter Isaac at the top of Mount Moriah.

Henry's encounter with stone idols occurs not in his father's store, but in Isabella's garden of statues, which turn out to be *copies* of great sculptures. When Isabella admits that the beautiful statues are not genuine, Henry's "face fell. 'Is something the matter?' she asks. 'Only that I couldn't tell the fake from the real.' 'Oh,' she insists, 'but many of the copies are exceedingly beautiful. . . It would take an expert to tell they weren't originals.'" To which Henry responds, "I guess I've got a lot to learn" ("The Lady of the Lake," in *The Magic Barrel*, 114). Just as Abraham's perceptiveness moves him closer to his fate, Henry's unperceptiveness, his inability to tell the real thing from a copy, determines the outcome of his romance with Isabella. In some respects Henry is almost a photographic negative of Abraham. Abraham *knew* idols were false; Henry does not know that Isabella is Jewish. Abraham had the courage to destroy all of his father's idols and to believe in God; Henry embraces statues and is too afraid to admit his own Jewishness, never considering the possibility that Isabella might be Jewish too.

Abraham's second trial found him imprisoned by Nimrod for ten years. Henry Levin, though not in a dungeon, had worked for years (we are not told how many) in Macy's book department, which seemed at the very least chafing and confining. A small inheritance enables him to quit his job and go to Paris, where he changes his name from the ethnic Levin to the more ambiguous, if ironic, Freeman. But because of the heat and tourists, "he felt he must flee" (99), whereupon he travels to Italy. Thus, he has enacted a third of Abraham's trials: to leave his land, change his name, and change his residence. But unlike Abraham's name change from Avram to Abraham, which brings him closer to G-d, Henry Freeman's name change signifies his desire to distance himself from his religion.

Henry's fourth trial, circumcision, figures into his relationship with Isabella as, when they are at the top of Mt. Mottarone in the Alps, he recalls that she may have seen him naked when they went swimming in the lake. At this point Freeman "felt constrained to tell her that circumcision was de rigueur in stateside hospitals; but he didn't dare. She may not have noticed" (119). Clearly, Levin has been circumcised in accordance with Jewish law, something that Freeman is prepared to disavow.

But the last and most demanding trial for Abraham (and Freeman) is the Akedah, the binding of Isaac at the top of Mt. Moriah. For the final test, G-d commands Abraham to take his son Isaac to "the land of Moriah; and offer him there for a burnt-offering upon one of the mountains which [I] will tell thee of." The Midrashic literature states that on the way, Satan tempts Isaac in the form of a young boy and then in the form of a gushing river, into which Abraham goes up to his neck, and says to G-d, "If Isaac drowns, who will sanctify your name?" At which point G-d shouts at Satan, who vanishes (*The Midrash Says*, 198–199). On the third day of their journey to Moriah, Abraham and Isaac ascend the mountain with wood for the fire, stones for the altar, and a knife. Isaac, seeing the knife and fire, asks his father where is the lamb for the burnt-offering? Abraham replies, "G-d will provide Himself the lamb for a burnt-offering." So they build the altar and Isaac binds his son. As the father "stretched forth his hand, and took the knife to slay his son, an angel of the Lord called out 'Abraham, Abraham!' And he said: 'Here am I.' And he said: 'Lay not thy hand upon the lad, neither do thou any thing unto him; for now I know that thou art a G-d-fearing man, seeing thou hast not withheld thy son from me.' And Abraham . . . beheld him a ram caught in the thicket by his horns. And Abraham offered the ram as the burnt-offering instead of his son" (Genesis 22:1–13).

Freeman has no living son to sacrifice, but his deceit and repudiation of his Judaism certainly cost him any future sons he might have had with Isabella. Rather, in Malamud's rendering of the Akedah, Henry Levin Freeman binds himself with lies and sacrifices his future with Isabella at the top of Mt. Mottorone. His sacrificial ram would have been the truth.

In place of Satan in the form of river and boy, Malamud employs Isabella's younger brother, Giacobbe (Jacob), to row Freeman to the island each time he wants to see his beloved. And rather than have Abraham nearly drown in the rushing river, Malamud has Freeman experience severe fatigue trying to row the boat himself. But to complete this part of the analogy with the Akedah, in place of Abraham's angel atop the mountain, Malamud casts Isabella, who tries repeatedly to get Freeman to admit that he is a Jew. She suggests, " 'Don't those peaks—those seven—look like a Menorah?' 'Like a what?' Freeman politely inquired. . . . 'Or do you see the Virgin's crown adorned with Jewels?' 'Maybe the crown,' he faltered. 'It all depends how you look at it'" (119). Henry's angel has tried, but Freeman does not realize that, as with Abraham, had he been prepared to risk losing his beloved, G-d would have provided for him. In yet another attempt to get Freeman to admit his Jewishness when they return from the mountain, Isabella confesses the truth about her family's name and position as caretakers of the grand estate. She again gives Freeman the opportunity to tell the truth, but he can only say, "I'm not hiding anything." "That's what I was afraid of," she replies (120).

The connection between Henry and stone idols is introduced when Freeman first sets eyes on Isabella: "It had momentarily seemed as though a statue had come to life, but Freeman quickly realized a woman was standing . . . watching the water" (102). From the beginning, this romance seems precarious, and the parallels between Freeman in a statuary garden and Abraham in his father's idol shop are uncanny. Abraham could distinguish God from stone idols; Freeman cannot distinguish a woman from a statue, an original statue from a copy, or a Jew from a non-Jew. In a sense, Henry worships his stone idols for the same reasons that the Aramites worshiped theirs—fear and, one could argue, ignorance. Interestingly, Freeman's description of Isabella's beauty notes that "her nose was perhaps the one touch of imperfection that perfected the rest—a trifle long and thin" (106). She has, it would seem, a Jewish nose, but Freeman does not pick up on it. After thinking to himself, "Had he, Oh G-d, at last met his fate?" (106), Isabella asks him three questions, the first in Italian, "Si e perduto?" (Are you lost?), "Are you an American?" and "Are you, perhaps, Jewish?" (106). Again he cannot seem to take a hint, and the Akedah of deceit begins. "He said, no, he wasn't . . . though he personally had nothing against them." He *had* met his fate.

Then, as he is about to kiss Isabella's hand, a "guide" appears, as if sent by G-d himself, yelling "waving his cane like a rapier" shouting "Transgressor" at Freeman (106). This guide turns out to be Isabella's father, who had earlier rowed Freeman to the island. He essentially spanks Freeman with his cane and sends him on his way. Immediately following this incident, as Freemen ponders a possible future with Isabella, he has "moments of grave doubt (and) wondered what *trials* [emphasis mine] he was in for if he went after her" (107), and he wonders why "she had asked him if he was Jewish. . . . But then he figured her question might have been a 'test' of some kind . . . to determine his eligibility" (108). Well, Freeman is right: he is in for trials and it was a test, to which he refuses to provide the correct answer.

The test of the question Are you Jewish? is simply a rephrasing of the test of sacrifice. Both requests demand and measure one's faith in and love of G-d. It is interesting to note that each time G-d calls Abraham, he replies, "Here am I," meaning, "I belong to you; I am here for you." The rabbis write that one of the principles derived from the Akedah is that "[i]t teaches us that someone who loves G-d must be prepared to give up for His sake whatever is most precious to him, even his own life or the lives of his children" (*The Midrash Says*, 204). In other words, in one's readiness and willingness to sacrifice the beloved, lies one's worthiness to keep the beloved. This is the trial that Henry Levin, who fancies that he is free to ignore his Judaism, fails.

It is no accident that Isabella's father is a guide and her family are caretakers. In the religious analogy, they also function as guides through and caretakers of Judaism, something that does not interest Henry Levin. As the story of yet another of Malamud's thwarted romances ends, the presence of G-d and stone intensifies. When Isabella says "goodbye" to Henry, he says, "I have come to marry you." The narrator then adds, "Then came the soft, inevitable thunder: 'Are you a Jew?' 'Why should I lie?' he thought. . . . But then he trembled with fear of at the last moment losing her." So he said, "'How many no's make never? Why do you persist with such foolish questions?' 'Because I hoped you were,'" she answers (122). Then, in a cruelly erotic move, she unbuttons her blouse, "arousing Freeman, . . .When she revealed her breasts—he could have wept at their beauty . . . —to his horror he discerned tattooed on the soft and tender flesh a bluish line of distorted numbers. 'Buchenwald,' Isabella said." She then tells him that she cannot marry him because, "We are Jews. My past is meaningful to me. I treasure what I suffered for." As he is about to tell her the truth, "grop(ing) for her breasts, to clutch, kiss or suckle them, she had stepped among the statues, and when he vainly sought her in the veiled mist . . . still calling her name, Freeman embraced only moonlit stone" (123). Here the story ends.

In what is perhaps a supreme irony, the Midrash tells us that Abraham and Isaac (Yitzchak) carried stones up to Mt. Moriah to build an altar for the sacrifice, and that Abraham set "up the stones with the exact same joy as a man who makes the wedding preparations for his son" (*The Midrash Says*, 198). The garden of statuary would no doubt have made a lovely place for a wedding, as that is where Henry first saw Isabella and mistook her for a statue/idol. It is most appropriate that Freeman is left embracing a symbol of what he does worship: the ability to pass for a Gentile, and by extension, the freedom to marry a Gentile. The moonlit stone he is left holding, therefore, harks back to the stone idols that Abraham destroyed in his father's shop. (Recall that this was Abraham's first trial.) Where Abraham smashed stone statues, Freeman literally embraces them. Where Abraham joyfully accepted the "signature" scar of circumcision, Freeman implicitly rejects what Isabella's branded numbers signify. Perhaps the Midrash on this story might read that had Levin remained true to Levin, he would surely have been a free man.

Malamud's treatment of the Holocaust may not satisfy Langer's conception of Holocaust literature, but it does sound some very human rings of truth with respect to post-Holocaust Jews, trying to live in that defining shadow. The one constant in these stories bespeaks the tragedy of compromising one's Jewish identity, either literally in name, or figuratively, in a foreign language, in hopes of succeeding in a non-Jewish society. Whether one is displaced by the Holocaust itself, as in the case of Oskar Gassner, or by simple geographical accident, as were Levitansky and Isabella, or by assimilation, as were Harris/Harvitz and Levin/Freeman, the consequences are tragic. Not true, although truth, indeed.

Works Cited

Benjamin, Walter. "The Task of the Translator." In *Illuminations*. New York: Schocken, 1955.

Langer, Lawrence L. "Malamud's Jews and the Holocaust Experience." In *Admitting the Holocaust*. New York: Oxford University Press, 1995.

Lasher, Lawrence. *Conversations with Bernard Malamud*. Jackson: University Press of Mississippi, 1995.

Malamud, Bernard. *The Stories of Bernard Malamud*. New York: Penguin. 1983. Parenthetical references in the text are from this edition.

———. *The Magic Barrel*. New York: Farrar Straus, 1958. Paranthetical references in the text are from this edition.

Weissman, Rabbi Moshe. "The Book of Beraishes." In *The Midrash Says*. New York: Benei Yakov Publications, 1980.

Chapter 14

BERNARD AND JULIET
Romance and Desire in Malamud's High Art

Alan Cheuse

In art, as in life, romance sometimes strikes when you least expect it. In Bernard Malamud's short fiction, it's also quite an anomalous occurence and a sometimes almost comical emotion in contrast to the pathos of his other motifs. It is expressed by a number of images so traditional—one of the most apparent being the attraction that moves from the image straight into the eye of the beholder with a certainty that we usually associate with the laws of physics—that the writer seems to have borrowed the motif quite unselfconsciously from some of the most important documents in the history of human affections. And though while most of the women who are the objects of the male characters' affections are represented without question as simple objects of sex and love, there is, over the long course of Malamud's storytelling career, a serious transformation that occurs in the attitude of his men toward their women, even if, ironically, the final, and most mature, love relationship takes the form of putative bestiality.

Take Rabbi Leo Finkle, for example. Having invited a matchmaker into his life in order to make an orderly search for an appropriate wife, he finds himself staring at a photograph left accidentally by Salzman the marriage broker in an envelope of proper prospects.

He gazed at it a moment and let out a low cry. . . . Her face deeply moved him. Why, he could not at first say. It gave him the impression of youth—spring flowers, yet age—a sense of having been used to the bone, wasted; this came from the eyes, which were hauntingly familiar, yet absolutely strange. He had a vivid impression that he had met her before, but try as he might he could not place her although he could almost recall her name, as if he had read it in her own handwriting. No, this couldn't be; he would have remembered her. It was not, he affirmed, that she had an extraordinary beauty—no, though her face was attractive enough; it was *something* about her moved him. . . . Her he desired. His head ached and eyes narrowed with the intensity of his gazing. . . . Only such a one could understand him and help him seek whatever he was seeking. She might, perhaps, love him. . . .

Love at first sight. And it occurs by means of the eyes. Although we don't usually think about Malamud's fiction as a repository of stories about physical love, this moment of peculiarly Malamudian amour also stands solidly in the tradition of European concepts of passionate desire. Think of how Dante describes his first meeting with Beatrice in *La Vita Nuova*. One look fixes him forever as her devoted love slave. And how does she first greet him when he sees her again in the higher spheres? By a piercing look! But this early Renaissance version of passionate love has its origins in the pagan notion of love as an oppressive condition in which the lover finds himself in the throes of emotions beyond his control.

Certainly for most of the second half of Malamud's story "The Magic Barrel" Leo Finkle would agree. Love takes him over, as a disease takes over the body and even the mind. He rushes off in search of Salzman. When he does not find him at home in his drab apartment, he rushes back to his own place, caught in that music, as Yeats would say, that works its way on the young and the impressionable, the melody and chords of romantic love. When he finally meets his match, the sky lights up in a Chagallian display of romantic, sexual fireworks: "Violins and lit candles revolved in the sky. Leo ran forward with flowers outthrust."

If this diagnosis of Finkle's condition seems paradoxical—it's classic, it's also romantic—that's only because Malamud himself, like any good modernist writer, draws his water from both wells. Consider, for example, such a classic scene as the man smitten as he observes the beloved at her bath, as in the myth of Diana. You'll recall a similar moment in *The Assistant* when Frankie Alpine works his way up from the basement of Morris Bober's store in the shaft of the dumbwaiter so that he can observe

Helen Bober in the bathroom. "If you do it," Alpine tells himself, "you will suffer." But after crossing himself, Frankie, turning himself into a classic voyeur, grabs the dumbwaiter ropes and pulls himself slowly up the shaft. "A light went on over his head," we're told. Then, leaning forward, "he could see through the uncurtained crossed sash window into the old-fashioned bathroom. . . ." Notice, among other things here, the double cross, as Frankie, for all of his naturalistic qualities as a low-life Peeping Tom, fulfills the requirements of the young man in love, laboring hard in order to reveal the depths and intensity of his passion. As Prospero says, "Light winning makes the prize seem light."

So let's watch Frankie Alpine as he spies on Helen Bober:

> Helen was there looking with sad eyes at herself in the mirror. He thought she would stand there forever, but at last she unzippered her housecoat, stepping out of it. . . . He felt a throb of pain at her nakedness, an overwhelming desire to love her. . . . Her body was young, soft, lovely, the breasts like small birds in flight, her ass like a flower. Yet it was a lonely body in spite of its lovely form, lonelier. Bodies are lonely, he thought, but in bed she wouldn't be. She seemed realer to him now than she had been, revealed without clothes, personal, possible. He felt greedy as he gazed, all eyes at a banquet, hungry so long as he must look. But in looking he was forcing her out of reach, making her into a thing only of his seeing, her eyes reflecting his sins, rotten past, spoiled ideals, his passion poisoned by his shame. . . .

The situation here is rich with allusions and transformations, both classic and romantic: Frankie's ascent from basement to higher up in the building, suggesting his rise in the world from criminal to shop-assistant, and his moral elevation from ignorant neighborhood thug to reader and thinker, though one wouldn't know it from his pathetic pose at the moment; and Helen's instant metamorphosis from neighborhood girl to object of mythological observation; and her body's transformation in pure metaphoric terms from human to animal and plant—her breasts to birds, her posterior to flower. There's also the classic trope of love fixing itself by means of the eyes. And an angular, almost geometrical modernist positioning, with Helen staring at her own eyes in the mirror in a self-conscious pose that is actually truly innocent because she was unaware that precisely at that moment Frankie Alpine is stealing his look at her. The classic transformation undergoes as well a modernist twist, since her change from girl to bird and flower takes place in an instant beneath his intense gaze, while Frankie's change from gentile to Jew articulated in the book's final paragraph needs the glacial force of the entire novel to make happen.

A number of Malamud's significant protagonists take walks on the wild side of love. S. Levin, in *A New Life*, for example, before entering into a more mature and devotional relationship with Pauline Gilley, falls quite easily into an affair with Nadalee, a student at the Oregon cow college where he has come to teach. The language in the scene of their tryst tells us something, as does the language in the voyeur scene in *The Assistant*, about how we are to read the overpowering emotions rampant in the scene.

Levin drives west to the motel belonging to Nadalee's absent aunt, "aimlessly on, in sadness contemplating all the failures of his life, the multifarious wrong ways he had gone, the waste of his going . . ." but, in a moment reminiscent of Dedalus's apprehension of the sea in the opening scene of *Ulysses*, he soon sniffs "a sea smell. Whirling down the window, he smelled again and let out a cry. . . . The ocean! . . . He beheld in the distance a golden lace of moonlight on the dark bosom of the vast sea. . . ." Liquid becomes the central metaphor of this discovery. "He saw himself as stout Cortez—Balboa, that is—gazing down at the water in wild surmise, both eyes moist. . . ." When he reaches the motel, he finds Nadalee waiting for him wearing "a sheer nightie . . ." He says to her, "I got lost." But "before he could say where or why, she had shucked off her garment and her gloriously young body shed light as he hungrily embraced it. . . ."

Interesting here that the language seems lively when it describes Levin's sight of the Pacific, and falls a little flat when it takes us into the sexual scene in the motel room. We might possibly say that when the character's heart isn't beating squarely behind his phallus, the writer loses some of the pleasure in the event. Though we should notice that the nose is becoming as important to love Malamud style as the eyes. But then there are moments that contradict this notion, as in the presumably hallucinatory pornographic vision of Yakov Bok's in *The Fixer* when lying at night in his cell he imagines a visit from Marfa Golov, the widow who has accused him of murdering her child for ritual purposes. Here it's mostly all done with the eyes. Bok sees her enter his cell and becomes a passive spectator to her striptease as she silently removes her clothes—"the white hat with cherries, the red rose scarf, green skirt, flowery blouse, cotton petticoat, pointed button shoes, red garters, black stockings and soiled frilly drawers. Lying naked on the fixer's mattress, her legs spread, she promised many goyish delights if he would confess to the priest at the peephole. . . ."

Sexual desire comes naturally by means of the eye to Roy Hobbs. When we first see him on the train in the opening of Malamud's debut novel he's stirred at once by a boarding passenger, "a girl in a dressy black dress. . . . Her face was striking [neat pun here, given Roy's profession, and the fate he is about to meet] and when she stepped up into the train her nyloned legs made Roy's pulses dance. . . ." Within a short while his desire leads to his wound as he makes his rendezvous in a Chicago hotel with this woman who is packing the gun with the silver bullets—in a scene where lust and water merge.

> Opening the door, he was astonished at the enormous room. Through the white-curtained window the sight of the endless dark lake sent a shiver down his spine. . . . Then he saw her standing shyly in the far corner of the room, naked under the gossamer thing she wore, held up on her risen nipples and the puffed wedge of hair beneath her white belly. . . .

When she fires the pistol at him at close range the bullet cuts "a silver line across the water. . . ."

Later in the book water and sex come together in a brief romantic encounter between Roy and Memo when they drive to Jones Beach. There's liquid in the sky as the night is "lit up by a full moon swimming in lemon juice, but at intervals eclipsed by rain clouds that gathered in dark blots and shuttered the yellow light off the fields and tree tops . . ." They don't reach the beach, stopping instead alongside a small stream where a sign announces that the water is polluted. They talk a while, stare at the water, finally kiss.

> He trapped her lips, tasting of lemon drops, kissing hard. Happening to open his eyes, he saw her staring at him in the middle of the kiss. Shutting them, he dived deep down again [more liquid metaphor]. Then she caught his passion, opened her mouth for his tongue and went limp around the knees. . . .

So there's as much sexual lip service as there are meetings of the eyes in this young writer's first novel where the tone still allows for the suggestion of something more than lust, that is, for romance. In the later novels, say, for example, *The Tenants,* the writer in middle age has much more on his mind than sex, sexual desire still plays an important part in the novel, but the senses shift away from the eye to the touch. Such matters Malamud describes rather explicitly as Lesser begins an affair with the black woman Mary Kettlesworth even as he falls in love with Willie Spearmint's young white girlfriend Irene. In bed with Irene we hear that "[t]hey kiss, grope, bite, tear at each other. He licks the floral scent of her flesh. She digs her nails into his shoulders. He is aroused by their passion." In a novel whose themes appear more interesting in the abstract than they

do in the execution, the writer seems to behave in similar fashion, stirred
by the prospect of writing about sex but not drawing us fully enough into
the scene itself.

Dubin's Lives is clearly not a young man's book. The motifs deal
deeply with the length of a life already mostly fully lived, and the sexual drive portrayed in its pages is not the hot ejaculatory rushing of a
neophyte in the throes of desire but the melancholy thrustings of a man
who seems himself on the downward slope of desire. Maturity may account for the fact that the descriptions of the couplings between Dubin
the fifty-eight-year-old biographer and the ex-student Fanny are the
most explicit in the Malamud canon even as the passages are punctuated
by annotative sentences about the meaning of the mixture of lust and desire. As in this scene toward the end of the book when ripeness is all
there is to their love affair:

> She glanced at him momentarily anxious as he took
> the water glass from her hand and held it as they kissed.
> Their first kiss, after a season of separation, loss, before
> renewing joy, hurt. Dubin set the glass down and began
> to unbraid Fanny's warm hair. She shook it out, heavy
> full. Her shoulders, breasts, youthful legs, were splen-
> did. He loved her glowing flesh. Fanny removed her
> heart-shaped locket and his bracelet, placing them on
> the bookcase near the dripping red candle. She kept the
> ruby ring on. Forcefully she pulled his undershirt over
> his head; he drew down her black underpants. Fanny
> kissed his live cock. What they were doing they did as
> though the experience were new. It was a new experi-
> ence. He was, in her arms, a youthful figure. On his
> knees he embraced her legs, kissed her between them.
> . . . Dubin slept with his arms around her; she with her
> hand cupping his balls. . . .

At the end of the novel, Dubin returns to his wife, his vitality
recharged by his exciting affair with Fanny, in a pose similar to the stylized
posture of Leo Finkle in the little Chagallian cameo in the sky above the
New York street where he meets his match. Leaving Fanny's bed and
house, Dubin runs up a moonlit road "holding his half-stiffened phallus in
his hand, for his wife with love. . . ." The comedy is ended with the hero
outthrust.

The human comedy, anyway.

But in Malamud's last completed novel, the allegorical post–nuclear
war fantasy *God's Grace*, the Malamudian sexual comedy continues by

other means, parodying the European romance tradition even as it breaks from it with a jarring sexual disjuncture. Cohn, the scientist hero, finds himself stranded on a Pacific island with only families of chimpanzees and baboons and gorillas as his company. Good intellectual that he is, he teaches the animals to speak. And because he worries about the demise of the human species, he eventually thrusts himself into a sexual situation with a female chimpanzee named Mary Madelyn who, while in estrus, with, as Malamud describes it, "the jeweled pink flower of her swollen sexual skin visible from the rear," gives off a "dense scent" that hits the wind like "a compound of night-blooming jasmine and raw eggs. . . ."

It's not only the chimps who seek her hungrily. Cohn, you'll recall, decides, as Malamud puns it, to "monkey with evolution," dressing the female ape in virginal clothing and then, one night, lifting her white skirt from the rear, "and with shut eyes, telling himself to keep his thoughts level," dipping "his phallus into her hot flower. . . ." There is "an instant electric connection" and Cohn parts "with his seed as she possessed it. . . ."

The intercourse between Cohn and Mary Madelyn is the most outrageous sexual coupling in all of Malamud's work—and it ranks along with Faulkner's scene of a Snopes standing on a stool behind a beautiful cow as one of the most outrageous romantic pairing in all American literature— yet it remains completely logical within the confines of the plot because of Cohn's desire to further the human species. Bestiality thus becomes a necessity in this odd futurist fable.

" 'I wov you,' " Mary Madelyn says to Calvin Cohn.

> He said he found her very engaging. She was even alluring these days, amiable brown eyes, silken black hair; her features approached human. Though Mary Madelyn could not be said to be classically beautiful—facts were facts—still beauty existed, derived to some degree from her intelligent, generous nature. She came to something. Having become aware of her quality, her spirit, Cohn thought, accounted for his growing feeling for her. . . . Sensing receptivity, Mary Madelyn presented herself to him, crouching low. . . .

So while there may not be any lit candles and violins revolving in the sky, as in a young man's passion, there is, from Cohn's side, the certain evidence of the cultivated affection of mature love. As Cohn considers it to himself, just before committing his seed for the hope of the future,

> If two daughters in a dark cave on separate nights, lay incestuously with their wine-sotted, love-groaning father,

why not Cohn, a clearheaded, honest man, lying with bio-
philial affection and shut eyes, against the warm furry
back of a loving lady chimpanzee who spoke English well
and was mysteriously moved by *Romeo and Juliet*?

A good question.

Chapter 15

BERNARD MALAMUD AND CYNTHIA OZICK
Kindred *Neshamas*

Evelyn Avery

Separated by gender, religious practice, and life style, Bernard Malamud and Cynthia Ozick would appear to share little but their accidents of birth and choice of craft as twentieth-century Jewish American authors. Indeed, they even define themselves differently since Malamud describes himself as a "writer who happens to be Jewish," while Ozick sees herself as a writer in the Jewish tradition.

Despite such differences, however, they share a deep respect, affection, and concern for each other's lives and writings as evident in their letters and interviews.[1] Moreover, their fiction reflects shared values, a common approach to their art, in spite of contrasts in style and subject matter. Linked by *Yiddishkeit*, compassion for the underdog, outrage against injustice, and commitment to truth, their fiction invites comparison. Works such as Malamud's "Silver Crown," *The Tenants, The Fixer*, and Ozick's "Pagan Rabbi," "Usurpation," "Mercenary," and *The Shawl* illuminate and enrich each other, verifying that their authors are kindred spirits.

Ozick's respect for Malamud's writing is apparent in "Usurpation," where she admits her envy of Malamud's "Silver Crown," which turns on magic, faith, and the possibility of redemption. The presence of Rabbi

Lifschitz, a questionable "miracle" worker, and his illusory silver crown ironically underscores the importance of faith and love, without which the miraculous is impossible. Since the crux of the story is an arid relationship between Albert Gans and his dying father, only love, an act of faith, can transform the son and save the father. Instead, the guilt-ridden, but shallow, Albert seeks a quick, cheap fix from Rabbi Lifschitz, who for a fee, will fashion a silver crown to heal the elder Gans.

Although the rabbi's intentions and the crown's existence are suspect, both Malamud and Ozick recognize their potential to inspire real magic, to alter Albert's feelings for his father and transmute hatred into forgiveness and even love. But in "The Silver Crown" there is no magic; the rabbi and the crown fail, for Albert's heart is bitter, his *neshama* merciless, as he curses his father. "He hates me, the son of a bitch, I hopes he croaks."[2] An hour later, Gans "shut[s] his eyes and expire[s]" (328). While Cecilia Farr argues that "trust in magic destroys faith and the father,"[3] the reverse is true in "The Silver Crown," where magic can only work if love, essential to faith, exists. Repeatedly the rabbi asks Albert whether he loves his father and "believes in God" (310). Repeatedly Albert is evasive, describing their relationship as difficult. Although the rabbi hardly looks or sounds prophet-like, his first name, Jonas (Greek for Jonah), suggests he has suffered and accepted God. While the rabbi may be a materialistic con man, he is capable of sacrifice and love, and qualified to instruct Albert. Thus, the Ganses' sterile relationship is counterpointed by the rabbi's bond with his retarded daughter. Described as a "bulky, stupefying, fifteen year old," with an "unfocused face" and garbled words, Rifkele lives with her father, whose magic she hawks in the street (308). In Albert Gans's eyes, she is disgusting, a freak who makes him question the rabbi's ethics and judgment, but ironically Rifkele uplifts Rabbi Lifschitz who views his daughter as God's perfect creation (310). In the end, rabbi and daughter "rush into each other's arms" when they witness Albert's blasphemy against his father. "Murderer," cries the rabbi as he and Rifkele embrace (328) and Albert flees with a "massive, spike-laden headache" instead of the silver crown (328). Without love, Malamud and Ozick both recognize, death ensues, with it life has meaning.

Although Ozick playfully considers brighter alternative endings with the father recovering, Albert reforming, or the silver crown materializing, her own stories are as magical and as "logically decisive" as Malamud's.[4] Thus, "The Pagan Rabbi" contains many of the "Silver Crown['s]" elements—obsessive emotion, absence of love, rejection of God's Law, and dire consequences. While teacher Gans cannot honor his father and seeks answers from a crown, Rabbi Kornfeld betrays his wife and seeks love from a tree, an act of suicide. A dialectic between man's soul and nature's sensuality, "The Pagan Rabbi" is a midrash on the dangers of paganism, the worship of the physical world, of hedonistic sexuality divorced from God and human love.[5] Relinquishing faith, love, and responsibility, the rabbi succumbs to the *yaisha hora*, the idolatrous evil impulse that Ozick repeatedly warns against in her fiction. On the surface, Rabbi Isaac Kornfeld seems very different from Albert Gans, one an orthodox rabbi, the other a secular Jew, but their self-indulgent natures are similar, incapable of sacrifice and love.

Nourished by the holiest literature and the most profound secular works, Rabbi Isaac Kornfeld, whose name paradoxically evokes the biblical and pastoral, rejects the Law for nature and seeks his soul in a tree nymph. In the process, he denies his wife and God, and in committing suicide, damns himself eternally. Like Malamud, Ozick depicts the dangers of idol worship, of investing faith and love in objects, whether a silver crown or a tree.

In a variation on the theme, both authors examine the impact of selfishness and crass ambition on a power struggle between Jews and blacks. Published a few years apart, Malamud's *The Tenants* (1971) and Ozick's *A Mercenary* (1974) seem to have usurped each other in their similar themes and conclusions. While settings, characters, and plot details differ, black and Jewish rivalry crushes friendship and eventually life itself. In both works the Jew dominates intellectually and culturally, threatening the black ego, until deposed by black rage.

Thus, in *The Tenants*, Harry Lesser, a published author struggling with his second novel, is challenged by Willie Spearmint, a self-taught black writer, who vies with him for literary supremacy and a Jewish woman's affections.[6] Because the Jew mentors the Black, correcting his grammar and critiquing his work, equality is impossible and violence inevitable.

Set against a jungle background in a crumbling tenement, the novel evokes the wilderness and passion of Africa where the Jewish intellect is no match for African fervor. In a Lesser dreamscape, he is married to Mary Kettlesmith by a tribal chief on the "dark continent" while his nemesis, Willie Spearmint, is simultaneously wed to Irene Bell (nee Belinsky) by a rabbi. Malamud's intentions seem clear. If ethnic differences can be muted, perhaps a clash can be avoided or better yet, if Jew and Black can wed professionally and romantically perhaps their people can thrive together. Unfortunately, even the dream ceremony is undermined by misunderstanding. In an increasingly nightmarish reality, the two writers stalk each other, driven by literary envy, romantic rivalry, and base fear until the verbal dueling erupts in violence with each attacking the other's most vulnerable site, Spearmint's brain and Lesser's manhood.

A pair of unequals, Black and Jew are doomed from the beginning, a truth Cynthia Ozick realizes in *Mercenary* where the settings alternate between Africa and New York, somewhat evocative of *The Tenants* except

that Africa is not just a dream, but an exotic-cannibalistic backdrop to the
deadly battle between Morris Ngambe, a prominent tribal member, and
his Oxonian assistant, Stanislav Lushinski, a Polish Jewish holocaust survivor. A paid diplomat for a tiny African nation, Lushinski enjoys the
tropical fruits including the plentiful "black-brown nipples." But despite
his privileged position, Lushinski cannot forget he is a Jew, although "he
was cold to Jews and labored to identify as an African."[7] Likewise
Ngambe, half of Luchinski's age, possessing an excellent British education and European experience, distrusts the West and Luchinski, but is attached to both.

The stage is set for the African and the Jew, both "impersonators," to
expose each others' real identities. In "New York, a city of Jews," Ngambe
views "their neighborhoods, their religious schools, their synagogues, so-
cieties and an avalanche of books" and then surveys nearby, "the streets of
Blacks, victims with African faces, lost to language and faith" (50). From
his perspective, the contrast is evident—economically, culturally, reli-
giously, the Jews are the "haves" and the Blacks, the "have nots." Nor can
individuals successfully reinvent themselves, especially when they possess the dense ethnic histories of the Holocaust or colonial experiences.
Thus, Ngambe and Luchinski are fated to play out their roles. Back in the
"white African villa," Luchinski receives a threatening note from Ngambe
who calls him a Jew, a traitor, and appeals to his mother's spirit to destroy
the imposter.

Although the tribal father heads the family and community, Ozick em-
powers Ngambe's mother, who, after her bizarre "unkosher" death, which
blends her nursing milk with blood, becomes a source of worship. Still
worse off, Luchinski had been orphaned when his aryan-looking, assimilated parents had been executed by Nazis, leaving Stanislav to fend for
himself. To survive, both youths had buried their pasts, donned masks,
and in effect attempted to exchange identities, but their behavior has been
no more than playacting.

In a Malamudian-style epigram, Ozick writes: "Every man at length
becomes what he wishes to victimize. . . . Every man needs to imperson-
ates what he first must kill" (51). Eerily reminiscent of *The Tenants*, *Mercenary* climaxes in an invocation to evil as Ngambe beseeches his "divine
mother" to return the Jew to "the merciless palms of [Polish] peasants and
fists of peasants under the rafters . . . , against the stone and under the
snow" (52). In short, the Polish Jew, dispatched by African sorcery, is
transported back to the Holocaust, to the Jewish identity and fate he
sought to escape.

Similarly, the Jew in flight is evident in Malamud's *Fixer* and Ozick's
The Shawl, both Holocaust nightmares, though the former is set in early-
twentieth-century Russia, while the latter occurs primarily in Miami, forty

years after the death camp experience. Commenting on *The Fixer*, Malamud acknowledged the Mendel Beilis case as the source for his novel but added that he "shap[ed] the whole to suggest the quality of the afflictions of the Jews under Hitler."[8] In short, *The Fixer* qualifies as Holocaust literature.

Although different ages, genders, and backgrounds, Rosa Lublin (*The Shawl*)[9] and Yakov Bok (*The Fixer*)[10] endure similar suffering and even possess comparable characteristics. Both have undergone terrible physical abuse, one in a camp, the other in prison. Rosa, raised in a prosperous, assimilated Polish Jewish family, is doubly bitter over her losses, while Yakov, extremely impoverished, yearns for wealth and the opportunity to assimilate into gentile Kiev. Both are arrogant, blaming others for their tragedies. Thus, Rosa believes her niece Stella responsible for her baby Magda's death while Yakov wrongly blames his wife Raisl for their childlessness. Both resist advice and comforting. Rosa accepts money from Stella but shuns her. Only reluctantly does she allow Simon Persky, a would-be friend, to enter her life. Likewise Yakov rejects his father-in-law's consoling words and initially condemns his wife when she visits the prison.

Of course both characters will change, mature, and accept responsibility for life. But before Yakov becomes a Jew, insisting on a public trial to clear his name and to expose Russian anti-Semitism, before he can do that, he must acquire courage to forgive his wife and acknowledge his fault in the failed marriage. He must become familiar with *Yiddishkeit* and credit the decency of some Russians. Since Rosa occupies a more circumscribed world than Yakov, her task is similar but more focused. Thus, she must relinquish the worn blanket that serves as her baby, admitting that Magda is dead, murdered in the camp. She must view her niece realistically and gratefully accept the overtures of other human beings who may come from "inferior" backgrounds, but who are "menschen."

In each work the protagonists are educated to become more understanding and virtuous. Clearly, Malamud and Ozick share the same values and speak the same language. Whether in "The Silver Crown," *The Tenants*, or *The Fixer*, the heroes struggle to control their basest instincts. When they fail, as in the instances of Albert Gans and Harry Lesser, we mourn with the author. When they succeed, as does Yakov Bok, we applaud their sacrifice and ultimate righteousness. As a longtime Malamud enthusiast, Cynthia Ozick expresses similar ideals. While some of her characters, Rabbi Kornfeld and Stansilav Luchinski, succumb to their passions, Rosa Lublin reminds us that transformation is possible even forty years after the Holocaust. Although Yakov Bok's fate is uncertain in the tsar's court and Rosa Lublin's future is somewhat problematic, we are reminded that their nobility resides in the struggle for freedom, an ongoing process.

At Bernard Malamud's funeral, a rather secular affair attended by hundreds, Cynthia Ozick mourned the loss of a great Jewish writer and friend. In the midst of the tributes to Malamud's genius, his contribution to literature, his personal relationships, Ozick rose and facing the mourners recited the Shéma, the holiest prayer in Jewish worship, which binds the Jew to God. Although she knew that Malamud was not observant, Ozick had to affirm that his *neshama* was Jewish, that Bernard Malamud was a member of the tribe. The mourners' surprised response assured her that the Hebrew prayer was not only fitting testimony but also a necessary reminder of Malamud's identity.[11]

Notes

1. Several Malamud-Ozick letters have been reprinted in *The Bernard Malamud Society Newsletter* 6 (1996). Telephone interviews between Ozick and Avery, December 1995 and August 1996.

2. Bernard Malamud, "The Silver Crown," in *The Stories of Bernard Malamud* (New York: Farrar, Straus, Giroux, 1983), 328. All subsequent references to this story are to this edition and are noted parenthetically in the text.

3. Cecilia Konchar Farr, "Lust for a Story: Cynthia Ozick's 'Usurpation' as Fabulation," *Studies in American Jewish Literature* 6 (1987): 90.

4. Cynthia Ozick, "*Usurpation* (Other People's Stories)," in *Bloodshed and Three Novellas* (New York: Alfred Knopf, 1976), 134. All subsequent references to this story and to "A Mercenary" are to this edition and are noted parenthetically in the text.

5. Cynthia Ozick, *The Pagan Rabbi and Other Stories* (New York: Schocken, 1976). All subsequent references to "The Pagan Rabbi" are to this edition and are noted parenthetically in the text.

6. Bernard Malamud, *The Tenants* (New York: Farrar, Straus, Giroux, 1971). All subsequent references are to this edition and are noted parenthetically.

7. See note 4 for citation on "Mercury."

8. Alan Cheuse and Nicholas Delbanco, *Talking Horse: The Life and Writing of Bernard Malamud* (New York: Columbia University Press, 1996), 89.

9. Cynthia Ozick, *The Shawl* (New York: Alfred A. Knopf, 1987). All subsequent references are to this edition and are noted parenthetically.

10. Bernard Malamud, *The Fixer* (New York: Farrar, Straus, Giroux, 1966). All subsequent references are to this edition and are noted parenthetically.

11. Ozick's description of the funeral appears in the letters and interviews cited in note 1.

Chapter 16

BERNARD MALAMUD AND HIS
UNIVERSAL *MENSCHEN*

Daniel Walden

Throughout his long creative career, from *The Natural* (1952) to *The People* (published posthumously), Malamud asked: How shall a man create for himself a new life? Through loneliness and suffering, through balancing the demands of passion and commitment, his characters respond, demonstrating what critics call "moral obligation." Characters as diverse as a Jewish grocer, his Italian assistant, a shtetl handyman, and an American baseball player struggle to become *menschen*, Malamud's common folk elevated by decency and morality. In his first novel, *The Natural*, Roy Hobbs, a young pitcher, is tested when he is shot by a crazed woman, survives, and makes a comeback fifteen years later as a Babe Ruth–type batter. On the way, however, he falls for a slut, then for a good woman, dallies with gamblers, leaving baseball honest but accused of throwing the crucial game.

Using real events, Malamud utilizes baseball history, American heroism, and individual morality to combat corruption in the "land of plenty." Against this backdrop, protagonist Roy Hobbs is the eternal quester, the character prominent in the mythic search for the Holy Grail. In *The Natural*, Roy and his homemade bat, "Wonderboy," conjure up the Arthurian sword, male potency, vitality and fertility, and undertake the journey to the "secret sources of life." Joining the last-place Knights, Roy singlehand-edly takes them into the pennant race but fails at the last moment when his lust for Memo tempts him to throw the game, ignore true love, and sacrifice honor. In wanting above all to be the best—he tells the good woman, Iris, "I'd a been the King . . . the best in the game"—he cheapens the status of a true hero. Indeed, when Harriet perceptively asks, "Is that all?" Roy is unable to understand the implication that a true hero is selfless while a self-centered, ego-centered "star" is not a true hero (33, 156).

Roy is a gifted natural who could have invigorated his team and American life, who could have had a fruitful relationship with a good woman, but whose fatal flaw was his inability to surmount his infantile yearnings. Blind to what could have been with Iris, attached to his own needs above all others, he is wounded by Harriet, used by Memo and the gamblers, and fails to grow significantly. Harriet Bird hates to see a hero succeed, Memo cares only about using her hero, while Iris hates to see a hero fail.

When Roy asks Iris why she has stood up for him at the game, her only answer is, "Because I hate to see a hero fail. There are so few of them." She adds, "Without heroes we're all plain people and don't know how far we can go." To this Roy responds, "I wanted everything." Iris's remark, "But I don't understand why you should make so much of that," emphasizes the point that if Roy had values he'd have understood, as she puts it later in the same conversation, that "[e]xperience makes good people better. . . . We have two lives, Roy, the life we learn with and the life we live with after that." Suffering is what brings us toward happiness. Unfortunately Roy cannot let suffering or life happen. "I am sick of all I have suffered," he says. "What I suffered," he insists, "I don't want any more" (150–158).

At the end, through Iris, Roy is entreated to win, to win for their boy, because he was meant to. But Roy, unaware of all the wrong things he has done in his life and tried to undo but cannot, breaks Wonderboy and strikes out the first time at bat in the last game. At his last at-bat, "in full armor, mounted on a black charger," facing a new young pitcher, Herman Youngberry, he strikes out with a roar. Though Roy threw the payoff money into the Judge's face, and called Memo a whore, it is too late. "He thought. I never did learn anything out of my past life, now I have to suffer again." No wonder the newspaper's headline reads: "Suspicion of Hobb's Sellout," and a kid cries, "Say it ain't true, Roy" (231–237).

If the "wasteland" in *The Natural* is Pop Fisher's New York Knights, the medieval Fisher King gives way to the quest for the Grail when Roy Hobbs, the heroic youth, disappoints the father figure by selling out. In *The Assistant* the parallel "wasteland" is the seedier side of New York City and Morris Bober is the honest, elderly "King" to whom Frank Alpine comes as a son who will bring life to the family. The essential difference between the two novels lies in the nature of suffering and loneliness experienced by the protagonists. Morris, a Jew who runs a mom and pop grocery and barely manages to survive, believes in the Law. "My father used to say to be a Jew all you need is a good heart." That is, "The important thing is the Torah. This is the law—a Jew must believe in the Law." What Morris means, as he explains to Frank, is "to do what is right, to be honest, to be good. This means to other people. . . . If you live, you suffer. . . . [in fact, he says calmly] I suffer for you" (123–125).

Frank Alpine, a Franciscan in spirit, starts out as a follower, a robber who tries to make amends. Having taken part in robbing Morris he gets a job as his assistant to expiate his sin by helping Morris. Falling in love with Helen, Morris's daughter, strengthens his resolve to help, but also leads to his desire to understand why an old man, beaten by events, struggles on, honest but poor. At the end, as the rabbi intones over Morris's grave, "He suffered, he endured, but with hope," Frank finally understands. Morris did what he had to do: that is, he suffered because he lived, because living meant more than taking or ego. Malamud understands that the Jew is a mythical man; as he put it, "All men are Jews." For Malamud what is supremely important is man's relationship to the Law, meaning doing what is right when it has to be done, no matter the suffering. Indeed, turning the figure around, through suffering—which Roy refuses and both Morris and Frank welcome—it is possible to mature, to grow, to that point where it is natural to do what is right, to be honest, to be good. This is what is meant by *menschlichkeit*; it is what Malamud means by the "Law."

This is also why in *The Fixer* Malamud approaches the universal through the particular better than in any other work. Speaking to the guard, Kogin, of the Law, he recites from the New Testament: "But it is easier for heaven and earth to pass away, than for one dot of the law to become void" (234). In the Judaic context, it was suggested, "Don't look for God in the wrong place, look in the Torah, the law," Shmuel tells Yakov (258). Most of all, Shmuel says, the Law is God, and even if God has been reduced to an idea, in the idea God exists and therefore embraces every facet of existence, whether personal, social, religious, or historical. The point is that *rachmones* (empathy) is necessary, mercy, not signs (257). The true miracle is belief. Without God we can't live. Without the Covenant we would have disappeared from history. As Bok learns from Ostrovsky, freedom exists in the cracks of the state, the law lives in the minds of men. As Bok put it to the Tsar, "what suffering has taught me is the uselessness of suffering" (333). Which means, he knows belatedly, that there is no such thing as an unpolitical man, especially a Jew (335). To paraphrase Spinoza, if the state acts in ways that are abhorrent to human nature it's the lesser evil to destroy it. "Long live revolution. Long live Liberty" (335).

The Natural shines forth when its elements of myth are found in the history of baseball. Roy Hobbs is a hero manqué, in the line of descent from Joseph Wood Krutch's *The Modern Temper*, where our suspicion of heroes is ascribable to the decline of Christianity and the work of Darwin and Freud. Roy is also caught up in our recent recognition that true heroes are hard to find, that we now call mere celebrities heroes, that hero worship or star worship can have catastrophic results.

Our need for heroes persists. But if the essence of a hero is that he must embody convincingly the best ideals of his culture, that he must do it in life, and that some part of the culture must be touched by his act(s), then baseball reflects those characteristics common to epic and tragedy: heroic fierce competition, honesty, and selflessness. But Roy Hobbs only appears to be, or promises to be, a true hero. A fierce competitor, he wants above all to be "the greatest there ever was in the game." That, unfortunately, is really all he wants. The result: a crazy girl shoots him and a "snappy goddess" uses him. Having survived a silver bullet, Roy calls the shooting a bit of bad luck. To survive Memo he succumbs to corruption, then changes his mind too late. In both cases he fails to learn from his experiences, from his suffering. In both cases he fails to act selflessly, to allow love to prevail. In the absence of a reasoned response, in the absence of the force that binds, he does not learn there could be an end to the evil and a beginning of good.

In *The Assistant*, Frank, through Morris, learns and can grow. Morris, one of the "little" men written about by Mendele, Sholom Aleichem, and Peretz, is acquainted at first with the pain that comes with poverty and psychic impotence. In admitting that he felt every *schmerz*, Morris defined the Jew as a suffering man with a good heart, one who reconciled himself to agony—for the sake of the Law, the Hebraic ideal of virtue. But Morris is also a compassionate and understanding man, though close to starvation himself. He gets up at dawn to sell a three-cent roll to a Polish woman. He accepts Frank Alpine and gives him an opportunity to redeem himself.

Frank, who begins by helping rob Morris, proceeds to pilfer from the cash register. He is a wanderer, a thief, an anti-Semite; he is also devoted to St. Francis. The grocery store is his prison, but it is symbolically the locus of his regeneration, his conversion to Morris's ideals and values, his conversion to Judaism, his love for Helen. He somehow realizes that he has to clean his own house first, "for whatever bad happened had happened wrong; to clean it out of his self and bring in a little peace, a little order" is necessary (69, 90).

That Frank is circumcised and converts to Judaism at Passover, and thus Easter, indicates that time is not accidental. Just as spring is the season when nature's renewal of life is most evident so it is the celebration of Jewish freedom and the resurrection of Christ. Frank experiences redemption or resurrection, from a self-centered, spiritually empty life to the promise of a new life. In one sense, as Jonathan Baumbach puts it, Frank's redemption was made possible by his uncompromising love for Helen, he is eager to be circumcised as a sign of "devotion and submission"—to Morris's Law and to Helen. The story of the power emanating from both Morris and Helen, that which leads to redemption, comes from the ability of Malamud's protagonists to give of themselves unselfishly, to love. In spite of a divided, contradictory, complicated, tempted soul, the divine force is still capable of binding the forces together. As Martin Buber has put it, "again and again innate grace arises from out of [the soul's] depths and promises the utterly incredible: you can become whole and one." Love redeems in Malamud's world, or at least love could or should redeem.

So it is also with Yakov Bok in *The Fixer*, whose attempt to find himself involves love and redemption. *The Fixer* is based on the life and trial in September 1913 of Mendel Beiliss in Kiev, Russia. Beiliss, an insignificant person, was tried for a so-called "blood libel," the ritual murder of a Christian boy whose blood was then to be used supposedly for ritual purposes. But Beiliss is a symbol of Russian Jewry which is being tried as a community. Yakov Bok's story becomes universal in its application precisely because the particular leads to the universal. Breaking the law by "passing," Bok lives in a *Judenrein* (forbidden to Jews) district; his attempt to survive leads to his accusations and trial. The extraordinary feat executed by Malamud, however, focuses on the nature of the guilt of Bok's oppressors and his attempts in jail to understand the purpose of God's covenant. He reads that "God talks. He has chosen, he says, the Hebrews to preserve him. He covenants, therefore he is. . . . But Israel accepts the covenant in order to break it. That's the mysterious purpose: they need the experience" (239–240). Indeed, "having betrayed the covenant with God they had to pay: war, destruction, death, exile—and they take what goes with it. Suffering, they say, awakens repentance, at least in those who can repent. And then God forgives them and offers a new covenant. This is his nature, everything must begin again" (240).

Through his trial and suffering Yakov has learned; the experience is his. The question is, what has he learned? Bok's answer starts with a question: "Have I only learned to know what my condition is—that the ocean is salty as you are drowning, and though you knew it you are drowned? Still, he goes on, "it was better than not knowing. A man had to learn, it was his nature" (315–316).

Malamud's myth-haunted novels, particularly *The Natural*, *The Fixer*, and *The Assistant*, deal symbolically with maimed "kings" or heroes whose flaws are self-interest and the inability to give wholly of themselves. Roy's insistence that he will gain fame and wealth by being the best leads his soon-to-be assassin Harriet Bird to ask: "Isn't there something over and above earthly things—some more glorious meaning to one's life and activities?" Frank Alpine's apparent necessity to "live like a prince" by stealing results in a reversal activated by Morris's life and values. Yakov Bok's denial of his Jewishness so that he might "pass" and thus work outside of the ghetto leads ultimately to a broadening of his moral education. In each case the moral and legal code is broken, with self-interest the motivating force. At the end "each eventually wins a moral victory over his old self through his concern for the larger unit of the group. In mythic terms of the regeneration he brings to society, he proves to be a true folk hero." What he has done selflessly has meaning to all.

It is likely that early in his life, as he grew up in Brooklyn, Malamud had an insight that became his governing assumption. His need, Philip Roth writes, was in fact "a need so harsh that it makes one ache even now to consider the sheer size of it. It was the need to consider long and seriously every last demand of an overtaxed, overtaxing conscience torturously exacerbated by the patterns of human need unabated." In Roth's eyes, Malamud was a man of stern morality who could act only as he was. In his most original moments when he renders in his grimly told, impassioned tales his deepest note, he remains true to what seems old and homely, matter-of-factly, touchingly unadorned poetry that makes things sadder than they already are.

Malamud believed that if a writer is lucky "serious things may seem funny," and in his best work, including *The Natural, The Assistant, The Fixer,* and the recent collected stories, "life to him [is] always on the edge of both tragedy and comedy, of reality and fantasy." Some humans are born whole, he knew, but "others must seek this blessed state in a struggle to achieve order." As Saul Bellow has written, perhaps order and love are the same thing. For Malamud, it is those "others" and their "struggle" that is the subject of his work, an epic of ordinary American life that is forever fantastic and extraordinary. In penetrating deeply into the particular, he exposed the universal. The moral obligation to be reborn through suffering, the chimera of love, the need to abjure the self's demands, are what unite Roy Hobbs, Frank Alpine, Morris Bober, and Yakov Bok. Malamud was, as were Shakespeare, Melville, Twain, and all great writers, a regional writer; he was also an American Jewish writer who was "a universal writer," to whom it mattered that his heroes tried, ultimately, to observe and honor their moral obligation. Asked in a 1974 interview to define what makes his characters Jewish, Malamud responded: "their Jewish qualities, the breadth of their vision, their kind of fate, their morality, their life; their awareness, responsibility, intellectuality, and ethically. Their love of people and God" (Leviant, 19). He might have been describing himself.

Works Cited

Aarons, Victoria. *A Measure of Memory in American Jewish Fiction.* Athens: University of Georgia, 1996.

Baumbach, Jonathan. "The Economy of Love: The Novels of Bernard Malamud," *Kenyon Review* 25 (Summer 1963).

Friedberg, Maurice. "History and Imagination: Two Views of the Beiliss Case," *Midstream* 12 (November 1996).

Friedman, Maurice. *Martin Buber: The Life of Dialogue.* Chicago: University of Chicago, 1955.

Hassan, Ihab. "The Qualified Encounter." In *Radical Innocence.* Princeton: Princeton University Press, 1961.

Hays, Peter. "The Complex Pattern of Redemption in *The Assistant,*" *Centennial Review* 13 (Spring 1969).

Krutch, Joseph Wood. *The Modem Temper.* New York: Harcourt, 1929.

Leviant, Curt. "Bernard Malamud: My Characters are God-Haunted," *Hadassah Magazine* 55, 10 (June 1974).

Malamud, Bernard. *The Assistant.* New York: Harcourt Brace, 1957.

————. *The Fixer.* New York: Farrar, Straus, Giroux, 1966.

————. *The Natural.* New York: Avon, 1952.

Roth, Philip. "Pictures of Malamud," *Sunday New York Times Book Review* (April 20, 1986).

Schulz, Max. "Bernard Malamud's Mythic Proletarians." In *Radical Sophistication.* Athens: Ohio University Press.

Walden, Daniel. "Where Have All the Heroes Gone?" *USA Today: The Magazine of the American Scene* 114 (January 1986).

Wasserman, Earl. "*The Natural*: Malamud's World Ceres," *Centennial* 9 (Fall 1965).

Weston, Jessie. *From Ritual to Romance.* Garden City, N.Y.: Doubleday, 1957.

Wetherby, W. J. "Blood Brother," *The Guardian* (20 March 1986).

Chapter 17

A KIND OF VIGILANCE
Tropic Suspension in Bernard Malamud's Fiction

Victoria Aarons

> He could see out but nobody could see in.
>
> —Bernard Malamud, *The Assistant*

At a crucial juncture in the short story "The Letter," the moment of reckoning we await in all of Malamud's fiction, a character stands alone at a crossroads, in this case, at a side entrance of a hospital whose psychiatric ward he inhabits. He stands at the gate, "in loose gray institutional clothes and canvas slippers,"[1] with a letter in his hand, a letter without words, blank, addressed to no one. Yet Teddy, whose fixed bearing calls to mind recurrent characters in Malamud's corpus of fiction, remains as if immobile at this nexus, an unlikely and unwitting locus of expectation and purpose, with the letter clutched in his hand as if it is a lifeline.

With this anticipatory frame, Malamud evokes a timeless moment of immediacy, the duration of which seems simultaneously uninterrupted, perpetual, for Teddy, standing before the gate, with his letter in his hand, "held it as he always held it, as though he had held it always" ("Letter," 156). This figurative gatekeeper stands as if arrested in time, and like the chiastic utterance that defines his hold on the letter, "as he always held it, as though he had held it always," he keeps time if only temporarily in check by maintaining a tightly constructed balance of redoubled association, both attenuated and suspended.

Like a crossroads, chiasmus positions us at a crossing. Derived from the Greek X, or crossover, the chiasmus as a rhetorical figure is essentially a spatial technique, a group of words balanced by their reversed order and arranged spatially around an implied center: "always held it . . . held it always." So the chiasmus is essentially a figure of repetition, since it consists of two phrases or clauses parallel in syntax, but it is also, and in Malamud's fiction much more interestingly, a figure of opposites, antitheses, because of the intrinsic reversal that defines the patterning of those phrases.[2] And it's at the center of the chiasmus, the place at which the implied crossing occurs, that we experience both juncture and disjuncture. For Malamud this spatial moment of tension becomes the ironic proffering of a choice, the action momentarily suspended in the doubling back of conditions, possibilities, revisions to the fate of his unsuspecting characters.

Such an ironic design, though ostensibly just a clever syntactic reversal, becomes, in Malamud's fiction, a medium of the ideological tensions and contradictions that characterize American Jewish fiction and its middle-class cultural milieu during the second half of the twentieth century. For Malamud, the chiasmus is shown to be a figure subtly insistent with ironic self-parody and narrative self-reflexivity characteristic of Jewish literature generally and Malamud's fiction in patterned particularity. In its ironic offering of choice, the chiasmus, distinctively so in Malamud's fiction, is suggestive of the paradoxical position of the American Jew, which might be expressed in the push/pull of the American-Jewish/Jewish-American dichotomy. And for Malamud this tension is central to his conception of the moral conditions of his characters, often displaced "old world" Jews (whether it be Schwartz the wandering Jewbird or Morris Bober the displaced grocer) who challenge traditional moral certainties, all the while clinging to them.

And it's curious that a figure essentially of repetition, suggestive of stasis, of inaction, the impossibility for change, should serve here to control its seeming opposite: the posing of choices, the positioning of alternatives, and through them the promise of change, conditions reversed, second chances. It is, after all, through the chiastic juxtaposition of the impossibly contrived conditions of his existence that Abramowitz, the "Talking Horse," can even begin to imagine another fate: "It's not what I am but what I wish to be. I wish to be what I really am, which is a man."[3] So in its "give and take," the imagined and the real, the chiastic structures would seem to forestall time, a literary "holding of breath," the final instant of suspension before the plunge. The moment of recognition, expressed chiastically, is, for Leo Finkle in "The Magic Barrel," the moment of reckoning, the point at which the future for him rests upon a movement back: "[I]t had come upon him, with shocking force, that apart from his parents, he had never loved anyone. Or perhaps it went the other way, that he did not love God so well as he might, because he had not loved man."[4] We seem to find in the chiastic structures both retreat and advance, where the one part of the chiasmus foils the other. And, in so doing, the one central stabilizing part of the chiastic structure stands alone, inert, stubbornly insistent on its repetitive hold: "I'm a slow learner. . . . I learn slowly."[5]

And so Teddy's relentless hold on the letter, in the story of the same name, would seem to suggest an unwillingness to part with it, a position as fixed and unchanging as that of his imposing vigil at the gate. Yet it's a letter that with some urgency Teddy wants mailed. And so he waits at the gate, both inertly waiting and lying in wait for the weary, duty-bound Newman, whose trips to the psychiatric hospital every Sunday to visit his father provide Teddy with the opportunity to make a seemingly simple request: "What about mailing my letter," becomes the Sunday refrain ("Letter," 156). His letter, however, remains unmailed. It does so because Newman, a character who in typical Malamudian fashion functions as impostor and foil to the imperfect yet uncannily prescient figure of Teddy, and who must pass Teddy's immovable vigilance at the gate, refuses to mail his letter. Despite Teddy's oracular perseverance—"Why don't you mail it? It won't do you any good if you don't" ("Letter," 157)—Newman's resolve not to mail the letter is as steadfast as Teddy's is to have him take it. And thus each man becomes the unwitting chiastic "other" of the one he so incompletely foils.

Newman is unwavering in his refusal to accept the letter, even in the face of the obvious—to take the envelope and inconsequentially put it in the mailbox—because, as he so ineffectually reiterates in a voice of rational authority only waiting to be undercut by Malamud, "There's nothing in it to mail" ("Letter," 157). So Teddy stands before the gate, "the arched iron-barred gate," both admitting and impeding entrance and exit, with his letter in his hand: "He held it as he always held it, as though he had held it always" ("Letter," 156). He stands arrested in time and in literary space, poised, ironically, for inaction, impeded by his delinquent other. Thus, like so many of Malamud's characters, the arresting figure of Teddy is, indeed, the keeper of the gate, whose very presence invites the kind of choice that Malamud's fiction demands of all his characters, a choice of conscience, of compassion, of responsibility to others.

Chiasmus thus creates the ironic ambivalence that governs the contours of character in Malamud's fiction. In, for example, Yakov Bok's disavowal of God, he is chastened by his father-in-law in this way: "Who are you, Yakov, Moses himself? If you don't hear His voice so let Him hear yours."[6] The linking term here is voice, a voice merged in the intimate relationship between human beings and God. Yet, at the same time, the tension emergent through the chiastic coupling reveals Yakov's failure, his presumptuousness in assuming his own importance. And so, while voice seems to yoke the two together, the fixer's importunity and God's mercy, it also, emphatically, separates them: it's God's silence that here emerges most powerfully; the burden of proof, as Yakov is reminded by the sententious closure that brings us out of the chiasmus, is not on God, but on his own compliance with the covenant: "When prayers go up blessings descend" (*Fixer*, 212).

Chiasmus, as Malamud persistently uses it, presents the reader with an ongoing, unfolding activity of perception designed to create particular, subtle effects, complex verbal relationships that expose character and that reveal the ironic, often darkly humorous, even despairing voice that permeates and controls so much of his fiction: "All I know is I've been here for years and still don't understand the nature of my fate; in short if I'm Abramowitz, a horse; or a horse including Abramowitz" ("Talking Horse," 329). The juxtaposition of the two elements of the chiasmus creates an ironic disparity, a tension that either explicitly or implicitly poses at once disunity, caused by the diametric reversal, and cohesion, caused by the conjoined proximity of the two terms or phrases read and understood as one unit. Thus, in its most explicit form, the chiasmus creates an antithesis by the stated inversion of key concepts. The chiasmus, thus, is used primarily as a foil, a figure suggestive, through its implied antithesis, of the synchronicity of the experience defined by the chiastic relations. But the chiasmus also can be more subtly implied in, for instance, the metaphorical juxtapositions made by a writer who turns a concept in on its own attempts at semantic and tonal balance—"The cello Dworkin passionately played played him"[7]—and who shows how one concept is identified with its apparent opposite in the juxtaposition.

Repetitive chiastic utterances reveal Malamud's complex, deeply ironic moral sensibilities, the rhetorical complexities of his moral vision. And, like his complex and varied moral vision, the chiasmus offers, not simple equivalents, but intertwined, reflexive, and often self-contradictory inverse structures, shapes of perception that refractively define both character and action. Thus, the characterization of Lesser in *The Tenants*, as a man who "lives to write, writes to live,"[8] identifies both Lesser's ethos and purpose, inseparable in their mutual design, a single obsession that defines him but that does so only by inviting its own negation.

The chiasmus thus both underscores because of its emphatic repetitive nature, but retracts, takes back in the reversal, since, as Malamud hastens to pronounce, "Lesser writes his book and his book writes Lesser" (*Ten-*

ants, 193). The chiasmus here is at once a validation and at the same time a correction, the "and" becoming an implied "but": "Lesser writes his book *but* his book writes Lesser." So a chiasmus, like a gate, admits but also refracts. And it's at the center of the implied crossing, the juncture at which the two phrases meet and turn, that reveals the weight, the heaviness of the trope itself and, for Malamud, the far more weighty and onerous ironic inseparability for which the chiasmus stands, poised much like the ironic presence, in "The Letter," of Teddy before the gate.

Ultimately, by employing the rhetorical figure of chiasmus, Malamud creates a sense of timelessness within fictions of temporal continuity: Teddy "held [the letter] as he always held it, as though he had held it always"; always holding it suggests an unfolding linear passage of time, but "as though he had held it always" characterizes a condition that pushes us back in time, reverses time's passage, obscures its privileged fictive status. Chiasmus at once arrests the linear unfolding of the narrative and suggests a nonlinear expansion of thematic elements through replay and ironic foreshadowing. Such figures, in effect, stop time, but they also, paradoxically, expand time through the textured repetition of key terms and names. This paradox creates an often-shadowy humorous tension, revealing Malamud's preoccupation with the ethical demands of endurance and forbearance and a timeless vigilance in the midst of faltering hesitation. "If you push time," we are forewarned in the short story "An Exorcism," "time pushes you."[9]

In fact, Malamud's works show a consistent preoccupation with the conditions of time, from the opening scene in *The Natural*, the train "that never stopped," propelling Roy through the "thundering" long tunnel, moving through time, yet "having no timepiece he appraised the night and decided it was moving toward dawn."[10] Time's movement here is undercut by Roy's unconsciousness of time, creating the narrative's dreamlike quality, in which time is always suspended, events repeated in fantastical and foreboding shapes. *The Natural* itself hovers between a mythic time of the heroic quest and a linear time of the baseball game, structured by the intrinsic thematics of its subject. Roy, brought up short in large part by the repetitive cycles of time, "through the nausea . . . remembered an old saying. He quoted, 'Woe unto him who calls evil good and good evil'" (*Natural*, 191). The very proximity of the two antithetical words, close in time and in space, suggests their uneasy alliance. The chiasmus here creates a kind of balancing act, in which each half of the chiasmus holds the other in check, removing us from the deceit of mythic time since it reminds us of the very real exigencies of time and circumstance. "In my dreams I ate, and I ate my dreams," the fixer sardonically contends (*Fixer*, 5). The eating in his dreams gives a false nourishment to the very real poverty expressed in the second half of the chiasmus: "I ate my dreams," food no more than the stuff of dreams, wished for, illusory, created out of sequence, out of time.

Arguably Malamud's most well-known chiasmus, one, I would add, that speaks to the heart of his fiction, comes from his paradigmatic Jewish character, Morris Bober, who is no less than the moral center of *The Assistant* and serves finally as the prototype for other Malamud heroes. When asked by Frank Alpine, a small-time hood, a lapsed Italian Catholic who futilely aspires to the goodness of Saint Frances, why the Jews suffer "so damn much," Morris Bober retorts: "I suffer for you. . . . I mean, you suffer for me."[11] Morris Bober's correction ("I mean") is rendered chiastically because it suggests the often unwitting but no less punctuated inseparability—by compulsion and choice—of Malamud's characters, and, in doing so, emphatically underscores what for Malamud is the inexorable connection between suffering and self-consciousness.

The suffering of these characters becomes interchangeable, because their lives are first circumstantially and then purposefully linked. The doubling implied structurally by the chiasmus anticipates the doubling of characters, frequent pairings in Malamud's fiction. The chiasmus here characteristically foreshadows the novel's ironic closure, where the one man will replace the other, where the "assistant" will emerge literally as the "grocer," "the one who had danced on the grocer's coffin" (*Assistant*, 280), but metaphorically as well, in a paradoxically redemptive act, inaugurated by "a pain that enraged and inspired him. After Passover he became a Jew" (*Assistant*, 297), a choice that defines his sense of a moral universe, a choice symbolic, here and elsewhere, of suffering and compassion. The chiastic utterance and structural reversal of the two men serve as the interpretive focus of the novel's universalizing the importance of suffering in the formation of moral consciousness, since Morris and Frank, in effect, suspend time by "writing each other twice," by negotiating their differences into their inevitably shared moral fate, their shared desire for redemption through suffering.

At the center of all Malamud's chiastic utterances is the necessity of moral choice, as accented by the syntactic structure of the chiasmus itself. Morris Bober's conviction that "I suffer for you . . . you suffer for me," reveals his empathetic pact with Frank Alpine, a choice taken up by the other man, since Frank essentially chooses to become Morris in a self-imposed and unrelenting covenant. The chiastic alteration of the key words offers an inherent choice, a choice implied in the structural antithesis that defines the sentence or paragraph, but—and here's the strength and core of the chiasmus—it's a choice that for Malamud is really not a choice, but rather an imperative, again emphasized by the carefully balanced structure of the chiasmus, contained in itself, closed on either end. The choice is more a charge, not unlike the first covenant an opportunity proffered to his characters to acknowledge the weight of their own moral destines.

"We doubt God and God doubts us," the Rabbi Lifschitz enigmatically reveals to the suspicious and stunned Albert Gans, who comes to the rabbi on a self-imposed but improbable mission to save his dying father.[12] In confirming the mutuality of doubt, the rabbi, of course, offers his reluctant disciple an "out" of sorts: "Of this kind doubts I am not afraid so long as you love your father" ("Crown," 313). The choice to affirm his love for his father, however, and thus, ironically, to compensate for God's doubts as well as our own, is too much for Albert, because, as we've suspected throughout the story, there is no love between father and son, the father's dying more a burden on Albert than it is a sorrow.

Like the much-beleaguered Newman in "The Letter," whose Sunday visits to his father in the psychiatric hospital are nothing more than a grotesque parody of the kind of connectedness and acknowledged consanguinity that Malamud insists his characters recognize, Albert's impenetrable avoidance of love suggests that the consequences of admitting familial connection are potentially too great. For such avoidance exposes the limitations drawn by its false sense of self-sufficiency, its own self-containment. At the conclusion of "The Letter," Newman is finally forced to disavow his father, as Albert Gans does at the conclusion of "The Silver Crown," when he disgorges his dutiful deceit and thus indicts himself: "He hates me, the son of a bitch, I hope he croaks" ("Crown," 328). Newman, similarly, denying his connection and thus his responsibility to his father, literally "walking away" at the end of the story, is summoned not by Teddy, this time, but by Ralph, Teddy's father: "Why don't you come back here and hang around with the rest of us," he asks, an invitation to recognize his own self-circumscribed failure ("Letter," 161). Ralph, at the story's close, replaces Teddy as the guardian of the gate, a comedic beacon, an immovable figure, whose presence both stands at and stands for a crossroads, a juncture that delimits choice, time, and reckoning. For the moment of choice is immediate and urgent for Malamud, a self-defining, time-expanding moment of human reckoning, but it is also the moment of recognizing that choice is thrust upon the "autonomous" moral agent, that "choice" marks the place where what's already past and irrevocable is revealed.

The immediacy and anticipatory nature of the figure chiasmus is suggestive and evocative of the oral intonations envisioned by the recurring subtleties of the trope. The patterned use of the chiasmus creates a distinctively oral quality in Malamud's fiction, which, in part, comes from the repetition of sound constitutive of the figure, but also is derived from the anticipatory nature and sense of urgency in the configuration of the trope. The chiasmus, perhaps much like any figure of repetition, creates a kind of "overhead" narrative. And, in this regard, the quiet immediacy of the chiasmus is shadowed by another rhetorical trope that patterns the structural design of Malamud's fiction: the figure polyptoton.[13] And while it is perhaps less arresting, less artful a figure, it is no less cunningly consistent with Malamud's voice and rhetorical design. In some ways, the polyptoton might be seen as a subset of the chiasmus, yet another figure of "addition," whose function is to emphasize through repetition.

Surely, Malamud characteristically employs simple figures of repetition: "the grocer . . . danced on the grocer's coffin," at the close of *The Assistant* (280). The unaltered and reiterated word here underscores the interchangeable relationship between the two men. But the deceptively simple repetition of a term, for Malamud, can also become the point at which the literal becomes metaphorical, becomes three-dimensional, as in Lesser's obsessive watchfulness in *The Tenants*: "Who could see a Black in all this black?" (*Tenants*, 58). The repetition of the linking term here, the word that speaks for the source of the heightened tension in the novel, creates a hypnotic, almost claustrophobic, effect, so much so that we are trapped inside Lesser's obsessions; there is, indeed, no way out because the enclosure of the language prevents passage. "I am not my brother's brother," Lesser feigns, but the enclosure of the repeated word circles back on itself and thus impedes the "out" that Lesser so desires.

But the characteristic use of the figure polyptoton, more than "saying the same thing twice," instead "rewrites" itself. The polyptoton, a repetitive figure at the word level, calls attention to itself by subtly altering its forms. In this line from *The Tenants*, in fact, the one word gives way to the other; what might in a different context be seen as simple repetition opens itself up to a more complex metaphorical reading, suggested by the trope: "Straining, he listened, and though he listened not to hear, heard the dulled clack of surely a typewriter" (*Tenants*, 26). Expositionally the polyptoton is a repetition of the same word or root of the word with different grammatical functions or forms, as we find in Malamud's understated description of the death of the pitcher in *The Natural*: "[T]he wall continued to advance, and though the redheaded lady of his choice was on her feet shrieking, Bump bumped it with a skull-braking band, and the wall embraced his broken body" (*Natural*, 65). We find these slight alterations in word forms—"Bump bumped"—throughout Malamud's fiction, which produce an almost lyrical rhythm to the prose, imperious as in "to mock the mocker"[14] ("Talking Horse," 346), hauntingly so as in this line from *The Natural*: "[S]he now mourned someone who even before his death had made her a mourner" (*Natural*, 69). These slight linguistic shifts, or twists—"mock," "mocker"; "mourned," "mourner"—become not unwelcome intrusions in Malamud's fiction, an unraveling of assurances given, claims made in haste, or unyielding utterance. The "turning of language" here, to borrow a phrase from Arthur Quinn (*Figures of Speech,* 98), seems to both arrest time and, ironically, create a sense of time unraveling: "Lesser knew the doorbell was ringing and went on writing. It rang insistently. It rings forever" (*Tenants,* 16)— "ringing," "rang," "rings."

At its most obvious, the polyptoton is a figure of emphasis and thus one of excess: "[O]ne [picture] was of Daddy grinning, who with a grin had (forever) exited dancing with his dancing partner" (*Natural,* 68–69); "At first he waited patiently. . . . He had waited and was still waiting. He had been born waiting" (*Assistant,* 162). But the real force of the figure is in its terse ellipses, in its minimalist constructions, paradoxically despite its repetitive function: "I'm frightened of the world. . . . It fills me with fright."[15] In its most subtle guise, the polyptoton ironically extends the meaning of the troped word through a repetition of sound or combinations of sounds: "not true although truth."[16] The altered yet repetitive word demands that we reassess its meaning, or that we acknowledge the possibilities for alternative meanings—"beyond belief believed"[17]—a linguistic bartering, an exchange or choice that is so characteristic of Malamud's form and thematic preoccupation.

The polyptoton, for Malamud, thus creates striking images, making fragments of the narrative stand apart from their surroundings; it calls attention to itself by its difference and thus extends its meaning in less obvious and certainly subtler ways. The variations of terms, in fact, redefine them: "Yet better look for something than just have it. The looking is the having" (*Tenants,* 226). And so, through the reconfiguring of the term, the word that becomes for Malamud the central defining feature of the passage, we are brought inside the impulses and obsessions, the motivations and yearnings of Malamud's characters: "Now that the imagination is imagining Lesser imagines it done" (*Tenants,* 4). But what is given, typically with Malamud, is taken back, as the polyptoton, like the chiasmus, shows us what Malamud's fictive world always does: that the apparently limitless plasticity or elasticity of language itself is often a seductive but incomplete buttress for the moments of uncertainty and the consequences of inaction that are constantly countered by the urgent and immediate placement of the rhetorical figures that fashion them.

In this way, those characters in Malamud's fiction, whose perspectives define the central ethical space within which all his characters must act, remain ever watchful. All are gatekeepers, literal or figurative, watching and catalyzing moments of moral reckoning, whether it's Teddy replaced by Ralph at the gates of the hospital in "The Letter," or Mendel who confronts the anthropomorphized figure of death waiting at the gate to the platform of the train station ("Idiots First"), or Leo, waiting in the hall, listening for some word from his son in "My Son the Murderer," or Morris

Lieberman who remains vigilant, riveted to the reports of the war on the radio in "Armistice."

Often such characters find themselves at a precipice, a point at which they must make such a choice, a choice whose chiastic tension reveals its exigency but also its impossibility. In the short story "Angel Levine," Manishevitz, besieged by pain and woe, his own and that of those he loves, in the face of the most peculiar black Jewish angel, is forced to make a choice, a choice from which there is no going back, an indelible commitment: "'I think you are an angel from God.' He said it in a broken voice, thinking, If you said it it was said. If you believed it you must say it. If you believed, you believed" ("Angel," 289). This passage moves performatively around its chiastic center: "If you said it it was said," a reversal that closes in on itself, that prevents outlet, that encircles the simple language of recognition and commits the speaker to its own circular logic. It's a linguistic move from the inside out, from hesitation ("in a broken voice, thinking"), to articulation ("he said it"), indecision to avowal, an affirmation that shelters belief, since the chiasmus "If you said it it was said" is ultimately replaced with "If you believed, you believed," simple repetition, no inversion. The matter of choice, of active and conscious choosing among juxtaposed elements—to believe or not to believe, to act or not to act—is fundamental to Malamud's vision of the human moral project. But it is framed, too, by the sense of the inevitability of its own reversal, of an almost naturalized sense of ethical disposition.

The chiastic structures in Malamud's fiction, then, invite, even in their implied antitheses, the recognition of a shared humanity, an envisioning of oneself in and through the other. A chiasmus can be both figure and trope. That is, it can manifest itself in both metonymic and metaphoric configurations. Arkin, in the short story "Rembrandt's Hat," in an attempt to come to terms with his unintentional slight of the sculptor Rubin, tries to imagine himself and the other man reversed, transformed so that the one man becomes the other: "Therefore, suppose Rubin was Arkin and Arkin Rubin."[18] The very structure of the sentence brings the two men together, literally and well as metaphorically, the two names, "Arkin Rubin," unmediated by intervening word or punctuation, the two men brought together for a provisional, arbitrary spatial moment in the course of a story whose actual linear unfolding ends much more ambiguously. Arkin's attempts to envision himself as his antagonist are ironically undercut by Malamud, since at the story's close, although the two men "stopped avoiding each other and spoke pleasantly when they met, which wasn't often," Arkin discovers Rubin, "regarding himself in the mirror in his white cap," the cap that was the ostensible source of so much trouble, worn "like a crown of failure and hope" ("Hat," 276). So, typically, we're not let off so easily. The chiasmus suspends time to allow possibilities for compassion and redemption, which are not bound by time and so are at best momentary and incomplete. And while the chiasmus presumes a dynamic relation among concepts, it is, after all, an unfolding and reiterative process of coming to terms with all-too-human contingencies. Related rhythmically as much as semantically to a chasm, then, the chiasmus represents, for Malamud, necessary leaps of faith, openings from whose depths one may find possibilities for an at least temporary redemption.

Or they may not. Kessler, in the short story aptly titled "The Mourners," bereft of his family, "never saw them . . . because he never sought them, and they did not seek him."[19] For Malamud, of course, this disavowal is the ultimate failure of the human moral conscience, made all the more real in the failure of the chiasmus itself, since Kessler, in sleet-driven isolation, bereft now not only of family but of shelter, sits alone on the side of the street where "people passing by skirted the pile of his belongings. They stared at Kessler and he stared at nothing" ("Mourners," 30). Here there is no reciprocity, the one half of the implied chiasmus standing alone, separated from its balancing other. And, in the world of Malamud's fiction, where there is no felt connection, its necessity is recognized in its motivating absence, as in this passage from *The Tenants*: "He felt, when he thought of it, a fear of the booming emptiness of the building where whole families had lived and vanished, and strangers came not to stay, but to not stay, a sad fate for an old house" (*Tenants*, 12). It is a fate "unfigured," undeterred.

Notes

1. Bernard Malamud, "The Letter," in *The Stories of Bernard Malamud* (New York: Plume, 1983), 156. Subsequent references are from this edition, identified as "Letter" in the text.

2. There are two books that I have found especially useful in identifying the complexities and diverse possibilities of the chiasmus: William J. Brandt's unfortunately out-of-print *The Rhetoric of Argumentation* (Indianapolis: Bobbs-Merrill, 1970), especially 160–163, and Arthur Quinn's delightful *Figures of Speech: 60 Ways to Turn a Phrase* (Salt Lake City: Peregrine Smith Bks., 1982), especially 93–95.

3. Bernard Malamud, "Talking Horse," in *The Stories of Bernard Malamud*, 348.

4. Bernard Malamud, "The Magic Barrel," in *The Stories of Bernard Malamud*, 135.

5. Bernard Malamud, "The Wig," in *Bernard Malamud: The Complete Stories*, ed. Robert Giroux (New York: Farrar, Straus and Giroux, 1997), 582.

6. Bernard Malamud, *The Fixer* (New York: MJF Books, 1992), 212. Subsequent references are from this edition, identified as *Fixer* in the text.

7. Bernard Malamud, "Zora's Noise," in *The People and Uncollected Stories* (New York: Farrar, Straus, Giroux, 1989), 244.

8. Bernard Malamud, *The Tenants* (New York: Farrar, Straus and Giroux, 1988), 23. Subsequent references are from this edition, identified as *Tenants* in the text.

9. Bernard Malamud, "An Exorcism," in *The People*, 211.

10. Bernard Malamud, *The Natural* (New York: Avon, 1952), 3. Subsequent references are from this edition, identified as *Natural* in the text.

11. Bernard Malamud, *The Assistant* (New York: Dell, 1974), 150. Subsequent references are from this edition, identified as *Assistant* in the text.

12. Bernard Malamud, "The Silver Crown," in *The Stories of Bernard Malamud*, 313. Subsequent references are from this edition, identified as SC in the text.

13. Once again, I have found the most clearly and expansively articulated definitions of this particular rhetorical figure and of the general function of repetition in William J. Brandt's *The Rhetoric of Argumentation*, especially 176, and Arthur Quinn's *Figures of Speech: 60 Ways to Turn a Phrase*, especially 73–77.

14. This trope, "to mock the mocker," is undoubtedly a pun, a play on the Yiddish "macher," the "doer" outdone. As Arthur Quinn points out, in *Figures of Speech*, the polyptoton often functions as a witticism or pun (see especially 77).

15. Bernard Malamud, "My Son the Murderer," in *The Stories of Bernard Malamud*, 91.

16. Bernard Malamud, "Man in the Drawer," in *The Stories of Bernard Malamud*, 212.

17. Bernard Malamud, "Angel Levine," in *The Stories of Bernard Malamud*, 285. Subsequent references are from this edition, identified as "Angel" in the text.

18. Bernard Malamud, "Rembrandt's Hat," in *The Stories of Bernard Malamud*, 275. Subsequent references are from this edition, identified as "Hat" in the text.

19. Bernard Malamud, "The Mourners," in *The Stories of Bernard Malamud*, 26. Subsequent references are from this edition, identified as "Mourners" in the text.

Works Cited

Brandt, William J. *The Rhetoric of Argumentation*. Indianapolis: Bobbs-Merrill, 1970.

Malamud, Bernard. *The Assistant*. 1957. Reprint, New York: Dell, 1974.

———. *Bernard Malamud: The Complete Stories*. Ed. Robert Giroux. New York: Farrar, Straus and Giroux, 1997.

———. *The Fixer*. 1966. Reprint, New York: MJF Books, 1992.

———. *The Natural*. New York: Harcourt, Brace, 1952.

———. *The People and Uncollected Stories*. New York: Farrar, Straus and Giroux, 1989.

———. *The Stories of Bernard Malamud*. New York: Plume, 1983.

———. *The Tenants*. 1971. Reprint, New York: Farrar, Straus and Giroux, 1988.

Quinn, Arthur. *Figures of Speech: 60 Ways to Turn a Phrase*. Salt Lake City: Peregrine Smith Books, 1982.

Part Four

ANNOTATED SELECT BIBLIOGRAPHY

ANNOTATED SELECT BIBLIOGRAPHY

Eileen H. Watts

Full-Length Studies

Abramson, Edward A. *Bernard Malamud Revisited*. New York: Twayne, 1993. Part of Twayne's "Revisited " series. Studies Malamud's novels in chronological order and his short stories in an attempt to examine the complete Malamud canon. Relies heavily on existing scholarship and for that reason is a useful resource.

Avery, Evelyn. *Rebels and Victims: The Fiction of Richard Wright and Bernard Malamud*. Port Washington, N.Y.: Kennikat Press, 1979. 116 pages. Examines depiction of blacks and Jews and their interaction in authors' seminal works.

Cheuse, Alan, and Nicholas Delbanco. *Talking Horse*. New York: Columbia University Press, 1996. 220 pages. Collection of Malamud's speeches, prefaces, interviews, journal notes, essays, and letters (most published for the first time) on the author's approaches to and development of his life and craft. The book is divided into four parts: "The Man and His Work," "The Man on His Work," "The Writer and His Craft," and "The Writer in the Modern World." Indispensable to anyone interested in how Malamud's intellect and imagination informed and created his fiction. His views on everything from the brevity of life to the state of the novel are invaluable to Malamud scholars and students. Chapters include "The Writer at Work," "Long Work, Short Life," "*The Natural:* Raison D'Etre and Meaning," "Why Fantasy?," "Source of *The Fixer*," "Beginning the Novel," "Psychoanalysis in American Fiction," "Jewishness in American Fiction," "Bennington Writing Workshops," and "The Writer in the Modern World," among numerous others.

Lasher, Lawrence, ed. *Conversations with Bernard Malamud*. Jackson: University Press of Mississippi, 1991. Collection of twenty-seven interviews (newspaper,

magazine, etc.) from 1958 to 1986 arranged chronologically. Framed by
Lasher's introduction and a concluding essay by Evelyn Avery. Includes
chronology of Malamud's life.

Sio-Castiñeira, Begoña. *The Short Stories of Bernard Malamud; In Search of Jewish Post-
Immigrant Identity.* New York: Peter Lang 1998. Extensive treatment of ten of
Malamud's hand-picked stories for Selected Stories anthology, organized
structurally by decade and collection (the 50's, *The Magic Barrel;* the 60's, *Idiots
First;* the 70's, *Rembrandt's Hat*). Approached thematically in terms of author's
premise that Malamud's Jews are each searching for his or her own necessar-
ily-lost Jewish identity, given the pressures of assimilation, the loss of Yiddish,
and the onslaught of American culture. Considers Malamud's purpose as
"show[ing] how American Jews make attempts to reconstruct their lost identities, either by avoiding both options of tradition and secularity, or by clinging to one of these options" (xiii). Sees Malamud's "personal anthology" as
answering the question of how Jews reinvent what being Jewish is in twentieth century America. Chapter 1 (*Magic Barrel* stories) deals with "characters
trying to find fulfillment in the context of family life" (9). Includes extensive
treatment of "The First Seven Years," "The Loan" and "Angel Levine." Chapter 2 (*Idiot's First* stories) discusses characters searching for "fulfillment in the
event of partnership (51). Groups stories according to those concerning race,
"Black Is My Favorite Color," "The Death of Me," "The Maid's Shoes;" "partnership outside the American context" (70), "Life Is Better Than Death;" and
partnership among people within the Jewish community, especially "The Jewbird." Chapter 3 (*Rembrandt's Hat* stories) explores their common theme as "a
mourning cry about human loneliness and alienation from the world" and
Malamud's implied "pessimism as to the possibility of communication among
human beings" (91). Notes that Malamud included seven of the eight stories
in *Rembrandt's Hat* for his anthology. Groups stories according to those involving loneliness in and alienation from family life ("My Son the Murderer,"
"The Letter," "A Silver Crown"); those struggling with "the existential vacuum" consequent to this alienation, isolation and failure to communicate, especially by the unmarried ("Man in the Drawer," "In Retirement," "The
Model," "Rembrandt's Hat"). Considers "Talking Horse," which concludes
Selected Stories, as marking the end of the anthology-as-journey toward identity. Analyzed in Freudian terms of id, ego and super ego. The "Conclusion"
deduces that the volume's twenty-five stories establish "the necessity for tran-
scendence and denouncing the sterility of a false 'freedom' that American
Jews have the illusion of enjoying, now that anti-Semitism is no longer an
enemy to fight" (137).

Articles/Chapters/Essays

Aarons, Victoria. "Malamud's Gatekeepers" The 'Law' and Moral Reckoning."
Studies in American Jewish Literature 18 (1999): 31–34. Argues that the following
characters are gatekeepers, positioned on metaphorical and literal thresholds
of variations of Kafka's "Law:" Teddy in "The Letter," standing at the hospital

gate; Mendel in "Idiots First," confronting Ginsberg at the train; Leo in "My Son the Murderer," watching and listening in the hall; Morris Lieberman in "Armistice" on guard for radio reports of the war; Salzman in "The Magic Barrel," chanting Kaddish while leaning against a wall; and Schwartz in "The Jewbird" perched at Cohen's kitchen window. Notes that in each story the main character is paired with another, through whose acknowledged suffering the former learns to recognize his own suffering. For example, Harvitz and Levitansky of "The Man in the Drawer" and Martin Goldberg and Oskar Gassner in "The German Refugee." Discusses the ways in which these character pairs dramatize the ambiguity and pliability of Malamud's reading of Kafka's immutable Mosaic Law. Suggests that Teddy's letter is "the letter of the law, the law reinterpreted and reinvented" (6), which is also characteristic of Mendel's law, "What it means human" ("Idiots First" 44), and that Ralph, Newman's father, replaces Teddy at the story's end, as gatekeeper. Sees structural reversal of character pairs (chiasmus) as Malamud's "master trope . . . the representative moment at which a choice must be made, but cannot really be made, a simultaneous opening and closing of the gate" (7). For example, Morris Bober's belief that "I suffer for you . . .you suffer for me" resonates with Frank Alpine's conversion to Judaism and physical substitution for Bober behind the grocer's counter. Argues that chiasmus in Malamud's work generates a verbal matrix that points the reader in the right interpretive direction. In "Rembrandt's Hat" for instance, "Therefore, suppose Rubin was Arkin and Arkin Rubin;" in "Talking Horse, Abramowitz does not know "in short if I'm Abramowitz a horse; or a horse including Abramowitz;" in "The Mourners," Kessler has lost his family, "never saw them . . . because he never sought them, and they did not seek him; and finally, when Kessler is out on the sidewalk, having been evicted, "[people] stared at Kessler and he stared at nothing." Along with characters as gatekeepers, these instances of verbal chiasmus, or its failure (Kessler stared at nothing), indicate the extent to which Malamud's law and so the measure of man's moral reckoning, hinges on humanity.

Abramson, Edward A. "Bernard Malamud and the Jews: An Ambiguous Relationship," *The Yearbook of English Studies* 24 (1994): 146–156. Discusses Malamud's Jews as metaphoric and largely emblematic of humanity. Examines the Jewishness of characters in *The Tenants*, *The Assistant*, *The Fixer*, and to lesser degrees several short stories. Concludes that Malamud's greatness is in his attention to the "human and humane," not in his attention to Jews or Jewishness.

———. "Experiments in Theme and Form: Five Malamud Apprenticeship Stories," *Studies in American Jewish Literature* 15 (1996): 49–60. Examines five stories collected in *The People and Uncollected Stories*: "Armistice," "The Grocery Store," "The Literary Life of Laban Goldman," "Benefit Performance," and "An Apology" in terms of their containing seeds that will find fruition in *The Assistant* and in *The Magic Barrel* stories. Some of these incipient themes include using stores as prison settings, and pairs of characters, one of whom tests the other in terms of morality and selflessness. in "Armistice (1940) Abramson finds numerous similarities to *The Assistant*, such as those between Morris Lieberman and Morris Bober, their sons, Ephraim (Bober's Ephraim is dead),

Leonard and Frank Alpine, and Gus Wagner and Ward Minogue, the last pair being the prototype of two characters whose relationship represents two sides of a moral issue. In "The Grocery Store" (1943) Abramson sees Sam Kaplan as Morris Bober's predecessor "in terms of his situation but not in terms of morality" (51). Sam's wife, Ida, also parallels Ida Bober (and Bessie Lieb in "The Loan"). In "The Literary Life of Laban Goldman" (1943) Abramson sees Laban as a precursor to Helen Bober and Frank Alpine; all three characters want American success and education. This story is seen as a description of "The tragedy of the pressures America imposes upon those who would suc- ceed" (53). "Benefit Performance" (1943), Abramson claims, is the earliest story to include Malamud's bittersweet humor. Maurice Rosenfeld (an unem- ployed actor in the largely defunct Yiddish theater) is disappointed in much the same way the Morris Bober is. "Both characters feel that values which they hold dear are not respected" (54). Another Ephraim (a plumber) appears in this story. Abramson links the theme of self-centeredness here to "The First Seven Years," "Angel Levine," and "The Last Mohican," particularly in terms of characters' being required to have "faith in an unlikely character" (56). In "The Apology" (1951) Abramson suggests that Bloostein is an earlier version of *The Assistant's* Breitbart, and sees Bloostein as "the model for later antago- nists" who are part of pairs of characters in which one must force the other to embrace ethical and humane values. Such pairings occur in "The First Seven Years," "The Mourners," "Angel Levine," "The Bill," "The Last Mohican," and finally proves unsuccessful in *The Tenants*. Abramson sees these early pairings as experiments in what would become one of Malamud's major patterns for the facilitation of moral growth.

Adler, Brian. "*Akedah* and Community in 'The Magic Barrel,' " *Studies in American Jewish Literature* 10,2 (Fall 1991): 188–196. Casts Salzman and Rabbi Finkle in the roles of Abraham and Isaac. Examines how the binding of Isaac (*Akedah*) informs the problematic binding of Finkle into the Jewish community.

Ashmead, John. "Bernard Malamud." In *American Writing Today*, ed. Richard Kostelanetz. Troy, N.Y.: Whitston, 1991, 155–165. Discusses three worlds in Malamud's work: Western humanism and its mythology, Jewish American and Yiddish culture, and nineteenth century American Romanticism. Intro- duces parallels between Malamud and Hawthorne, Cooper, Melville, James, Poe, and others.

Avery, Evelyn. "Remembrances of Malamud: 1972–1986." In *Conversations with Bernard Malamud*, ed. Lawrence Lasher. Jackson: University Press of Missis- sippi, 1991, 145–151. Narrative of some of Avery's conversations and corre- spondences with Malamud.

———. "Malamud and Ozick; 'Kindred Neshamas.' " *Studies in American Jewish Literature* 18 (1999): 31–34. Asserts that despite obvious personal differences (gender, religious practice, lifestyle, how each defines him-herself relative to being a writer and being Jewish) Malamud's and Ozick's fiction confirm their writers' kindred spirits. Sees Yiddishkeit, compassion for the underdog, out- rage against injustice, and commitment to truth" as issues common to Mala- mud's "The Silver Crown," *The Tenants*, and *The Fixer*, and Ozick's "The Pagan

Rabbi" and "Usurpation," "A Mercenary" and "The Shawl," respectively. Whereas "Usurpation" is the reverse of "The Silver Crown," "The Pagan Rabbi" includes the former story's main elements: "obsessive emotion, absence of love, rejection of God's law and dire consequences" (32). Focuses on *The Tenants* and "A Mercenary" as treatments of selfishness in the arena of Black-Jewish relations, noting that in both works "the Jew dominates intellectually and culturally, threatening the black ego, until deposed by black rage" (32). In both novel and story, Black and Jew expose one another's real identity. Explores the issues of identity, especially the "Jew in flight" in *The Fixer* and "The Shawl," as both are "Holocaust nightmares. Yakov must finally become a Jew through his suffering, and Rosa must give up her blanket that substitutes for the dead Magda, to "gratefully accept the overtures of other human beings who may come from 'inferior backgrounds,' but who are 'menchen' " (34). Sees in all of these works confirmation that "Malamud and Ozick share the same values and speak the same language," as all of their heroes grapple nobly to overcome their "basest instincts," and to achieve freedom. Concludes by reporting that at Malamud's funeral, Ozick stood and recited the "Shéma," reminding the mourners that the soul ("neshama") of the non-observant Malamud was indeed Jewish, and thereby connected to all Jews.

Baris, Sharon Deykin. "Intertextuality and Reader Responsibility: Living On in Malamud's 'The Mourners.' " *Studies in American Jewish Literature* 11, 1 (Spring 1992): 45–61. Applies reader-response approaches to suggest that the story challenges its readers to become responsible humane mourners. Places story in line with Melville's "Bartleby, the Scrivener" and Crane's "The Blue Hotel," and presents connections between language, action, and responsibility.

Beck, Rosemarie. Letters to Bernard Malamud. Berg Collection, New York Public Library.

———. "In My Studio." *Arts Annual* (1961), 61–64.

Bryant, Earle V. "Malamud's 'Idiots First,' " *The Explicator* 55, 1 (Fall 1996): 43–45. Suggests that Ginsburg's perplexing *Gut Yuntif* (Happy Holiday) greeting to Mendel refers to Mendel's impending death, as death is a type of holy day. Argues that this reading confirms Ginsburg's identity as The Angel of Death.

Buchen, Irving H. "Malamud's *God's Grace*: Divine Genesis, Mortal Terminus," *Studies in American Jewish Literature* 10, 1 (Spring 1991): 24–34. Philosophizes on Malamud's treatment of man and God as imperfect artists, and on the novel's problematic and disturbing conclusions.

Chard-Hutchinson, Martine. " 'A Lost Grave' by Bernard Malamud: Ambiguity as Topos." *Studies in American Jewish Literature* 17 (1998): 103–108. Posits ambiguity as the dominant mode for narrator and main characters Hecht and Goodman, and as a governing pattern in "A Lost Grave" (in Malamud's posthumous collection *The People and Uncollected Stories*). Distinguishes two types of narrative ambiguity, one obvious, the other, subtle, consisting of "repetitive patterns, stylistic shifts, especially those involving symbols and puns" (104). Suggests that "this is where meaning has to be recaptured" (104). Objective reality and subjective fantasy in the story are analyzed in terms of further constituting or complicating ambiguity. Finds repeated words and puns to be "distorted echoe[s] which reveal the ambiguous relationship between physical and sentimental space as well as the permanent shift from objectivity to subjectivity" (1050. Points out secondarily, Freudian concepts of "The repression of ungratifying conjugality . . . [and] the subsequent transfer on to the image of a virtual couple, that of Goodman and his secretary" (105). Notes the story's motif of dampness and rain to include Hecht's "wet spot on his pillow" upon waking from a dream in which he had searched in vain for his late-wife's grave. Interprets this ambiguity between sleep and waking, dream and reality as Malamud's desire to explore the unconscious. Suggests that the second half of the story is "spiritually-oriented" consequent to Goodman's reversal from mysterious caretaker to detective who "guides Hecht toward spirituality" (106). Moreover, Hecht and Goodman reverse roles; Goodman now speaks and Hecht listens. Ambiguity, however, enters the story here when narrative and character voices dissolve into each other, and it is difficult to tell who is speaking. Concludes that the paradoxes of dream as "reality's best friend" and the cemetery as the place of insight are Malamud's paths to truth. On Rosh Hashanah Goodman reveals to Hecht that his late-wife's grave has been found, suggesting that the new year's symbol of renewal is coterminous with Hecht's finding "his true self" (107). Sensitively sees in this story, written barely one year before the ailing Malamud died, the author's attempt "to grant himself" a "fairly ambivalent respite," as "only ambiguity could enable him to face death and to mock her at the same time" (107).

Dessner, Lawrence Jay. "Malamud's Echoes of Hawthorne's 'Young Goodman Brown.' " *Notes on Contemporary Literature* 29: 2 (March 1999): 6–8. Discusses ways in which the objective and the imaginary in "The Magic Barrel," "The Silver Crown" and "Angel Levine" are similar to their treatment in "Young Goodman Brown." Draws parallels between Malamud's ambiguity as to Salzman's "powers," Rabbi Lifschitz's "magical powers," and Levine's angel-status, and Hawthorne's Brown. For example, Leo sees loaves of bread in the sky, Manischevitz sees a black feather fall and turn to snow, and Brown sees a pink ribbon fall from the sky, grasps it, and knows it is the same one his wife had worn that evening. Concludes by noting that Malamud's stories end happily; Hawthorne's unhappily.

Freese, Peter. "Surviving the End: Apocalypse, Evolution, and Entropy in Bernard Malamud, Kurt Vonnegut, and Thomas Pynchon," *Critique* 36, 3 (Spring 1995):163–176. Presents and compares three "end of the world" narratives: Malamud's *God's Grace*, Vonnegut's *Galapagos*, and Pynchon's *The Crying of Lot 49*. Suggests that all three novels "treat death in order to explore the possibilities of rebirth and envision destruction only to discover the means of renewal." Argues that *God's Grace* is "an ironically inverted retelling" of Noah, and versions of Adam sans Eve and a frustrated Moses trying to civilize his people. But most significant, Cohn is Abraham to Buzz's Isaac. Here, however, the son sacrifices the father to complete the self-destructive cycle of man to make "room for a new cycle of evolution." George-the-gorilla's "long kaddish" at the novel's end signals that the father's sacrifice was not for nought and that saying Kaddish for a dead "father" marks some existence of continuity and perhaps a new beginning. Considers that *God's Grace* is also a version of *Robinson Crusoe*. Cites several references to Defoe's novel, including Malamud's epigraph, but points out that unlike Robinson, Cohn has no society to which to return. Sees additional parallels between Cohn-Buzz and Prosper-Caliban, especially evoking Miranda's "O brave new world, that has such people in't." Finally, sees the novel as an allegory of Jewish-Christian relations. Traces biblical and historical allusions in characters' names: Calvin Cohn, Bunder (bund meaning covenant) Kuhn, and argues that the fable remains enigmatic despite all the illuminating parallels. Suggests that the novel is irreducible to one allegory because "Cohn is not only a failed rabbinical student but also a learned scientist." Thus, he experiences things in terms of "biblical archetypes" and "experiments in evolutionary advancement." Sees *God's Grace* as a running commentary between evolutionists and creationists. Notes that Malamud drew on Goodall's *In the Shadow of Man* and Johanson and Edey's study *Lucy: The Beginnings of Human Kind*, which tells the story of Louis Leakey's dig in immoral Tanzania where he named one of the prehistoric skulls he found George, the name of Malamud's Kaddish-reciting gorilla. Also discusses the metafictional aspect of the novel in terms of its being "about the limits of and power of storytelling and . . . Language," noting that in the novel life imitates stories and that Buzz learns that "everything gets to be a story because God is "made of words." Examines Vonnegut's *Galapagos* and Pynchon's *Lot 49* in comparison with Malamud's accomplishment in *God's Grace*.

Furman, Andrew. "Imagining Jews, Imagining Gentiles: A New Look at Saul Bellow's *The Victim* and Bernard Malamud's *The Assistant*," *Studies in American Jewish Literature* 16 (1997): 93–102. Departs from Roth's thesis in "Imagining Jews" concerning *The Victim* and *The Assistant* to argue that in the former, Jew and Gentile exhibit the same dialectical responses to one another: "trepidation and aggression, prejudice and good will," and that Leventhal is not *The Victim's* "sole exemplar of moral conscience."In terms of *The Assistant*, argues that Helen and Ida's practicality steers the novel away from moral allegory by challenging Morris's "ethical Jewhood." Suggests that *The Victim* actually explores how a Jew should live in an anti-Semitic world, and depicts Leventhal and Allbee not as opposites but as men equally susceptible to "evil impulses and equally accountable for their actions." Sees the same similarity with respect to Morris Bober and Frank Alpine. Points out that in *The Assistant* Morris's fellow Jews are as guilty of prejudice as the Gentiles are (e.g., Nat Pearl calls Alpine a "dago"). Argues that *The Assistant's* Jews are neither its sole sufferers nor its sole victims, and that immoral Jews succeed (Karp) where the moral fail (Bober). Cites Helen as victim of Bober's moral suffering to ground it in reality. Maintains that Malamud's "society" punishes the moral and rewards the immoral.

Giroux, Robert. "Introduction." In *Bernard Malamud, The Complete Stories*. New York: Farrar, Straus and Giroux, 1997, ix–xv. Loving and gentle tribute recounting Malamud's publishing history and friendship with Giroux at Harcourt, Brace and then at Farrar, Straus and Giroux. Includes biographical sketch of Malamud's family members, his early jobs (such as a civil service post checking estimates of drainage ditch statistics in 1940), where some of the stories and novels were written, and the prodigious list of Malamud's awards, prizes, and honors. Explains that the stories are printed in order of composition rather than publication and introduces the experimental forms of "In Kew Gardens" and "Alma Redeemed," which Malamud called "fictive biographies" and "biographed stories." Mentions that only one story, "Suppose a Wedding," is in dramatic form, and that another, "A Confession of Murder," was the first chapter of an abandoned novel. Reveals that "Steady Customer," written in 1943, had been recently discovered in *New Threshold* . Cites Flannery O'Connor, Richard Gilman, Cynthia Ozick, and Daniel Stern on Malamud's writing and status as an American Master.

Gorg, Claudia. "Jewish-Gentile Relations and Romance in *The Assistant*," *Studies in American Jewish Literature* 14 (1995): 58–63. Works out the Frank-Morris/ Frank-Helen relationships in terms of parallels and repetitions. Points out that Morris and Frank have a father-son/ teacher-student relationship symbolic of Judaism's being the "father" of Christianity. Notes that being Jewish means suffering for others and questions the sincerity of Frank's conversion. Suggests that the novel's few romantic scenes are overshadowed by the difficulties of Frank and Helen's relationship and that in both the Frank-Morris and Frank-Helen relationships, getting close to the other is difficult, but that the novel implies that barriers of prejudice can be surmounted by affection.

————. "Bernard Malamud's 'The German Refugee.' " *Studies in American Jewish Literature* 18 (1999): 18–22. Presents the story as graduate-student/English-tutor Goldberg's unfolding lesson on the nature and depth of "Oskar's actual defeat" beyond the linguistic, financial and cultural displacements suffered by immigrants. Author cogently explains Oskar's loss of identity as no longer a German Jew, but only a Jew: "The Nazis have redefined him . . . This leaves him in a terrible predicament because his native language is German, the basis of his professional success as a journalist" (18). Moreover, when Oskar curses the Germans as "Pigs mazquerading as peacogs" his simultaneous contempt for and dependence on the German language is revealed in the thickly accented English. Points out the prison imagery used to describe Oskar's attempts at English; e.g., "handcuffed and tortured English," "tormented English." Notes that when Oskar tries to characterize all Germans, including his wife, as Nazis, he feels overwhelming guilt when he discovers his wife had converted to Judaism before being slaughtered by the Nazis. Interprets his wife's note asserting that she has been faithful to him for 27 years, as his final and crushing defeat, for Oskar must now consider himself the prejudiced spouse, not his wife, and realize that he has "betrayed the idea of humanity," (21) which is what he so treasured in Whitman's poetry. Concludes that this compounded guilt leads Oskar to suicide. Explains that Oskar's bequeathing his possessions to Goldberg insured that the tutor would read Oskar's mother-in-law's letter recounting her daughter's conversion. Ends by portraying the story as one in which two strangers "meet by chance" and become intertwined: "The very minute a person opens himself towards a fellow-man, he is bound to his fellow man." The examples of the wife, Oskar and Goldberg "illustrate the central philosophical idea of the story: the brotherhood of men" (22).

Grobman, Laurie. "African Americans in Roth's *Goodbye Columbus,* Bellow's *Mr. Sammler's Planet,* and Malamud's *The Tenants,*" *Studies in American Jewish Literature* 14 (1995): 80–89. Discusses the portrayal of African Americans in three novels stressing their stereotypical characterizations. Notes that the Jew and African American in each work are alienated from the larger society, but that in *Goodbye Columbus* Roth (ab)uses the black child immorally by not portraying him in depth and by using him only as an agent by which Neil realizes his own humanity. Argues with Barry Gross's justification of Roth's use of blacks, insisting that "the reading audience can and should hold (writers) to certain standards of morality." Bellow's portrayal of a black pickpocket in *Mr. Sammler's Planet* is also criticized as stereotypical. Readings by Gross and Robert F. Kiernan are given fair airings, but are taken to task for not finding fault with Bellow's use of the black pickpocket as "an emblem rather than a whole human being." Malamud's depiction of Willie Spearmint in *The Tenants* gets higher marks for portraying "the African American with more humanity." After presenting Cynthia Ozick's interpretation of *The Tenants* in "Literary Blacks and Jews," however, Grobman disagrees, seeing Lesser and Willie as fellow writers first and as Jew and black, second. Concludes by calling on Jewish writers to do more than simply reflect the world, but use their fiction to improve the relationship between Jewish Americans and African Americans.

Hanson, Philip. "Horror and Ethnic Identity in 'The Jewbird,' " *Studies in Short Fiction* 30, 3 (Summer 1993): 359–366. Finds parallels between "The Jewbird" and historical changes in the American Jewish Community of the 1960s. Analysis is further informed by correspondences to Poe's "The Raven" and to Bakhtin.

Lainoff, Seymor. "Prison as Metaphor in the Fiction of Malamud, Singer and Roth." *Modern Jewish Studies* 11:3–4 (1999): 64–69. Locates the vacillation in Jewish American novels between assimilation and traditional Jewish life on Nietzsche's Dionysian and Apollonian spectrum; the former correlates with "the tragic hero's unbridled energy at the beginning of the drama," the later with "the restrained and limiting wisdom the hero achieves at the end" (64). Studies prisons in Malamud's *The Fixer,* Singer's *The Magician of Lublin* and Roth's *The Anatomy Lesson* as metaphors for the heroes' modes of moving from the Dionysian to the Apollonian and thereby variously confronting their Jewish pasts. Concludes that all three prisons, in Malamud, the prison of exile; in Singer, "shutting out of all lust and impulsiveness;" in Roth, "the prison of neurosis; (paralysis) the inability to turn back or move forward," (69) represent variant ways of dealing with one's Jewish past.

Langer, Lawrence L. "Malamud's Jews and the Holocaust Experience." In *Admitting the Holocaust.* New York: Oxford University Press, 1995, 145–155. (Reprinted from *Critical Essays on Bernard Malamud,* ed. Joel Salzberg. New York: G.K. Hall and Co., 1987.) Locates Malamud in the tradition of writers for whom suffering nourishes the soul. Questions why Malamud has touched only "peripherally" on the Holocaust "and how, when, he has approached it, has he reconciled its atrocities with his determination to illuminate the human?" Suggests that

Malamud's fictional world is alien to the one that produced the Holocaust, and that by reducing the Europe of 1911–1943 to focusing on one person, Malamud "transforms (it) into a story of the affirmation of private dignity that elevates the ordeal to tragic dimensions." Contends that Yakov Bok's situation and response to it falls far short of the dehumanizing death camps. Sees Bok's suffering in the line of prison literature of Dostoevsky, Koestler, and Solzhenitsyn. Seems to attack *The Fixer* and *The Assistant* for not being realistic in their portraits of anti-Semitism and Jewish suffering, that is, realistic in terms of institutional state-sanctioned anti-Semitism and death camp suffering. Malamud's anti-Semites (Black Hundreds, Ward Minogue, Frank Alpine) "afflict only private fates, providing a mere flickering prelude to the incomprehensible fiery doom that consumed European Jewry decades later." Compares Bok's dream of talking with the Tsar with Tevya's efforts to engage God in dialogue, and claims that to a great extent Bok's misery was a consequence of his own choices, unlike the misery inflicted on Europe's doomed Jews. Sees *The Assistant* as presenting the Jew as a victim of twentieth-century anti-Semitism. Finds egregious fault with critics who see metaphors for the Holocaust in Morris Bober's grocery store-prison and leaking gas stove. Claims that seeing such metaphors "is to abuse metaphor and to distort one-half of the comparison." Finds short stories "The Loan" and "The Last Mohican" to be instances of Malamud's more fully realizing "the dilemma of confrontation between Holocaust survivor and the vain, insensitive American Jew." Suspects that Malamud's treatment of the Holocaust was minimal because its atrocities are so at odds with his own "impatience at the modern devaluation of man."

Lasher, Lawrence M. "An Early Version of Malamud's 'The German Refugee' and Other Early Newspaper Sketches," *Studies in American Jewish Literature* 12 (1993): 94–108. Reprints and discusses six 1940 newspaper sketches by the youthful Malamud and identifies them as his earliest published writings, aside from his boyhood juvenilia. Most of Lasher's attention is given to "The Refugee," "an interesting skeleton version of 'The German Refugee,' published some twenty-three years later."

———. "Plenty of News: Bernard Malamud's 'The Letter,' " *Studies in Short Fiction* 31, 4 (Fall 1994): 857–866. Goes beyond domestic father/son readings of "The Letter" to articulate the larger political meaning of how the twentieth century's wars have devalued human life and so risk destroying the human race. This message is the metaphoric content of the four-page blank letter that Ralph and Teddy, both veterans and inmates of a mental hospital beg Newman to mail. Newman refuses because he, a nonveteran, does not understand the message. Analyses and interpretation of story's structure, economy of language, and use of past and present tense.

Luftig, Victor. *Seeing Together: Friendship between the Sexes in English Writing from Mill to Woolf*. Stanford: Stanford University Press, 1993.

Lyons, Bonnie. "The Contrasting Visions of Malamud and O'Connor," *Studies in American Jewish Literature* 12 (1993): 79–86. Defines the contrasting works of O'Connor and Malamud as a "dialogue of opposing ideas and strategies." Arguing that their "best work—their stories—reveal themselves in light of each other"—the bulk of the article is a close, contrasting reading of "The Magic Barrel" and "A Good Man is Hard to Find" in which the author finds fundamentally "opposing visions." If life, in Malamud's story, seems "an inexhaustible mysterious and rich magic barrel," O'Connor's vision is one "peopled by blind, self-righteous, morally dead, ordinary people and desperate, murderous misfits."

———. "The Female Characters in Bernard Malamud's Stories." *Studies in American Jewish Literature* 17 (1998): 129–136. Analyzes Malamud's choice of stories in *The Stories of Bernard Malamud* in terms of those dealing with male/male character interplay, male/female interplay, and the predominance of the quest motif relative to each. Notes that many of the stories are "spiritual success stories" that teach and inspire, and whose characters transcend their poverty and loneliness. Looking through a "feminist lens," the author finds no "positive female characters" in Malamud's stories; the women are not questers. Summarizes the eight stories that have male/female interplay: "Take Pity," "Black Is My Favorite Color," "The German Refugee," "The Maid's Shoes," "In Retirement," "God's Wrath," "Life is Better Than Death," and "The Model." Notes that seven of these eight "are about failure to break through," i.e., stories about failure, for which "Take Pity" is the model. Moreover, in each male/female story, the sexual relationship also always fails. Proceeds to explore the nine stories which deal with male/male relationships, in which one male facilitates some positive (moral, psychological, spiritual) development in the other. These stories include: "The First Seven Years," "The Mourners," "Idiots First," "Angel Levine," "The Last Mohican," "Rembrandt's Hat," "The Magic Barrel," "The Man in the Drawer," and "Talking Horse." Concludes that Malamud's favoring of male/male relationships as those which enable men to grow, and his portraits of male/female relationships as failures give Malamud his measure. Moreover, because there is no female character in Malamud's self-selected stories as "wonderfully human, deeply Jewish [and] finally mysterious [as] Salzman" the author argues "that his (Malamud's) art is diminished by this limitation" (136).

Malamud, Bernard. Letters to Rosemarie Beck. Berg Collection, New York Public Library.

Mandel, Siegfried. "Bernard Malamud's 'Alma Redeemed:' A Bio-fictional Meditation," *Studies in American Jewish Literature* 14 (1995): 39–45. Suggests that in Malamud's fiction the Jew who has no connection to his Jewish historical and communal past is essentially dead. Notes that as part of his experimentation with fictive-biographies Malamud found in Mahler a "ready-made Jewish renegade." Provides the biographical points of contact between Alma's and Gustav's lives and "Alma Redeemed." Suggests that the converted-Catholic Mahler is a version of Harry Freeman (né Levin) who lies about his Jewish identity to the luscious Isabella del Dongo ("The Lady of the Lake"), only to find that she is Jewish and will not marry a non-Jew. Discusses Alma's admiration of Nietzsche and Wagner, her attraction to Jewish geniuses and Mahler's anti-Semitism. Suggests that in "Alma Redeemed," "Kew Gardens," and other works of "experimental fiction," Malamud obliterates "the lines between biography and fiction to allow an interplay between facticity and the creative imagination."

Morisco, Gabriella. "Bernard Malamud e la critica anglo-americana negli anni ottanta," *I Lettore - di - Provincia*, 48100 Ravenna, Italy (Dec. 23, 1991):82, 99–104. Overview of American literary criticism on Malamud to 1980.

———. "Bernard Malamud: An American Reading of Feodor Dostoevsky," *Studies in American Jewish Literature* 14 (1995): 14–27. Summarizes list of readings or versions of Dostoevsky's works in works by Bellow, Kazin, Wallant, Howe, Mailer, and Rahv. Suggests that *The Assistant* is an ironic reading of *Crime and Punishment* and examines "a complex pattern of references and coincidences" between the two consisting of "explicit and implicit quotations, reversals of meanings and ellipses, parodies and highly allusive sign languages." Argues that both novels are driven by the themes of guilt and punishment, and by "the theme of meeting." Points out that *Crime and Punishment* begins with Raskolnikov's *personality*, whereas *The Assistant* begins by focusing attention "on the victim of the crime," and that Dostoevsky's tone is dramatic, whereas Malamud's is alternatingly comic and pessimistic, i.e, ambiguous. Concludes that Malamud's narrative compared with Dostoevsky's turns dramatic pathos upside-down. Sees the theft scene for example as a "masterpiece of *reductio ad absurdum* of Dostoevsky's dramatic scene." Suggests that Frank is compared with St. Francis of Assisi and "the idea of Napoleon." Points out that Frank's reading of *Crime and Punishment* (at Helen's request) marks the meeting between Frank and Raskolnikov in terms of reading, and is indicative of "Frank's moral metamorphosis." Argues that the role of savior, which Dostoevsky assigns to Sonia, the prostitute, falls to Morris Bober, a thinly veiled version of Martin Buber, and that Buber's *I and Thou* informs the relationship between Frank and Bober. That is, Frank learns that suffering has value only in terms of one's relationship with others. Suggests that Frank's moral choice "merges St. Francis of Assisi's spirituality with Bober/Buber's ethics of suffering, merges two religions (the Christian and the Jewish) with two kinds of mysticism (the Franciscan and the Chassidic)." Compares Frank's ritual circumcision to Christ's stigmata and notes that at the ends of *The Assistant* and *Crime and Punishment* spring arrives and both Frank and Raskolnikov read the Bible.

New, Elisa. "Film and the Flattening of Jewish-American Fiction: Bernard Malamud, Woody Allen, and Spike Lee in the City," *Contemporary Literature* 34, 3 (Fall 1993): 425–449. Argues that *The Tenants* pushes the limits of the urban novel into the realm of the cinematic. Suggests that the black/white stereotypes that paralyze writers Spearmint and Lesser are best rendered in the novel's translation of film's flattening qualities. Woody Allen and Spike Lee's movies are used as comparative examples of novelistic urban films.

Nilsen, Don L. F. "Humorous Contemporary Jewish-American Authors: An Overview of the Criticism." *MELUS* 21, 4 (Winter 1996): 71–101. Summarizes recent literary scholarship examining the use of ethnic humor in contemporary Jewish-American literature. Critical treatment of the works of Woody Allen, Saul Bellow, Stanley Elkin, Allen Ginsberg, Fran Lebowitz, Bernard

Malamud, Philip Roth, J. D. Salinger, and Mort Sahl is presented. Also examines scholarly critiques comparing these and other Jewish American authors.

Ohana, Yolanda. "An Interview with Bernard Malamud: A Remembrance," *Studies in American Jewish Literature* 14 (1995): 64–71. In this January 1984 interview, Malamud discusses why he resists interviews ("My work comes first. You live for posterity"), his literary influences (Henry James, Faulkner, Dostoevsky, Chekhov, among others), and his insistence that "the most satisfying response to my fiction is an active imagination." In this respect, he is pleased that he has forced the reader to find his own ending for *God's Grace*. Malamud also reflects on Art, how he writes, the importance of being influenced by past and present literatures, and confirms the connection between Raskolnikov and Frank Alpine (explored by Gabriella Morisco in "Bernard Malamud: An American Reading of Feodor Dostoevsky," above). Malamud discusses the difficulties in writing *The Fixer*, his "research" trip to Kiev, and plans for a book with a woman hero. The only question he refused to answer was, "Do you believe in God?" His reply: "I won't answer. It's a much too personal question."

Parrish, Tim. "Women in the Fiction of Bernard Malamud: Springboards for Male Self-Transformation?" *Studies in American Jewish Literature* 16 (1997): 103–114. Treats the depiction and function of women in terms of their mediation of male heroes' conflicts in "The Model," "The Girl of My Dreams," "The Magic Barrel," and *The Assistant*. Subsidiary discussions of women in *The Natural* and *Dubin's Lives*. Suggests that in "The Model" Mrs. Perry reverses the artist/model relationship when she observes that Elihu is no artist. In so doing, she forces Elihu to see himself differently and allows her to object to his reification of her. Argues that Mrs. Perry is the only Malamudian female character with "the eloquence to object to her own representation" (excepting Helen in *The Assistant*). Suggests that the Elihu/Mrs. Perry relationship is emblematic of the Malamud/female character relationship, proving "that Malamud could imagine a compelling female perspective." Observes that this story's conclusion is typical of Malamud in that the male character's work is completed "at the expense of the female character's reality." "Girl of My Dreams" also involves a male artist, a writer, whose conflicts are resolved by means of a woman, Olga. Here, however, Olga, or Mitka's idealization of her, inspires him to keep writing, whereas Mrs. Perry causes Elihu to stop painting. Remarks that Olga's story stops when Mitka has no further need for her. Considers Malamud's female characters as "moral markers against which the male protagonist measures himself." In "The Magic Barrel" Stella is seen as the agency of Salzman's and Leo's restoration; Lily as agency for Leo's recognition that he does not love G-d. Observes that Lily too disappears after her purpose has been served. Sees Helen in *The Assistant* as "Malamud's most fully drawn female character. Argues that her thematic function is to combine the roles of Lily and Stella in "The Magic Barrel," vis à vis Frank. Discusses Helen's control in terms of her sexuality and, observes that like Helen of Troy, two men covet her, Frank and Nat. Notes that for Roy Hobbs and William Dubin as well as for Frank Alpine, women are forces to be feared and desired. Sees Helen as agent of Frank's "moral transformation" and his circumcision upon converting to Judaism as a response to his raping her; she calls him an "uncircumcised dog." Even though Helen is Frank's ideal, she contradicts that ideal by being "the voice of material reason." Notes that Helen seeks to give meaning to her late father's life, thereby becoming an extension of Morris's and of Frank's lives. Observes that many of Malamud's male characters resolve their conflicts by means of mediating women.

Pinsker, Sanford. "Cityscape as Moral Fable; The Place of Jewish History and American Social Realism in Bernard Malamud's Imagination," *Studies in American Jewish Literature* 14 (1995): 28–38. Suggests that Malamud converted what is traditionally thought of as cityscape by internalizing it or making it psychological or historical. Distinguishes Malamud's cityscapes from those of Cahan, Ornitz, Michael Gold, Henry Roth, and Daniel Fuchs. Argues that Malamud's fictions make the provincial and local into the universal and "morally significant" by means of "collapsing history and cityscape . . . in tales that move steadily toward the condition of moral fable." In "The Magic Barrel" this is accomplished by moving Finkle from the urban realm to an internalized "cityscape"—"an interior condition set into motion [as] he opens himself to eros." Suggests that Finkle, unable to love, dissolves into archetype as the story unfolds in the larger context of "Western love." Concludes that "The Magic Barrel" is set in the cityscape of New York City and in Finkle's "New York heart." Contends that Malamud's fiction is most modern when he conflates "landscape and psychological condition, [wrenches] expectation and outcome, [and alternates] currents of social realism and imaginative fancy." Examines *The Assistant* as a case of "cityscape as psychological condition" and unravels numerous instances of doubling in the novel. Discusses *The Fixer* as "an example of history internalized." Concludes by maintaining that Malamud's "modernist experimentation" changed "our definition of cityscape" and altered our understanding of "the relation of moral fables to essentially realistic fictions."

Purcell, William F. "The Demands of Love: The Ending of Bernard Malamud's *The Assistant*," *Notes on Contemporary Literature* 23, 5 (November 1993): 4–5. Reviews various critical speculations about the "future" of the Frank/Helen relationship in order to argue that it is precisely the indeterminacy of the relationship that is the point of the novel since it defines Frank's genuine conversion: "to have taken the story further would have detracted from its moral impact."

Ross, Michael L. "Brief Roman Candles: Wharton, Huxley, and Malamud." In *Storied Cities: Literary Imaginings of Florence, Venice, and Rome*. Westport, Conn.: Greenwood Press, 1994, 265–282. "A Great Tradition Travestied: Fidelman in Florence" (101–108) examines "A Pimp's Revenge" from *Pictures of Fidelman* in terms of the play between the city of Florence and Fidelman's growth as artist and man. Suggests that Fidelman's experience in Florence clarifies his illusions about life and art. "Glass Menageries: The Venice of Hecht and Malamud" (173–186) treats Venetian motifs in Hecht's "The Venetian Vespers" and in "Glass Blower of Venice" from *Pictures of Fidelman*, focusing "on the Venetian clash between fact and fantasy." Sees Malamud as inverting the tradition of "Venetian melancholy" resulting instead in laughter. Argues that Fidelman in Venice is an inverted version of Mann's Gustave Aschenbach (*Death in Venice*). Sees Venice for Fidelman as a city marking the beginning of experience, and not, as has been historically the case, the end of it. "Brief Roman Candles: Wharton, Huxley, and Malamud" (265–282) examines Wharton's "Roman Fever," Huxley's "After the Fireworks" and Malamud's "Behold the Key." Sees "Behold the Key" as exploring "the potential for farce" in the differences between New York and Rome in terms of time (Romans seem obsessed with it). Suggests that "The Last Mohican" is about "an American's discovery of Rome and of himself [including Fidelman's] relation to his racial and cultural past, and his personal responsibility for the tragic facts of modern history." Casts Fidelman as "the Eternal Jew" in the Eternal City, doing what Jews do—flee. Sees Rome as providing Fidelman with "the Roman knowledge to stop running from himself and his human responsibilities."

Ruotolo, Lucio. "Bernard Malamud's Rediscovery of Women: The Impact of Virginia Woolf," *Twentieth Century Literature* 40 (Fall 1994): 329–341. Argues that Malamud found in the life and works of Virginia Woolf the woman's way of experiencing the world that he felt he lacked. Demonstrates parallels between Woolf and the female characters of "In Kew Gardens" (a fictionalized Woolf herself), "Alma Redeemed" (Mahler's wife), and "A Wig." Suggests that Malamud's teaching of a course on Woolf in 1979 was more than simply preparation for these short stories, but led him to a new theory he called "autobiographical essence," which, Ruotolo posits, Malamud had intended to apply in a larger work.

Safer, Elaine B. "The Allusive Mode, The Absurd, and Black Humor in Bernard Malamud's *God's Grace*," *Studies in American Humor* 7 (1993): 104–117. Noting that there is a tension in much of Malamud's work between the positive, humanistic vision and "an angry, ironic side that is fraught with absurdist humor," Safer argues that "*God's Grace* is the most violent and bleak expression of black humor anywhere in Malamud's fiction." That absurdist black humor arises, she says, out of a virtual parody—or deconstruction—of "the biblical works that Cohn praises and the Jewish humanism that he stresses. Focusing on Malamud's parodic versions of the biblical dialogues between God and Moses, the verbal text of the Passover Seder, the dialogues between Abraham and God in Genesis, and the Kaddish, Safer concludes that the novel fulfills its aim as "a visionary tale with a prophetic warning" primarily through its "grim humor."

Salzberg, Joel. " 'The Loathly Landlady;' Chagallian Unions, and Malamudian Parody: 'The Girl of My Dreams Revisited," *Studies in Short Fiction* 30, 4 (Fall 1993): 543–554. Argues that the story parodies both the Quest Romance and "Loathly" or transformed lady of Arthurian legend and Chagall's bridal imagery.

———. "The Rhythms of Friendship in the Life of Art: The Correspondence of Bernard Malamud and Rosemarie Beck," *Salmagundi* 116–117 (Fall/Winter 1997): 61–124. Includes Salzberg's introduction and the texts of some thirty-one letters between Malamud and Rosemarie Beck between 1959 and 1969. Introduction describes the nature of the twenty-seven-year correspondence and friendship between Malamud and Beck, "a little-known, New York–based painter who still exhibits and gives lectures on painting." Salzberg reports that in 1990 Beck gave the entire correspondence (some 165 letters and thirty-two postcards from Malamud, and her 153 letters and nine postcards to him) to the Berg Collection of the New York Public Library. The letters chosen by Salzberg for this article deal with the meaning of friendship for Malamud and reveal his methods of composition: "I am enormously conscious of form, the right place for the right idea, and it is form that I breed by ideas for," and his self-doubt. Salzberg also illustrates the ways in which Malamud and Beck were effectively one another's cheerleaders, believing in one another's talents, coaching one another to keep at it. Writer and painter also engaged in sometimes irritating criticism of one another's work, but the friendship endured. See Salzberg's entry in this work, *The Magic Worlds of Bernard Malamud.*

Singh, Sukhbir. "The Moral Survivor, Bernard Malamud." In *The Survivor in Contemporary American Fiction, Saul Bellow, Bernard Malamud, John Updike, Kurt Vonnegut, Jr.* Delhi: B.R. Pub., 1991, 83–127. Detailed analysis of heroes' moral failures, growth, and successes in *The Natural, The Assistant, A New Life,* and *The Fixer.* Traces Malamud's heroes as weak individuals whose struggles can evince moral victories and a humanity of which the characters seem otherwise incapable.

Sio-Casteñeira, Begoña. " 'The Jewbird:' Bernard Malamud's Experiment with Magical Realism." *Short Story* 6:1 (Spring 1998): 55–64. Claims that Malamud's success lay in rendering "the realistic in fantasy . . .and the fantastic in everyday life" (55). Structures her argument on Chanady's three requirements for magical realism: "the juxtaposition of the natural and the supernatural on the same textual level, the resolution of the antinomy between both worlds, and the authorial reticence" (57). Cites Malamud's natural treatment of Cohen and of Schwartz as fulfilling the first requirement; the reader's suspension of judgment in realistically considering Schwartz as a legitimate character, as fulfilling Chanady's second requirement; and the absence of narrative intrusions into the story, as satisfying the third requirement for magical realism. Suggests that magical realism is an appropriate place for Malamud to search for his Jewish identity. Schwartz is an authentic Jew; Cohen, an inauthentic or existential Jew. Interprets magical realism's ability to synthesize opposites as an appropriate vehicle for depicting these conflicting tendencies in the modern Jew.

Sloan, Gary. "Malamud's Unmagic Barrel," *Studies in Short Fiction* 323, 51 (Winter 1995): 51–57. Argues that Salzman is an ordinary man who wanted Leo for his son-in-law from the outset, and that by forcing Leo to see her in comparison to other women, gets his wish. Traces how Salzmane ensures that Leo will be disenchanted with other women, particularly Lily, and how he "correctly packages Stella." Suggests that there is nothing magical at all about Pinya Salzman and that his ploy to get Leo to marry Stella is a carefully choreographed affair. Reads Salzman's Kaddish as a prayer for the romantic illusions soon to be destroyed by marriage.

Spevack, Edmund. "Racial Conflict and Multiculturalism: Bernard Malamud's *The Tenants*," *MELUS* 22, 3 (Fall 1997): 31–55. Frames Black-Jewish conflict depicted in *The Tenants* in terms of current multicultural-versus-mainstream-American divides. Begins with W. E. B. DuBois, Henry Louis Gates Jr., and Gerald Early on problems of ethnic differences, multiculturalism, and the political goals of postmodernism, respectively. Observes that since literature has been the battleground for these conflicts/campaigns, the divergences between Jewish American and Black American writers is significant. Questions whether Jews and Jewish writers who have completely assimilated into the American mainstream still retain the status of "oppressed minority" in the sense that Black Americans are. Sees Harry Lesser as assimilated Jewish writer and Willie Spearmint as writer of a Black literature that "is not of assimilation, but in many ways that of establishing difference, separation, and cultural resistance." Explores whether or not Malamud was restating separatist sixties views of Blacks and Jews in *The Tenants* or whether he was suggesting that Blacks do have their own form of expression. Moreover, questions whether *The Tenants* "anticipates the multiculturalism and canon debates of the 1980s and 1990s." Notes that the purpose of and audience for Harry Lesser's novels are problems of love and people like himself—mainstream, educated intellectuals. Whereas the purpose and audience for Willie's work are to vent his anger and share experiences common to people like himself—poor, uneducated, underprivileged black men who have used crime as a means of survival and have spent time in prison. Suggests that Willie has discovered what Gates found in slave narratives, "the direct relation between freedom and discourse." Willie is writing to "write himself out of slavery . . . and into being." Cites Early in seeing Willie's writing as a postmodern and multicultural art that will ultimately free his race. Considers Malamud's artistic conflict in *The Tenants* as representing that between Jewish American writers and Black American writers. Notes that in 1971 Malamud had already "recognized the problem of literary dominance and subordination." Argues that Willie prefigures Gates's admonition to Blacks that they define themselves before others define them. Speculates that Willie is modeled after Amiri Baraka/LeRoi Jones, Black poet and dramatist. Suggests that Gates et al. are represented by Willie and that Arthur Schlesinger Jr. et al. are represented by Lesser. Looks to Todorov for any hope of resolution in terms of "a well-tempered humanism." Discusses "Angel Levine" and "Black Is My Favorite Color" to chart Malamud's dwindling optimism for Black/Jewish relations, which reaches its nadir in the catastrophic ending of *The Tenants*. Suggests that Willie is Malamud's assessment that Black writers in 1971 were at "a different stage in development." Yet the question of whether Black writers should attempt to assimilate "to adopt the forms of white literary tradition remains open." Discusses the novel's multiple endings as alternative resolutions to Black/Jewish relations. Cites Kernan in suggesting that *The Tenants* asks whether the contemporary novel can still accommodate the realities in which Willie must live. Concludes by agreeing with Malamud, that mercy or "the moral concept of mercy" is the "basic precondition for the construction of a new national synthesis," but, also like Malamud, concedes that its prospects are grim.

Steed, J.P. "The Spirit in All Things: The Search for Identity in Malamud's 'Angel Levine.' " *Studies in American Jewish Literature* 19 (1999): 11–17. Treats the issues of identity and belonging using as a springboard Malamud's oft-quoted statement, "All men are Jews except they don't know it." Analyzes "Angel Levine" in terms of an ironical identity quest, in which Manischevitz's belief in the Black angel Levine's Jewishness facilitates his belief in his own Jewishness. Argues that Manischevitz's remark at the story's end that "There are Jews everywhere" can be understood to mean that "there is Jewishness everywhere" (12). Thus, this statement applies ironically to Manischevitz himself, that is, to those who are Jews already. Maintains that the story "is primarily an exploration of the religious aspect of this metaphor of 'Jewishness'—the idea that an element of divinity exists in all men" (12). Considers Manischevitz's acceptance of Levine's divinity as a catalyst for and mirror of Manischevitz's own divinity/Jewishness/identity. Thus, the author investigates Jewishness as metaphor in this story and its link with divinity, leading to Manischevitz's epiphany of divine identity. Points out that Manischevitz's lack of identity is foregrounded in his visits to Harlem, where he feels out-of-place everywhere but at the Black tailor's shop and at the store-cum-synagogue. Argues that Manischevitz's acceptance of Levine's divinity "creates the same link between Jewishness and divinity that had previously been created by Levine" (15). Interprets the illusory changing of the black feather into white snow as Malamud's signal that color is only external, and what had previously served to alienate Manischevitz from Levine (i.e., color) is now used to signify their community; both are Jewish and both are divine.

Sullivan, Mary Rose. "Malamud in the Joycean Mode: A Retrospective on 'The Magic Barrel" and "The Dead," *Studies in American Jewish Literature* 14 (1995): 4–13. Examines parallels between "The Magic Barrel" and "The Dead" stemming from both stories' use of epiphany and their formal designs. Points out that both stories concern tradition-bound cultures' propensities for stifling rather than encouraging life. Joyce and Malamud wrestle with "the struggle of the life-wish against the death-wish," but also share structural elements, such as specific imagery and death dirges at their stories' ends. Suggests that in Joyce "hope succumbs ineluctably to fear and inertia," but that in Malamud, hope triumphs and "leads to some form of life-enhancing connectedness." The two stories also share similar types of narrators, winter imagery, and both make use of epiphany. In this last respect, Sullivan sees Malamud most clearly adapting Joyce's technique employed in "The Dead." She goes on to draw analogies between Gabriel and Leo arguing that Malamud condenses the many steps of the Joycean process of disillusion into one encounter with one woman—Lily. However, while Gabriel seems to surrender Gretta and his world at the end of "The Dead," Leo seizes the world, running toward Stella at the end of "The Magic Barrel." Closely compares "The Magic Barrel"'s ending with Salzman's reciting Kaddish. Suggests that Salzman could be mourning the altered perception of himself in Leo's eyes, from "Wonder-Rabbi" to "ordinary suffering" man. Alternatively, Salzman could be mourning the old Leo, who no longer exists, or simply "the world's woes." Points out that father-figure Salzman has no counterpart in "The Dead," but connects Salzman instead to Leopold Bloom (after establishing Malamud's links to Joyce in *A New Life*), who represents "a humanistic Jew," and who fulfills Malamud's "idea of humanism." Points out that Bloom ends his meeting with Stephen by "chanting a fragment of the Jewish prayer for the dead," and maintains that Bloom's Kaddish has more in common with Salzman's than does Gabriel's dirge in "The Dead." Sees "The Magic Barrel" as Malamud's "Kaddish for an honored literary father."

Walden, Daniel. "The Bitter and the Sweet: 'The Angel Levine' and 'Black Is My Favorite Color,' " *Studies in American Jewish Literature* 14 (1995): 101–104. Provides background of Malamud's knowledge of and interest in Blacks. Notes that "The Angel Levine" was written in the fifties when Black-Jewish relations were strong, and that "Black Is My Favorite Color" was spawned by the sixties when Black-Jewish animosity was strong. Argues that in order to relieve his Job-like suffering, Manischevitz in "The Angel Levine" must make a leap of faith and believe that a Black man is a Jewish angel. "It depends on the tailor's ability to extend his idea of Jewishness. . . ." In contrast, "Black Is My Favorite Color" (1963) sees Nat Lime extending himself to the Black community repeatedly only to be rebuffed, violently at times, over and over again. Distinguishes this story's realism from "Angel Levine's combination of fantasy and realism." Suggests that, unlike Manischevitz, who had to learn that Jews are everywhere, Nat must accept that "the black world is a closed world to him." Concludes by proposing that by 1970–1971 Malamud knew that Blacks were not "interested in acceptance at the expense of identity."

Watts, Eileen H. "Jewish Self-Hatred in Malamud's "The Jewbird,' " *MELUS* 21 (Summer 1996): 157–163. Argues that "The Jewbird" opens with an allegory of the diaspora and immigration quotas within which issues of Jewish anti-Semitism and self-hatred are raised. Schwartz, the Jewbird, represents new, unassimilated immigrants; Cohen, the penthouse-renting frozen food salesman into whose kitchen Schwartz flies, stands for the self-hating assimilated Jew who is ashamed of and embarrassed by unassimilated Jews. Suggests that the interaction between Schwarz and Cohen lays bare the political, social, and psychological fallout of assimilated Jew as good tenant, unassimilated Jew as bad, and Gentile as landlord. Also suggest that tenancy is one of Malamud's central metaphors for Jewishness in that tenancy corresponds uncannily to the Jews' status in America and indeed throughout the diaspora. Roth's "Eli, the Fanatic" is discussed as a corollary treatment of assimilated Jews' self-hatred directed at Hasidim.

———. "The Art of Racism: Blacks, Jews, and Language in *The Tenants*," *Studies in American Jewish Literature* 15 (1996): 42–48. Suggests that the novel is an antidote to theories that assume that art and reality are mutually exclusive. Examines the ways in which *The Tenants'* structural and linguistic components echo its subject: stormy Black-Jewish relations, here played out in the contexts of tenancy, writers writing, and sex. Claims that Malamud has sculpted the novel's formal conventions and finessed language's conventions to both express and correspond to the ugly, and sometimes chaotic, reality of racism and anti-Semitism. Explains the problematic multiple narrators and narratives in the book about a man writing a book about a man writing a book in terms of Malamud's desire to demonstrate "The truth in unimpeachable form;" namely, that art is inextricably bound to and shaped by the sexual, social, economic, and political realities of the writer's life. The resulting novel yields a text in which we are not always sure who is talking, a difficulty that Watts claims is a literary analogue of Yeats's last line from "Among School Children:" "How can we know the dancer from the dance?" Art and the reality that has molded the artist are indistinguishable. The artist, like the dancer, is so much embodied in his art that we cannot tell the teller from the tale. Sees the novel's vile scatological cursing and typographical gimmicks as Malamud's proof that real life determines how writers use language and even typography. Considers the novel's four endings in light of "inconclusive experiences" (cf. Conrad's *Heart of Darkness*) arguing that multiple endings imply multiple beginnings—alternating despair and hope, and in fact, shadowing the on-again/ off-again history of Black-Jewish relations.

Zucker, David J. "Abraham, Isaac, and Malamud," *Conservative Judaism* 45, 4 (Summer 1993): 66–75. Examines versions of the Abraham-Isaac story in "Idiots First," "The Silver Crown," and *God's Grace*.

———. "Malamud as Modern Midrash," *Judaism* 43, 2 (Spring 1994): 159–172. Argues that Malamud's writing is a "figurative parallel" to the function and content of Midrashim. Distinguishes three types of Midrash (*Aggadot*): 1) "*Aggadot* that are related to biblical narrative"; 2) "Historical *aggadot* which tell of post-biblical personalities and events"; and 3) "Ethical-didactic *aggadot* which offer guidance and outline principles in religious and ethical thoughts." Using this framework, Zucker relates biblical midrashim of Jacob and Rachel to "The First Seven Years," "Job" to "Angel Levine," Isaac to *God's Grace*"; the postbiblical characters of Elijah to "Angel Levine" and "The Silver Crown," The Angel of Death to "Idiot's First"; the ethical-didactic themes of "Ethics of the Fathers" (*Pirke Avot*) to "The Lady of the Lake," and the directives that one "[s]trive to be a good person, to judge all people in the scale of merit and to have a good heart" to "The German Refugee," *The Assistant*, and *A New Life*. Suggests that Malamud, literally teacher in Hebrew, lived up to his name and created midrash in his work.

Victoria Aarons, Professor of English at Trinity University, is the author of *A Measure of Memory: Storytelling and Identity in American Jewish Fiction*, which received a 1996 *Choice* Award for an outstanding Academic Book. She has also written a number of essays in scholarly journals and edited collections on American Jewish literature.

Edward A. Abramson is Senior Lecturer in American literature, in the Department of American Studies, at the University of Hull, in England. He has also been a visiting Professor of English at the College of William and Mary, in Virginia. In addition to numerous articles and reviews on literary subjects, particularly American Jewish literature, he has published: *The Immigrant Experience in American Literature* (1982), *Chaim Potok* (1986), and *Bernard Malamud Revisited* (1993).

Alan Cheuse is a fiction writer and essayist, the author of three novels, among them *The Light Possessed* and *The Grandmothers' Club*, several collections of short stories, and a memoir, *Fall Out of Heaven*. His short fiction has appeared in such publications as *The New York Times*, *The Chicago Tribune*, *The Dallas Morning News*, *Redbook*, and *The San Diego Reader*, among other places. With Nicholas Delbanco, he edited *Talking Horse: Bernard Malamud on Life and Work*. With Caroline Marshall, he edited two short story anthologies, *The Sound of Writing* and *Listening to Ourselves*. The latest collection of his short stories is *Lost and Old Rivers*. Cheuse lives in Washington, D.C., teaches in the writing program at George Mason University, and serves as book commentator for National Public Radio's evening news-magazine *All Things Considered*.

Nicholas Delbanco is the Robert Frost Collegiate Professor of English Language and Literature at the University of Michigan, where he also directs the Hopwood Awards Program. The author of twenty books of fiction and non-fiction, his most recent titles are *The Lost Suitcase: Reflections on the Literary Life* (non-fiction) and the novel *What Remains*. He is also the co-editor, with Alan Cheuse, of *Talking Horse: Bernard Malamud on Life and Work* (Columbia University Press).

S. Lillian Kremer is the author of *Witness Through the Imagination: The Holocaust in Jewish American Literature* (Wayne State University Press, 1989), and *Women's Holocaust Writing: Memory and Imagination* (University of Nebraska Press, 1999). The latter volume explores women's Holocaust experience in fiction by émigrés writing from memory and native-born Americans working from research and the imagination. Kremer is also the author of numerous journal articles and essays in collections on American literature. She is a professor of English at Kansas State University where she teaches American literature, American ethnic literature, and Holocaust literature and film.

Paul Malamud is Bernard Malamud's son. At present, he lives in Washington, D.C., and works for the U.S. State Department in the Office of International Information Programs.

D. Mesher is a professor of English and Coordinator of the Jewish Studies program at San Jose State University. He has published more than a dozen essays on various Jewish writers, including several on Malamud, as well as a bibliography of Sephardic authors writing in English.

Cynthia Ozick, distinguished American novelist, short story writer and essayist has won numerous awards and honors including the American Academy of Arts Award for Literature, several O. Henry First Prizes for fiction, Guggenheim and National Endowment for the Arts Fellowships and recognition from Jewish heritage groups. Her five novels and three collections of novellas and stories, which include *The Pagan Rabbi*, *The Cannibal Galaxy*, *The Messiah of Stockholm* and *The Shawl*, are rooted in Jewish experience and universal themes, which have received broad critical acclaim.

Sanford Pinsker is Shadek Professor of Humanities at Franklin and Marshall College. He writes widely on Jewish-American literature and culture for journals such as *Tikkun*, *Midstream*, *Partisan Review*, *The Georgia Review*, *Sewance Review*, *The Virginia Quaterly* and others. His books include *The Schlemiel as Metaphor*, *Bearing the Bad News*, and *Studies of Philip Roth, Cynthia Ozick*, and *J.D. Salinger*.

Karen Polster is a doctoral candidate of the University of California, Riverside. Her work has appeared in *Contemporary Jewish-American novel-*

ists: A Bio-Critical Source Book, edited by Joel Shatsky and Michael Taub. She has also contributed a number of articles to *Studies in American Jewish Literature* and *Yiddish.* She is currently completing a dissertation entitled *Twentieth Century Immigration Literature and the Borderlands.*

Joel Salzberg is an Emeritus Professor of English at the University of Colorado at Denver. Author of *Bernard Malamud: A Reference Guide,* editor of essay collections on the fiction Bernard Malamud and J.D. Salinger's *Catcher in the Rye,* Salzberg's writing has appeared in such journals as *Studies in the Novel, Studies in Short Fiction, Salmagundi* and *Studies in American Jewish Literature.*

Daniel Stern is the Cullen Distinguished Professor of English in the Creative Writing Program at the University of Houston and the author of nine novels, four books of short stories, a play and several screenplays. He has been the recipient of the International Prix Du Souvenir for his novel, *Who Shall Live, Who Shall Die,* the Academy of Arts and Letters Rosenthal Award for his short stories, *Twice Told Tales,* and several O. Henry Prizes for the short story. His stories have been dramatized on National Public Radio and Public Television.

Daniel Walden published *On Being Jewish* in 1974, *Twentieth Century American Jewish Fiction Writers* in 1984, and is now working on *Conversations with Chaim Potok.* He has published more than 70 articles and has been the editor-in-chief of *Studies of American Jewish Literature* since 1975.

Eileen H. Watts has published articles on Bernard Malamuc in *Melus* (Multi-Ethnic Literature of the United States) and *Studies in American Jewish Literature,* and on Malamud and Kafka in the forthcoming *Modern Jewish Studies Annual* for 2001. Her work has also appeared in *American Imago, Modern Language Studies* and *The Journal of Psychology and Judaism.* She has served as bibliographer for the Bernard Malamud Society since 1993, and teaches at the Torah Academy of Greater Philadelphia.

Editor

Professor of English, Coordinator of Jewish Studies, Evelyn Avery offers courses in American, Ethnic-American and Jewish literature at Towson University in Baltimore, Maryland. She is the author of *Rebels and Victims: The Fiction of Richard Wright and Bernard Malamud,* and numerous articles and essays on American Jewish literature. As a founder of the Bernard Malamud Society and co-editor of the *Malamud Newsletter,* she views her work as the inspiration for *The Magic Worlds of Bernard Malamud.*

INDEX

Proper names within quotation marks are fictional characters

213